Matthias T. Frank

Knowledge-Driven Harmonization of Sensor Observations

Exploiting Linked Open Data for IoT Data Streams

Knowledge-Driven Harmonization of Sensor Observations

Exploiting Linked Open Data for IoT Data Streams

by
Matthias T. Frank

KIT Scientific Publishing

Karlsruher Institut für Technologie
Institut für Angewandte Informatik und Formale Beschreibungsverfahren

Knowledge-Driven Harmonization of Sensor Observations:
Exploiting Linked Open Data for IoT Data Streams

Zur Erlangung des akademischen Grades eines Doktors der Ingenieurwissenschaften von der KIT-Fakultät für Wirtschaftswissenschaften des Karlsruher Instituts für Technologie (KIT) genehmigte Dissertation

von Matthias T. Frank, M.Sc.

Tag der mündlichen Prüfung: 6. Oktober 2020
Referent: Prof. Dr. York Sure-Vetter
Korreferent: Prof. Dr. Stefan Zander

Impressum

KIT Scientific Publishing

Karlsruher Institut für Technologie (KIT)
KIT Scientific Publishing
Straße am Forum 2
D-76131 Karlsruhe

KIT Scientific Publishing is a registered trademark
of Karlsruhe Institute of Technology.
Reprint using the book cover is not allowed.

www.ksp.kit.edu

Print on Demand 2021 – Gedruckt auf FSC-zertifiziertem Papier

ISBN 978-3-7315-1076-5
DOI 10.5445/KSP/1000128146

Knowledge-Driven Harmonization of Sensor Observations

Exploiting Linked Open Data for IoT Data Streams

Zur Erlangung des akademischen Grades eines
Doktors der Ingenieurwissenschaften
(Dr.-Ing.)

bei der Fakultät für Wirtschaftswissenschaften
des Karlsruher Instituts für Technologie (KIT)

genehmigte
DISSERTATION

von

M.Sc. Matthias T. Frank

Datum der mündl. Prüfung: 6. Oktober 2020

Referent:	Prof. Dr. York Sure-Vetter
Korreferent:	Prof. Dr. Stefan Zander
Prüfer:	Prof. Dr. Orestis Terzidis
Vorsitzender:	Prof. Dr. Maxim Ulrich

Abstract

The rise of the Internet of Things (IoT) leads to an unprecedented number of continuous sensor observations that are available as IoT data streams. It seems to be obvious to employ this new source of data for better founded decision support in various domains. However, harmonization of such observations is a labor-intensive task due to heterogeneity in format, syntax, and semantics. We therefore aim to reduce the effort for such harmonization tasks by employing a knowledge-driven approach. In order to avoid having to build up a new knowledge base for each harmonization task, we pursue the idea of exploiting the large body of formalized public knowledge represented as statements in Linked Open Data (LOD) for this purpose.

This approach reveals three challenges: *i*) we have to establish trust for at least a subset of LOD in order to ensure that statements employed for the harmonization process are consistent and trustworthy, *ii*) we have to handle sensor observations contained in IoT data streams with respect to the dimensions of volume, veracity, velocity, and variety and *iii*) we have to address varying data requirements that are given for varying use cases and target decision support systems (DSSs). We address these challenges by *i*) enabling knowledge workers to collaboratively curate and annotate knowledge and leverage it using common knowledge published as LOD, *ii*) mapping key-value tuples of observations contained in IoT data streams to meaningful and validated triples on-the-fly, and *iii*) providing dynamic harmonization workflows that automatically adapt to the requirements of different data consumers based on the context knowledge of an observation.

Our approach is evaluated within the domain of geographical information systems (GISs). The results show that *i*) the informative value of knowledge bases can be leveraged by LOD if knowledge about schema and provenance is evaluated precisely, *ii*) mapping, transformation, and validation of continuos environmental observations can be efficiently provided using current stream processing technologies and *iii*) machine learning algorithms are suited to dynamically compose efficient preprocessing workflows that meet varying requirements of various data consumers.

Acknowledgements

According to the PhD regulations, a PhD thesis has to demonstrate the applicant's ability to carry out independent scientific work. Scientific work (which is far more than this thesis can represent) depends of course also on external factors, as the research environment, advisors, reviewers, critics, supporters, fellows, funders, partners, community, or the social and professional foundation that was granted to us. I would therefore like to take the opportunity to express my gratitude to all the people and organizations who made that possible.

First of all, I would like to thank Prof. Dr. **Stefan Zander** (Darmstadt University of Applied Sciences), who opened up the world of scientist to me. Starting with his role as adviser for the TGL-Seminar during my master's degree, he also agreed to supervise my master's thesis, introduced me to the Rudiverse, entrusted me with research projects, supported me with my publications, and served on the *doctoral committee* as co-referent. In this context, my gratitude also goes to Prof. Dr. **Rudi Studer** (KIT), who built an open, friendly, creative and productive environment in semantic web research, gave me the opportunity to participate in his group as a research scientist, and supported my early work as PhD student with his valuable feedback. Following seamlessly I would like to thank Prof. Dr. **York Sure-Vetter** (KIT), who agreed to continue Rudi's legacy, took over the role as advisor for my PhD project, and softly transformed the Rudiverse to a Yordiverse. I am deeply grateful for all the advice and insights that he gave me during my years as a doctoral student, and also for his support in sharpening my research, for his motivation to run the 'Badische Meile', and for serving on the doctoral committee as referent, despite his duties as director of the National Research Data Infrastructure (NFDI). Furthermore, I thank Prof. Dr. **Orestis Terzidis** (KIT), and Prof. Dr. **Maxim Ulrich** (KIT) for completing the doctoral committee.

In perfect complement to the aforementioned advisors and members of the doctoral committee, I would also like to thank my *research fellows* from the Yordiverse for their participation and their valuable feedback. I especially thank Dr. **Dominik Riemer**, Dr. **Viliam Simko**, Dr. **Patrick Philipp**, and Dr. **Nelly Frank** for their commitment as mentors and reviewers in the context of my doctoral project.

When it comes to *research environment*, my thanks also go to **FZI Research Center for Information Technology** and all the people who work hard every day to make FZI a great place to work, research, learn, and develop. This goes beyond doing research and writing a PhD thesis and also covers aspects of industrial development, organizational structure, and shaping the collaboration. With all the dynamics in research, certain constants gain special significance. I therefore thank **Heike Döhmer** for supporting the research division Information Process Engineering in such a good manner, keeping the group together and happy, giving the newcomers a warm welcome, and staying in touch with the alumni.

The privilege of doing research is not a matter of course, nor is research free of charge. I would therefore like to thank the **Federal Ministry for Economic Affairs and Energy** (BMWI) for *funding* the research projects CultLab3D and SeRoNet and also the **Federal Ministry of Education and Research** (BMBF) for funding the research project BigGIS. All these projects were important parts of my scientific work, especially due to the great project partners we had and also the opportunities to evaluate my own research approaches.

For the *professional foundation* required for my PhD project, I thank the passionate instructors of **Siemens Professional Education** Stuttgart, who supported me in starting my career as a business IT specialist. I also thank the teachers of **Oscar-Walcker-Schule** Ludwigsburg, who spend their evenings and saturdays in order to enable second-chance education. My thanks also go to **Karlsruhe University of Applied Sciences** and its professors for enabling me to study Business Information Systems for my Bachelor and Master degrees, including semesters abroad in Singapore, India, and Taiwan. And again to the BMBF for funding my studies.

For the *social foundation* required for my PhD project, I deeply thank my parents **Johanna** and **Reinhard** for conveying their values to me, always serving as a role model, and supporting me wherever my journey took me. I thank my siblings **Daniel**, **Tabea**, **Kornelius**, and **Marie-Ann** for the continuous and active exchange and also my mother-in-law **Bububatma** for her love and for providing a research environment abroad. And to conclude: My biggest thanks go to my beloved wife **Dilbara** and my wonderful daughter **Ayana** for making my life worth living.

Matthias T. Frank, October 2020, Karlsruhe

Contents

1

Introduction to Knowledge-driven Harmonization

In Chapter 1, we motivate our field of research and point out the addressed *challenges*. In order to define the scope of this thesis, we introduce *research questions*, *hypotheses*, and *contributions*. Further, we introduce the structure of this thesis, including the overall approach and data used for the evaluation.

1.1 Challenges of Knowledge-driven Harmonization

Popularity and pervasiveness of sensor *observations* available on the internet are continually growing. It therefore seems likely to employ this new source of information for better founded decision support in various domains. However, harmonization of such observations is a labor-intensive task due to heterogeneity in format, syntax, and semantics. We therefore aim to reduce the effort for such harmonization tasks by employing a *knowledge*-driven approach. To avoid rebuilding knowledge bases for each harmonization task, we propose to exploit the large body of formalized public knowledge represented as statements in *Linked Open Data (LOD)*[1].

In this thesis we are pursuing the idea of exploiting LOD for automated and meaningful harmonization of heterogenous sensor observations contained in *IoT data streams*. We aim to reduce the effort for labor-intensive data harmonization

[1] Key terms emphasized in Section 1.1 such as *knowledge, observation* or *Linked Open Data*, are defined in Section 1.2. In addition, a glossary is provided at the end of this thesis.

tasks and enable *decision support systems* (*DSSs*) to provide decision support based on well-founded observations. For the evaluation within this thesis, we apply this approach to the domain of *geographical information systems* (*GISs*) and identify restrictions that have to be considered when applying the approach to other domains. By exploiting new sources of knowledge about objects on the earth's surface described as LOD, we also obtain additional information about the environmental context of an observation. The increasing availability of both, tuples of environmental sensor observations and triples of explicit modelled knowledge published as LOD are the foundation for a new generation of GISs. For the intended knowledge-driven harmonization of sensor observations, we have identified the following three main challenges:

Challenge 1: Inconsistency in LOD. There is a large body of formalized public knowledge represented as statements in LOD [Bizer et al. 2009; Hausenblas 2009; Heath and Bizer 2011]. These statements are modelled as triples that provide explicit semantics for subject, predicate, and object. As an example, the triple `wd:Q1040 rdfs:label "Karlsruhe"@de`[2] states that entity with identifier (ID) 'wd:Q1040' has a label which is represented as literal with language code 'de'. Therefore, such statements provide distinct and machine interpretable semantics that allow for automated evaluation and reasoning on formalized knowledge. We therefore propose the idea of exploiting LOD in order to provide explicit semantics for sensor observations. However, when exploiting LOD for meaningful observations, we have to ensure that statements employed for the harmonization process are consistent and trustworthy. Due to the open-world assumption of LOD, trust has to be established within a dedicated context, for example a *corporate knowledge graph*. Challenge 1 is further discussed in Section 3.1.2.

Challenge 2: Ambiguous key-value tuples in IoT data streams. The second challenge addresses the lacking semantics of various sensor observations. Publicly available IoT data stream of environmental observation stations are continually growing in popularity and pervasiveness. Examples are public observation stations for traffic noise or air pollution, but also private observation stations or other weather stations which publish their observations continuously in a machine processable format on the internet. Preferentially, these observations are also

[2]In this example, resources are represented by QNames as described in Section 2.3.2.

available as web application programming interfaces (APIs) or directly subscribable as IoT data stream. However, most of these sensor observations consist of ambiguous key-value tuples that do not contain any explicit semantics. Without explicit semantics, these values are meaningless [Brown 2013; Sapot 2016]. They can also not be evaluated on-the-fly or dynamically transformed to fit varying requirements of various DSSs. We therefore need a further understanding of data and a corresponding data transformation that can be applied on IoT data stream. Challenge 2 is further discussed in Section 4.1.2.

Challenge 3: Varying requirements of data consumers. Well-founded observations are the basis for meaningful decision support. However, sensor observations have to fit the requirements of varying DSSs in order to gain value. For example, the quality of the decisions made from a GISs depends heavily on the quality of the geospatial data provided [Sholarin and Awange 2015]. The geospatial data provided must therefore be 'accurate, complete, consistent and up-to-date' [Sholarin and Awange 2015] with respect to the decision supported. Because of the open-world assumption mentioned in Challenge 1, completeness assertions are not possible for LOD. Also, the heterogeneity of various sensor observations hinders to integrate these observations directly for decision support. We therefore have to find a solution that evaluates sensor observation data automatically and addresses the requirements of various DSSs. These requirements depend on the quantities, units of measurement, and granularity of observations that are needed for a certain use case, but also on the data formats that are supported by a DSS. Therefore, a dynamic harmonization approach is required to feed various DSS with heterogenous sensor observations. Challenge 3 is further discussed in Section 5.1.2.

1.2 Terms and Definitions

For a consistent naming within this thesis, we define key terms in Section 1.2. Additional terms are introduced within the respective sections. In addition, a glossary is provided at the end of this thesis.

Knowledge: We define knowledge as a theoretical understanding of a subject, formalized as explicit statements about this subject. Knowledge-based systems apply knowledge acquired through learning, where learning includes both instruction and experience [Ackoff 1989]. According to the data-information- knowledge-wisdom (DIKW) hierarchy[3], there can be no knowledge without information and no information without data [Ackoff 1989; Rowley 2007]. The product of sensor observations can be considered as raw data, whereas information is extracted from data by analysis in order to gain value [Ackoff 1989]. In the DIKW hierarchy, knowledge builds the foundation for wisdom. However, wisdom does also include ethical and aesthetic values which are unique and personal and therefore differentiate human from machines [Ackoff 1989]. As the representation and organization of knowledge is central to this thesis and builds the foundation for the approaches we discuss in Chapter 3, Chapter 4, and Chapter 5, we dedicate Chapter 2 exclusively to this topic.

Observation: An observation is the act of measuring or otherwise determining the value of a property [Cox 2013]. It includes method, time, place and result of determining the value. In the context of this thesis, we employ numerical values observed by a sensor. Those often heterogenous values have to be harmonized before being evaluated by a DSS which requires homogenous messages. For this purpose, we employ context knowledge to add explicit semantics to observation messages from heterogenous sensors.

Linked Open Data: LOD refers to the global 'web of data', which is described and interlinked in meaningful and machine-processable ways and follows well-defined grammar and language constructs [Hebeler 2009, p. 5]. Berners-Lee introduced the first idea of LOD in 2007 [Berners-Lee 2007] and concretized it with the definition of LOD in 2009 [Berners-Lee 2009]. However, data publishers have to determine which vocabularies should be used to describe the semantics of the data, which hinders the efficient use of LOD. The Linked Open Vocabulary (LOV) initiative therefore offers an observatory for the ecosystem of reusable linked vocabularies [Vandenbussche and Vatant 2014]. The concept of LOD is further discussed in Section 2.4.2.

[3] Ackoff also introduces 'understanding' between knowledge and wisdom for the DIKW hierarchy, however, this additional layer is omitted in recent definitions [Rowley 2007].

IoT data stream: As the Internet of Things (IoT) is basically 'empowered by sensors, identifiers, software intelligence, and internet connectivity' [Jamali et al. 2020], data streams of sensor observations are available on the internet. We refer those data streams as IoT data streams.

Corporate knowledge graph: As mentioned in Challenge 1, statements in LOD follow the open-world assumption [Baader et al. 2003]. Relying on statements retrieved from LOD could therefore cause inconsistency for further processing steps. To address this issue, we define a *locally closed environment* [Doherty et al. 2000] that contains a validated subset of LOD to ensure the trustworthiness of triples that can be considered as ground truth. In the remainder of this thesis, the locally closed environment that contains the validated subset of LOD is referred to as *corporate knowledge graph* (*CKG*) [Bellomarini et al. 2017]. We define a corporate knowledge graph as a knowledge graph which is completely under control of a single organization. Such an organization could be an enterprise, non-governmental organization (NGO), civil service, or any other kind of organization that pursues knowledge managed. The concepts of open-world assumption, locally closed environment, and corporate knowledge graphs are further discussed in Section 2.4.3.

Decision support system: A DSS is defined as a special type of information system (IS) that is used to condense and prepare information for decision support in various domains. They need to be flexible and adaptable to accommodate changes in both the environment and the user's decision-making approach [Sprague 1980]. Although research on DSSs has been going on for decades, service-oriented DSSs that enable efficient and effective decision making processes by exploiting appropriate data converted to meaningful information are still gaining in importance due to the increasing amount of data available [Demirkan and Delen 2013].

Geographical information system: A GIS is defined as a DSS that specializes in capturing, storing, retrieving, processing, analyzing and visualizing geospatial data to support decision-making [Sholarin and Awange 2015]. Traditional data input for GISs are points, polygons, or a matrix of numbers that represent objects on the Earth's surface at a fixed point in time [Cowen 1988]. In contrast to that, continuos sensor observations provide the additional dimension of time to GIS data. GISs that evaluate observations from IoT data streams based on their context knowledge are considered as a new generation of GIS in the remainder of this thesis.

To address the challenges identified in Section 1.1, we introduce research questions, hypotheses, and contributions in Section 1.3.

1.3 Research Questions, Hypotheses, and Contributions

In order to define the scope of this thesis, we pose *research questions*, derive *hypotheses*, and introduce our respective *contributions* in Section 1.3. Figure 1.1 outlines the general structure of research questions, hypotheses, and contributions covered by this thesis.

1.3.1 Research Questions

The aim of our work is to combine IoT data streams of publicly available environmental observations with the explicit semantics described as LOD in a meaningful way. We are researching whether this new approach will reduce human effort for sensor data harmonization and simultaneously improve the quality of DSSs by providing conclusions based on well-founded observations. As a consequence, our work addresses the following principal research question:

How can Linked Open Data be exploited for a knowledge-driven harmonization of sensor observations?

This principal research question is broken down into the following three sub-questions which are answered in Chapter 3 to Chapter 5 as shown in Figure 1.1.

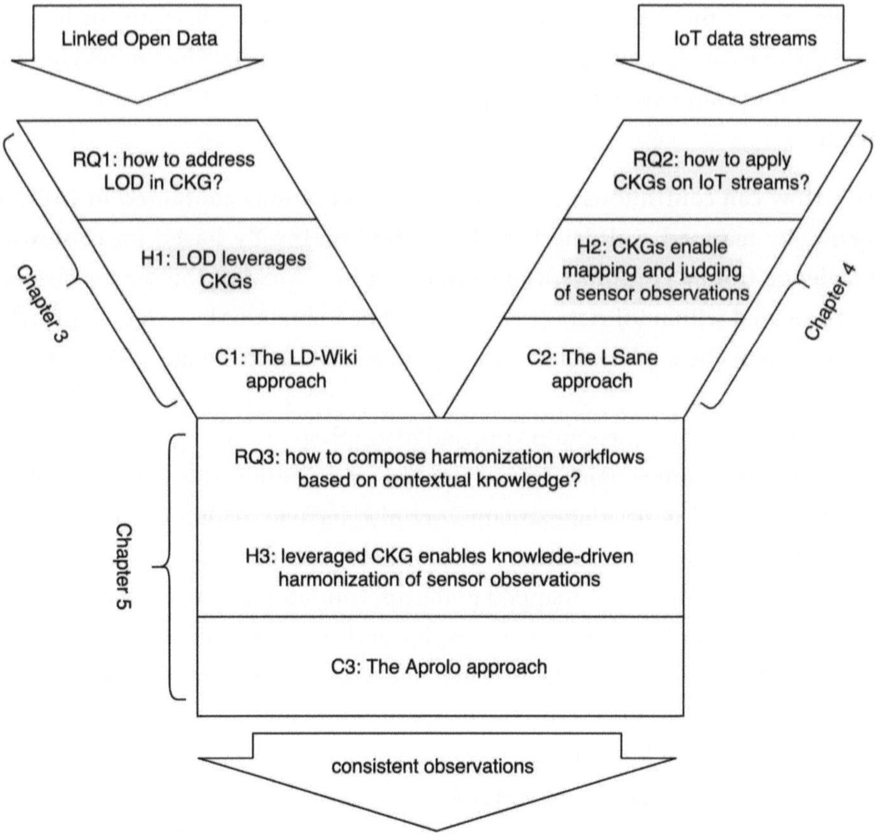

Figure 1.1: General structure of research questions (RQ), hypotheses (H), and contributions (C) covered by this thesis in order to exploit Linked Open Data for automated and meaningful harmonization of heterogenous sensor observations contained in IoT data streams.

RQ1: How can Linked Open Data be exploited as a lever for the knowledge contained in corporate knowledge graphs?. As pointed out in Challenge 1, we have to ensure that statements employed for the harmonization process are consistent and trustworthy. When exploiting LOD for that purpose, trust has to be established within a dedicated context due to the open-world assumption[4] of LOD. Such a dedicated context could be provided by a corporate knowledge graph. In order to employ LOD for environmental sensor observations, we therefore first

[4]The differences of open-world assumption, closed-world assumption, and locally closed environment are further detailed in Section 2.4.3.

have to answer the research question of identifying and sufficiently addressing the challenges in exploiting Linked Open Data as a lever for the knowledge contained in corporate knowledge graphs. Research question RQ1 is answered in Chapter 3.

RQ2: How can continuous environmental observations contained in IoT data streams be mapped, validated, and enriched on-the-fly based on contextual knowledge from a corporate knowledge graph?. Most of the sensor observations provided within IoT data streams consist of ambiguous key-value tuples that do not contain any explicit semantics as pointed out in Challenge 2. We therefore aim to combine tuples of continuous environmental sensor observations with according triples of a corporate knowledge graph in order to gain observations with explicit semantics. For a knowledge-driven harmonization of sensor observations contained in IoT data streams, we also have to evaluate and transform observations on-the-fly if needed. As a potentially high frequency of heterogenous observations has to be mapped to the appropriate statements, the process of harmonization tends to result in a complex and computationally intensive task. We therefore have to answer the research question of how a stream of continuous environmental observations can be mapped, validated, and enriched on-the-fly based on contextual knowledge from a corporate knowledge graph. Research question RQ2 is answered in Chapter 4.

RQ3: How can harmonization workflows for sensor observations be composed automatically based on the contextual knowledge of an observation?. In order to address different data consumers with varying requirements as mentioned in Challenge 3, data harmonizing workflows have to be composed dynamically. Those workflows have to meet the relevant requirements with respect to the supported data format, quantities, units of measurement, as well as the time and space granularity of observations selected for a certain use case. We therefore investigate how preprocessing workflows for environmental observations can be composed automatically based on the contextual knowledge of an observation. Research question RQ3 is answered in Chapter 5.

1.3.2 Hypotheses

From the research questions in Section 1.3.1, we derive the hypotheses presented in Section 1.3.2. For the general research question, we derive the following general hypothesis:

Linked Open Data provides sufficient knowledge to automate the harmonization of sensor observations.

We expect that DSSs that rely on this new generation of GISs will provide better founded conclusions due to amount and proven quality of involved observations in combination with the provided context knowledge. This principal hypothesis is broken down into the following three sub-hypotheses which are tested in Chapter 3 to Chapter 5 as shown in Figure 1.1:

H1: The comprehensive knowledge which is provided as Linked Open Data can be exploited to leverage the knowledge represented in a corporate knowledge graph. In order to exploit the comprehensive knowledge retrieved from LOD, we have to ensure that this knowledge can be used as a lever for the knowledge represented in corporate knowledge graphs. If the benefit of such an approach is greater than its implementation effort, we consider this hypothesis to be confirmed. If the implementation effort exceeds the benefits, we consider the hypothesis to be refuted. We test hypothesis H1 in Section 3.6.

H2: A well-curated corporate knowledge graph enables automated mapping, validation, and enrichment of ambiguous sensor observations based on explicit semantics. IFor knowledge-driven harmonization of continuous sensor observations contained in IoT data streams, we have to ensure that the knowledge provided by a corporate knowledge graph enables meaningful mapping, validation, and enrichment of ambiguous sensor observations on-the-fly. If the knowledge provided by a corporate knowledge graph can be employed in this way, we consider hypothesis H2 to be confirmed. If the harmonization without additional inputs is not possible or the total processing time increases to more than a cycle duration of the IoT data stream, we consider hypothesis H2 as disproved. We test hypothesis H2 in Section 4.6.

H3: Contextual knowledge of observations makes it possible to meet the requirements of different data consumers automatically. I Varying DSSs and other data consumers of homogenized observation messages may have different requirements on format and representation of those observations. We hypothesize that a set of semantic transformation rules retrieved from a corporate knowledge graph enables dynamically composed data processing workflows that meet such requirements on demand. If it is possible to compose such workflows automatically based on the knowledge of a corporate knowledge graph, we consider hypothesis H3 to be confirmed. If the composition without additional inputs is not possible, we consider hypothesis H3 as disproved. We test hypothesis H3 in Section 5.6.

1.3.3 Contributions

This thesis contributes approaches and implemented systems to work through the research questions posed in Section 1.3.1 and support the evaluation of the derived hypotheses as introduced in Section 1.3.2. In Section 1.3.3, we introduce the following contributions as shown in Figure 1.1:

C1: The *LD-Wiki*-approach: integrating LOD in corporate knowledge graphs. I The proposed approach aims to overcome the limitation of ambiguous schema definitions in various corporate knowledge graphs as identified in Challenge 1 (inconsistency in LOD) and provides an alignment to a common schema definition by supporting the annotation of organization-specific schema knowledge with the common and well-established terminology of LOV [Janowicz et al. 2014] within semantic wiki systems. Based on the resulting extended and interlinked schema knowledge, additional statements about a concept can be queried directly from LOD and integrated within a semantic wiki system. In order to contribute to the domain of semantic wiki software, we propose a generic extension for wiki systems that allows to leverage the semantic statements of a wiki with statements from LOD. Contribution C1 is broken down into the following sub-contributions which are detailed in Section 3.1.3:

C1.1 Provide a mechanism to suggest and curate LOD resources that match the organization-specific concepts described in a wiki system.
C1.2 Identify *statements that are redundant* within the corporate knowledge graph federated of statements from a semantic wiki and LOD.
C1.3 Identify *statements that are inconsistent* within the corporate knowledge graph federated of statements from a semantic wiki and LOD.
C1.4 Identify *statements that are likely missing* according to schema knowledge in order to describe concepts within a semantic wiki.
C1.5 Estimate *trust for statements* used within a semantic wiki, including statements derived from LOD.

C2: The *LSane*-approach: linked stream annotations for mapping, validation, and enrichment of observations. I The proposed approach aims to master the challenge of ambiguous key-value tuples in IoT data streams as identified in Challenge 2. In order to contribute to the domain of semantic sensor observations, we propose a semantic stream processing framework that maps observation messages to explicit semantics, validates each message, and enriches them with further statements based on collaboratively created annotations provided by domain experts. Contribution C2 is broken down into the following sub-contributions which are detailed in Section 4.1.3:

C2.1 Map sensor observations on-the-fly to explicit semantics.
C2.2 Validate sensor observations on-the-fly based on explicit semantics.
C2.3 Enrich sensor observations on-the-fly based on explicit semantics.

C3: The *Aprolo*-approach: self-learning preprocessing workflow for linked observations that dynamically employs a set of predefined actions in order to meet varying requirements on demand. I The proposed approach aims to master the challenge of varying requirements of data consumers as identified in Challenge 3. In order to contribute to the domain of automatically composed preprocessing workflows for GISs, we propose a self-learning preprocessing workflow for linked observations that dynamically employs a set of predefined actions in order to meet varying requirements on demand. Contribution C3 is broken down into the following sub-contributions which are detailed in Section 5.1.3:

C3.1 Explicitly define possible states of observation messages for GIS in a machine interpretable way.
C3.2 Explicitly define the target state for all observations as required by a data consumer.
C3.3 Explicitly define actions and apply these actions to messages in order to change their state.
C3.4 Provide an algorithm to learn the most efficient sequence of actions to reach a certain target state.

The overall approach for answering the research questions is introduced in Section 1.4.

1.4 Overall Approach

The work presented in this thesis covers the process of semantic data preparation of environmental observations from semantic mapping of key-value tuples received by environmental observation stations, mapping to triples with explicit semantics, validation of semantic triples and semantic enrichment by inferring new triples. An overview of the overall approach is depicted in Figure 1.2.

Linked Data Wiki (LD-Wiki): We propose an approach that enables knowledge workers to collaboratively curate knowledge of LOD in a locally closed and quality ensured environment. It aims to complete context knowledge of trusted triples within a corporate knowledge graph by leveraging them with LOD. For the overall approach, LD-Wiki provides metadata M, rules R, and shapes[5] D_{MT} to enable knowledge-driven harmonization of sensor observations. The LD-Wiki approach is described in detail in Section 3.3. An exemplary implementation is introduced in Section 3.4.

Linked Stream Annotation Engine (LSane): For mapping tuples of environmental sensor observations contained in an IoT data stream to triples with explicit semantics and provide enrichment and validation for those triples based on semantic annotations, we propose LSane. LSane subscribes to IoT data streams and

[5]In this thesis, the term *shape* stands for a meta description of messages in order to define restrictions that have to be fulfilled for valid messages of a certain message type.

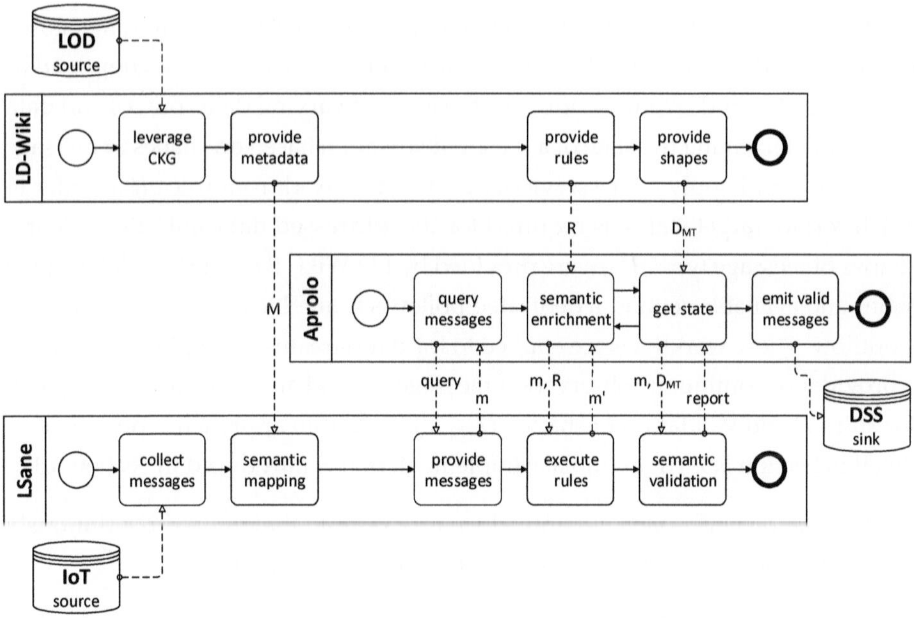

Figure 1.2: Overview of the overall approach: LD-Wiki exploits Linked Open Data to leverage a corporate knowledge graph. LSane collects messages m from an IoT data stream and maps those messages to explicit semantics based on metadata M provided by LD-Wiki. Aprolo queries for messages in LSane as needed for a certain task. Based on rules R and shapes D_{MT} provided by LD-Wiki, Aprolo orchestrates the enrichment and validation of messages in LSane and emits valid and consistent messages to a data sink, e.g. a DSS.

maps each message of an IoT data stream to explicit semantics based on metadata M. Those mapped observations are provided for other services which query for messages as needed for a certain task based in the context knowledge of an observation. Further, LSane provides an execution environment to apply rules R on messages m and receive enriched messages m'. Similar to the execution environment for rules R, LSane also provides validation reports for messages m based on provided shapes D_{MT}. The LSane approach is described in detail in Section 4.3. An exemplary implementation is introduced in Section 4.4.

Automated processing of linked observations (Aprolo): Environmental sensor observations are available in varying formats and representations due to the heterogeneity of sensors and data providers. In addition, varying data sinks such as DSSs have different data requirements. In order to meet those requirements, we introduce workflows of loosely coupled micro services which can be composed as needed on demand. Aprolo addresses the issue of varying data sources and data sinks by determining the state of a sensor observation based on shapes of message types D_{MT} and apply micro services as actions derived from rules R in order to reach certain target states as required for the addressed data sink. Rules R and shapes of message types D_{MT} are provided by LD-Wiki. Based on the determined states and available actions, a dedicated policy is trained to compose an adequate workflow. Those workflows are applied to IoT data streams by employing LSane as a provider of continuous observation messages m and an execution environment for rules R and validation of shapes D_{MT}. The Aprolo approach is described in detail in Section 5.3. An exemplary implementation is introduced in Section 5.4.

To evaluate our approach, we introduce an example that is used continuously within this thesis and the according evaluation setup in Section 1.5.

1.5 Evaluation of the Overall Approach

In Section 1.5 we introduce data and setup to evaluate the overall approach introduced in Section 1.4 and answer the research questions posed in Section 1.3.1.

1.5.1 Evaluation Data

For the empirical evaluation against real-world data, we introduce two exemplary observation messages which are used continuously for the evaluations in Section 3.5, Section 4.5, and Section 5.5. For these examples, we use data published by two different data providers, namely Landesanstalt für Umwelt Baden-Württemberg (LUBW)[6] as a representative for public environmental observation providers and the senseBox project[7] as a representative for an initiative of collecting environmental observations of private sensing devices. Both types of messages consist of ambiguous key-value tuples that do not contain any explicit semantics as pointed

[6]https://www.lubw.baden-wuerttemberg.de
[7]https://sensebox.de/en/

out in Challenge 2. The first example in Code Example 1.1 shows an observation message emitted by LUBW. The second example in Code Example 1.2 shows an observation message emitted by a senseBox device.

```
{
  "no2":61,
  "ozn":10,
  "luqx":0,
  "latitude":48.18169,
  "height":510,
  "so2":0,
  "station":"DEBY189",
  "pm10":0,
  "timestamp":1516191751218,
  "longitude":11.46445
}
```

Code Example 1.1: Message of an observation as received from LUBW as a representative of public environmental observation stations.

The shape of the observation message in Code Example 1.1 is characterized by a set of ten key-value pairs of observed values and metadata. The implicit semantics of observed values can not be evaluated without the knowledge of a domain expert. Besides observed values, the observation message does also contain spatial and temporal information. The spatial information is given as latitude and longitude for the World Geodetic System 1984 (WGS84) and the temporal information as milliseconds since 1/1/1970.

```
{
  "title": "Temperatur",
  "unit": "C",
  "sensorType": "HDC1008",
  "icon": "osem-thermometer",
  "_id": "59ec966d49f6f80011c1239a",
  "lastMeasurement": {
    "value": "7.98",
    "createdAt": "2018-01-18T13:02:14.330Z"
  }
}
```

Code Example 1.2: Message of an observation as received from a senseBox device as representative of private environmental observation stations.

In contrast to Code Example 1.1, Code Example 1.2 contains only one observed value together with an ISO 8601 timestamp and some addition metadata. Both types of message have in common that they are provided as JavaScript Object Notation (JSON) messages with key-value tuples. Also, both message types provide timestamps and geographical coordinates for the WGS84 system.

Although only one representative of each type is shown, we use IoT data streams of continuous observation messages that have the same shape but different values. The introduced exemplary types of observation messages are chosen because they illustrate examples for all three challenges identified in Section 1.1:

- **Challenge 1:** strings that represent common concepts which can be expected to be described as LOD, rather than proprietary concepts.
- **Challenge 2:** observation messages which are consumable as IoT data streams and contain a set of ambiguous key-value tuples.
- **Challenge 3:** variety in structure, quantities, units of measurement, and granularity which has to be addressed when harmonizing those messages for varying data consumers.

1.5.2 Evaluation Setup

Using the the common evaluation data introduced in Section 1.5.1, we work through research questions RQ1, RQ2, and RQ3 for the empirical evaluation. Irrespective of the common evaluation data, we have to prepare a dedicated evaluation setup for each research question in order to test hypotheses H1, H2, and H3. The setups are introduced as follows:

Evaluation setup for Research Question RQ1: The evaluation setup for RQ1 performs a field study. We investigate the results of public SPARQL Protocol and RDF Query Language (SPARQL) endpoints that serve LOD when querying for concepts for a corporate knowledge graph. We also evaluate the coverage of concepts referred in Code Example 1.1 and Code Example 1.2. The evaluation setup for RQ1 is discussed in detail in Section 3.5.

Evaluation setup for Research Question RQ2: In order to prepare the evaluation for RQ2, we use a data set of 10,000 precached observation messages in the shape of Code Example 1.1 and Code Example 1.2. This data set is used to carry out an empirical evaluation based on real data. Because of the precached messages, we are able to reproduce the exactly same stream of observation messages and perform a controlled laboratory evaluation to investigate the runtime behavior of the system. In multiple cycles, we map each tuple of each observation message to a triple with explicit semantics and also validate those triples. The evaluation setup for RQ2 is discussed in detail in Section 4.5.

Evaluation setup for Research Question RQ3: The evaluation setup for RQ3 performs a controlled laboratory evaluation. It employs observations of Code Example 1.1 and Code Example 1.2 that are mapped to triples with explicit semantics as input. Based on these semantics, the system infers the state of the observation data and applies actions in order to achieve a certain target state. For comparability reasons we test both, random application of actions as well as training and execution of a dedicated policy. The evaluation setup for RQ3 is discussed in detail in Section 5.5.

With this evaluation setup, we intent to show 1) to which degree LOD can be exploited as a lever for CKGs (Contribution C1), 2) how efficient a CKG can be employed to map, validate, and enrich messages of IoT data streams (Contribution C2), and 3) to which degree semantics of messages enable an automated harmonization (Contribution C3).

1.6 Previous Publications

The core contributions of this thesis are peer-reviewed and published as follows:

Leveraging knowledge graphs with LOD (Chapter 3): We have shown how the Open Annotation Data Model can be used to interlink formalized knowledge with LOD in order to complete context knowledge in [Frank and Zander 2016a]. For completing context knowledge for robotic components and capabilities, we have published a survey in [Zander et al. 2017]. In [Frank and Zander 2017c], we have introduced our approach of Linked Data Wiki, which is further discussed in [Frank and Zander 2017b] and [Frank and Zander 2017a]. The most important publication on leveraging knowledge graphs and completing context knowledge was published in the Communications in Computer and Information Science (CCIS) series [Frank and Zander 2017a]: *The Linked Data Wiki: Leveraging Organizational Knowledge Bases With Linked Open Data.*

Knowledge for IoT data streams (Chapter 4): In [Zander et al. 2016a], we have shown how the utilization of IoT devices in general can be enhanced by using ontological semantics. Focused on environmental sensors, we have shown in [Frank and Simko 2018] how collaboratively created annotations can be exploited to map messages of tuples with environmental sensor observations in data streams to triples with explicit semantics. Based on this approach, we have shown in [Frank et al. 2018] how observations that are mapped in such way can be continuously enriched and validated based on further annotations.

Knowledge-driven automation of data harmonization (Chapter 5): For the dynamic integration of big spatio-temporal data, we have introduced an approach based on collaborative semantic data management in [Frank 2016]. In [Frank and Zander 2016b], we have discussed how smart web services can be employed for a loosely coupled architecture of reusable components for the automated preprocessing of sensor observations in GISs.

1.7 Structure of this Thesis

This thesis is structured as follows: Chapter 1 and Chapter 2 are preliminaries. Chapter 3 to Chapter 5 are the the main chapters that address the three research questions of Section 1.3.1 and cover the main contributions as illustrated in Figure 1.1. A conclusion is given in Chapter 6, followed by bibliography, lists of figures, tables, code examples, and abbreviations, as well as the glossary. The remainder is structured as follows:

Chapter 2: Foundations of knowledge representation and organization. In Chapter 2 we lay the foundations for the approaches we discuss in Chapter 3, Chapter 4, and Chapter 5. In particular, we introduce the work that has been done in the fields of knowledge representation, description logic, semantic web technology and its organization in the forms of ontologies, LOD, completeness assertions, semantic rule languages, and assertion of trust for retrieved triples.

Chapter 3 to Chapter 5: Findings for answering the research questions. In Chapter 3 to Chapter 5, we present our findings for answering research questions RQ1, RQ2, and RQ3. This involves testing hypotheses H1, H2, and H3 respectively. Each of these chapters is structured as follows:

1. *Introduction of the research question:* In Section 3.1, Section 4.1, and Section 5.1, we motivate research questions RQ1, RQ2, and RQ3 respectively. We further detail the challenges as well as our contributions to address these challenges.
2. *Literature review:* The first step on answering the research questions is to review the literature of related work. This is done for each research question separately, following the same methodical approach. For each review, we provide a concept matrix according to Webster and Watson [Webster and Watson 2002] in Section 3.2, Section 4.2 and Section 5.2. The symbols used within a concept matrix are explained in Table 1.1.
3. *Approach:* We detail requirements and propose architectures for the approaches LD-Wiki, LSane, and Aprolo in Section 3.3, Section 4.3, and Section 5.3.
4. *Implementation:* Implementations of the approaches are detailed in Section 3.4, Section 4.4, and Section 5.4 respectively.
5. *Evaluation:* Based on the introduced implementations, we provide an evaluation for each research question in Section 3.5, Section 4.5, and Section 5.5.
6. *Conclusion:* We conclude our findings for research questions RQ1, RQ2, and RQ3 in Section 3.6, Section 4.6, and Section 5.6 respectively.

Chapter 6: Conclusion and outlook. In Chapter 6, we conclude this thesis with a summary of results and an outlook on future work.

Legend to the Symbols	
✓	The examined papers of the approach mention the criterion as supported or the context suggests it as supported. The papers do not necessarily describe their solution in detail.
(✓)	The examined papers of the approach mention the criterion, but the provided solution is incomplete or different from the description of the criterion.
?	The examined papers of the approach do not mention the criterion and we do not know if it is supported.
–	Either the examined papers of the approach mention the criterion as not supported or the criteria is not in the focus of the examined papers and thus it is probably not supported. *It is important to notice that the approach might support the criteria nevertheless.*

Table 1.1: Explanation of used symbols for the tabular categorization of analyzed works. These symbols express the degree to which a certain aspect has been fulfilled by a specific work.

2

Foundations of Knowledge Representation and Organization

In Chapter 2 we lay the foundations for the approaches we discuss in Chapter 3, Chapter 4, and Chapter 5. In particular, we introduce the work that has been done in the fields of knowledge representation, description logic, semantic web technology and its organization in the forms of ontologies, LOD, completeness assertions, semantic rule languages, and assertion of trust for retrieved triples.

2.1 Knowledge Representation

The research field of knowledge representation (KR) deals with the formal representation of knowledge about real-world subjects. However, it is not possible to completely 'know' a real-world subject, because we can never capture all perspectives and interpretations of it [Bergman 2018]. The rule of KR is therefore to 'describe the richness of the natural world' [Davis et al. 1993] and ensure that our immediate representation of subjects is in close correspondence to the according real-world subject [Bergman 2018]. In the following, we give an overview of the definition, representation, and identification of subjects as they are used to represent knowledge for this thesis:

Definition of Knowledge: Ackoff defines knowledge as know-how which enables the transformation of information into instructions [Ackoff 1989]. However, Rowley points out that definitional statements about knowledge are complex and imply 'extended definitional discussions on the nature of knowledge, its various representations and manifestations, and philosophical debates on the nature of knowledge' [Rowley 2007]. A full discussion and definition of the concept of 'knowledge' is therefore not covered by this thesis. For practical reasons, we define knowledge in this thesis as a theoretical understanding of a subject, formalized as explicit statements about this subject. Such formalized statements represent explicit knowledge as residing in documents, databases and other recorded formats in contrast to implicit or tacit knowledge as embedded in the individual [Rowley 2007]. Furthermore, it cannot always be ensured whether these formalised statements are true or false. Keeping in mind the triangle of reference[1] [Ogden et al. 1923] shown in Figure 2.1, we are also not able to draw a direct relation from a symbol to a real-world subject. We rather try to find symbols that represent the concept of a real-world subject at best. Neither does the formal representation of a concept modify the real-world subject, nor does the real-world subject influence the formal representation of its concept.

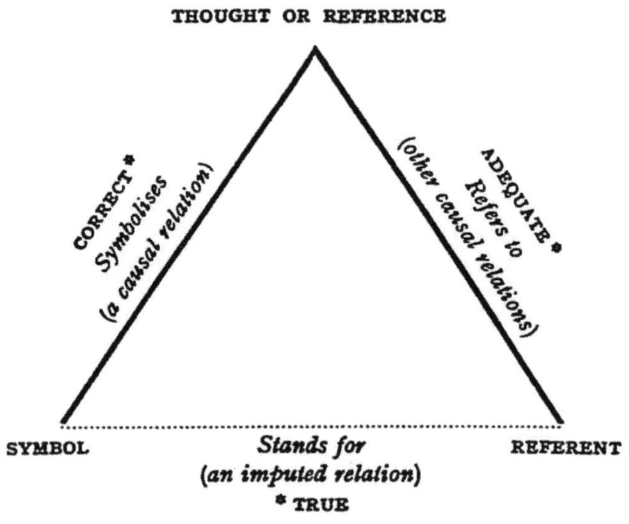

Figure 2.1: Triangle of reference by Ogden and Richards [Ogden et al. 1923]: Symbol and referent have no direct connection.

[1] Also often referred to as triangle of signification [Ogden and Richards 1956].

Formal Representation of Concepts: A concept is defined as the set of statements that every human associates with a real-world subject [Ogden and Richards 1956]. It is to be assumed that the set of statements associated with a real-world subject is varying for every human, wherefore no unique overall concept can be applied to a real-world subject. To still allow for a common understanding of real-world subjects, we have to find a formal representation that covers at least the most relevant statements commonly associated with that subject. Therefore, within the scope of this thesis, we define a concept consistent with [Klyne and Carroll 2004] as the subset of formal statements $\mathbb{RDF} = \{(s, p, o) : s \in Subject, p \in Predicate, o \in Object\}$ that are commonly shared within individual concepts of that subject. Further, we distinguish concepts that apply to the understanding of a subject within an organization including unpublished statements and concepts that are derived from openly available statements.

Identifier of Concepts: Technically, we use Uniform Resource Identifiers (URIs) as further discussed in Section 2.3.2 to uniquely identify each concept. Using URIs rather than arbitrary textual labels, we can ensure that a unique URI does not represent varying concepts. However, as concepts in contrast to real-world subjects are not necessarily unique and could be defined independently by varying authors, multiple URIs may refer to the same subject. This leads to redundant definitions of the same concept among varying sources.

2.2 Description Logic

Knowledge representation alone is not a sufficient basis for knowledge-driven data harmonization. According to Sowa, 'knowledge representation formalisms are useless without the ability to reason with them' [Sowa 2000]. If we want to deal with truth-preserving operations over symbolic structures, we have to consider the domain of logic [Brachman and Levesque 2004]. A logical formalism for knowledge description is provided by description logic (DL). A *knowledge base* in DL consists of a Terminological Box (TBox) that introduces the terminology and the Assertional Box (ABox) that contains assertions about named individuals [Baader et al. 2003, p. 50]. For this thesis, we refer to the knowledge base definition by Breitman et al.:

> 'A knowledge base is a set of axioms and assertions, written using a specific language. The terminology, or TBox, of the knowledge base consists of the set of axioms that define new concepts. The world description, assertional knowledge, or ABox of the knowledge base consists of the set of assertions. The TBox expresses intentional knowledge, which is typically stable, whereas the ABox captures extensional knowledge, which changes as the world evolves.' [Breitman et al. 2007, p. 41]

The schema of a knowledge base in DL is therefore the TBox, which provides a common terminology and is described as follows:

> 'DLs and their semantics traditionally split concepts and their relationships from the different treatment of instances and their attributes and roles, expressed as fact assertions. The concept split is known as the TBox (for terminological knowledge, the basis for T in TBox) and represents the schema or taxonomy of the domain at hand. The TBox is the structural and intensional component of conceptual relationships.' [Bergman 2009]

In addition to the schema, knowledge bases in DL as well as ontologies of the semantic web provide individuals, or instances. These individuals are not part of the schema and are therefore considered separately [Bergman 2018, p. 254]. In DL, the set of individuals is know as ABoxes which is described as follows:

> 'The second split of instances is known as the ABox (for assertions, the basis for A in ABox) and describes the attributes of instances (or individuals), the roles between instances, and other assertions about instances regarding their class membership with the TBox concepts. Both the TBox and ABox are consistent with set-theoretic principles.' [Bergman 2009]

In addition to the definition given above, automated interpretation of statements also requires rules that extend the knowledge base to a *rule knowledge base* which is defined as *'a triple $K = (T, A, R)$, where T is a TBox, A is an ABox, and R is a set of rules written as inclusion axioms'* [Baader et al. 2003, p. 78].

2.3 Basics of the Semantic Web

In this thesis, we aim to exploit knowledge that is represented using semantic web technologies. Therefore, we introduce the idea of the semantic web in this chapter and also show how to identify, describe and query resources on the semantic web.

2.3.1 Introducing the Semantic Web

The idea of a semantic web was introduced by Berners-Lee et al. in 2001. In their paper, they draft the semantic web as an extension of the World Wide Web (WWW) in which information is provided with a well-defined meaning in order to enable computers and people to work better in cooperation [Berners-Lee et al. 2001]. Therefore, the aim of the semantic web is to find ways and methods to represent information in such a manner that enables machines to use information in a way that seems to be useful and meaningful to human being, rather than enabling machines to understand the meaning of information [Hitzler et al. 2008, p. 12]. Other definitions describe the semantic web as a web of data which is described and linked in ways to establish context or semantics which follows defined grammar and language constructs [Hebeler 2009, p. 5]. In addition to the term 'semantic web', Sir Tim Berners-Lee as the inventor of the WWW coined the term Giant Global Graph (GGG) [Berners-Lee 2007] for the web of data constructed with the Resource Description Framework (RDF) in order to draw a distinction to the WWW constructed with the Hypertext Markup Language (HTML). Table 2.1 lists some basic differences between these two concepts. For building the semantic web, resources have to be identified and also described. An introduction to identifiers of the semantic web is therefore given in Section 2.3.2.

	Web of Documents	Web of Data
Tim Berners-Lee:	"World Wide Web"	"Giant Global Graph"
Transmission of:	Documents (HTML)	Data (RDF)
Client:	HTML Browser	Linked Data Browser
Navigation:	Hyperlinks	RDF Links

Table 2.1: Web of Documents vs. Web of Data.

2.3.2 Identifying Resources

One of the first steps towards the semantic web is to define unique identifiers for all distinct resources that should be used for building statements. During recent decades, a couple of identifiers which are used in the context of the web have been established. Some of them, which are relevant to this thesis, are described below.

The *URI* is used to identify web resources. On the one hand, these are pages on the web, which are provided by a web server on the WWW. On the other hand, web resources may also be other files, web services or e-mail recipients. In Request for Comments (RFC) 1630 of June 1994 URI is still defined as 'Universal Resource Identifier' [Berners-Lee 1994]. However, in later publications it is defined as 'Uniform Resource Identifier', as it is in the latest definition in RFC 3986 of January 2005. The five basic elements of a URI are in hierarchical order scheme, authority, path, query and fragment. However, only scheme and path are mandatory whereas path may also be an empty path [Berners-Lee et al. 2005a]. The common usage of a URI with a fragment identifier is also denoted as URI reference (URIref) [Breitman et al. 2007, p. 59]. However, as an exact determination between URI and URIref is not essential within this thesis, URIrefs are not explicitly stated in the following. Some examples of how to build a URI using different URI schemes derived from [Berners-Lee et al. 2005b] and [Breitman et al. 2007, p. 59] are shown in Table 2.2.

scheme:	[authority]	path	[?query]	[#fragment]
foo:	//example.com:123	/over/there	?name=ferret	#nose
urn:		example:animal:ferret:nose		
ftp:	//ftp.mysite.com	/files/foobar.txt		
http:	//www.mysite.com	/pub/foobar.html		
mailto:		em@we.org		

Table 2.2: Structure of a URI.

The *Uniform Resource Locator* (*URL*) is a special subtype of a URI, which addresses the functional requirements for locating resources on the web. This applies in addition to the identification of the resource and the primary access mechanism, such as the network location. The syntax and semantics for URL are defined in RFC 1738 from December 1994 [Berners-Lee 1994] for the first time.

Uniform Resource Name (*URN*) is another subtype of URI with the schema *urn:*. It is location-independent, globally unique and must be preserved, even if the resource itself is no longer available or exists. The URN Syntax is defined in RFC 2141 from May 1997 [Moats 1997]. However, URN is also the name given to any other URI, which has the property 'name' [Berners-Lee et al. 2005b].

The *Universally Unique IDentifier* (*UUID*) has been developed by the Open Software Foundation. It is unique across time and space and has a length of exactly 128 bits. RFC 4122 from July 2005 [Leach et al. 2005] defines a URN namespace for UUIDs. The advantage of UUIDs is that they can be generated in large quantities using an algorithm and they are also independent of a central registry. Therefore, UUIDs can also be used as transaction IDs.

The *Internationalized Resource Identifier* (*IRI*) is a supplement to URI, which allows in contrast to the URI to use characters from the unicode defined by the International Organization for Standardization (ISO) 10646 standard in addition to the characters defined as the American Standard Code for Information Interchange (ASCII). It is defined in RFC 3987 from January 2005 [Duerst and Suignard 2005]. Since allocation of IRI exist on URI, IRI can also be used instead of URI.

A classification of the different identifiers is shown in Figure 2.2. The subtypes of URI are expressed as subsets (solid circle), whereas the IRI as an extension of URI is expressed as an superset (dashed circle).

As absolute URIs may be long and complex, it could be disruptive to human users to have many of them within a document. Therefore, it is possible to state hierarchical URIs relative to a base URI and write only the distinctive part of the URI [Segaran et al. 2009, p. 64]. This part is known as the 'local name' which is unique within its namespace. In this case, there is no need to state scheme and authority part for each local name. Even some parts of the path may be skipped if they are part of the base URI [Hitzler et al. 2008, p. 28]. The base URIs

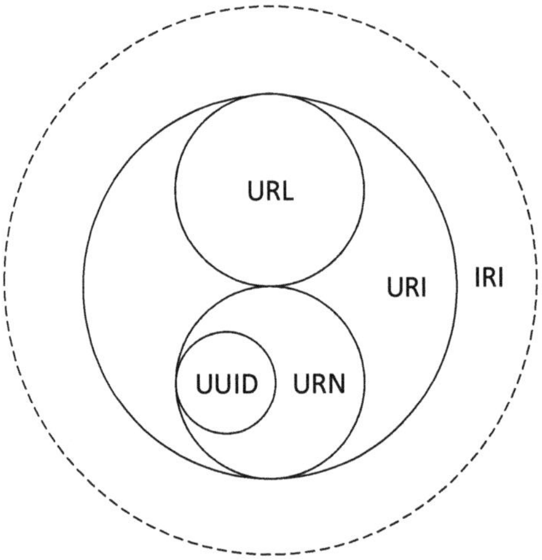

Figure 2.2: Classification of resource identifiers.

can be abbreviated by a user defined prefix. This prefix is only defined within an application and may have a completely different meaning in other contexts. However, it is recommended to select abbreviations that are easy to read and that refer the human reader to what they abbreviate [Hitzler et al. 2010, p. 26]. Identifiers of the form 'prefix:name' are also known as qualified names (QNames) [Breitman et al. 2007, p. 60] or more general, Compact URI expressions (CURIEs) as a superset of QNames [Birbeck and McCarron 2009].

In the context of this thesis, base URIs are called namespaces. These namespaces are identified by a prefix which is unique at least within the scope of this thesis. Namespaces and their abbreviations are introduced in the corresponding sections of this thesis.

2.3.3 Describing Resources

Information resources within the semantic web are described using RDF [Schreiber and Raimond 2014]. Whereas traditional HTML-documents are optimized for human users, RDF-resources are designed to be consumed and interpreted by machines. Each distinct resource is uniquely identified by an URI as stated in Section 2.3.2. Therefore, these resources can be published and reused many times.

RDF provides an approach to model knowledge for the semantic web as a graph. Resources are described by statements consisting of subject, predicate and object in accordance with the definition in Section 2.1. The predicate of such a statement can be considered as the property of a subject and the object of the statement as the value of that property [Breitman et al. 2007, p. 62].

Resources that are identified by a URI are named URI-resources, as the URI does henceforth represent that resource [Hitzler et al. 2010, p. 76]. However, as these URIs are still names and not necessarily references as stated in Section 2.3.2, Berners-Lee distinguishes between browsable and non-browsable RDF-graphs. He defines an RDF-graph as being browsable, if the server returns any RDF statement in which a looked up URI-resource appears as either subject or object [Berners-Lee 2006]. As an example, if the server returns the statement `wd:Q1040 rdfs:label "Karlsruhe"` for the URI resource `wd:Q1040`, this RDF graph is considered searchable because `wd:Q1040` appears as the subject of this statement.

In RDF, predicates are always URI-resources. Subjects and objects can be URI-resources as well, but also blank nodes (bnodes). In contrast to nodes described as URI-resource, bnodes have no global identifier as introduced in Section 2.3.2. They are therefore also known as 'anonymous nodes' [Segaran et al. 2009, p. 67] and can not be identified on the web. They rather have a local ID only for the use within the local context. This local ID may also vary on each serialization of the graph. Therefore, bnodes are only used as helper resources with a simply structural function [Hitzler et al. 2010, p. 43].

Besides URI-resources and bnodes the object of a statement in RDF could also be a simple literal value. As long as no datatype is defined for a literal in RDF, they are called untyped literals and are always interpreted as strings. Literals are not eligible to be the origin of edges in an RDF graph, that means we cannot use a literal as subject to make direct statements about it [Hitzler et al. 2010, p. 24]. Therefore, the statement `"Karlsruhe"ex:isLabelOf wd:Q1040` is not a valid statement in RDF. However, a literal value can have a type (e.g. integer, boolean, string) or a language (e.g. English, German) associated with it [Segaran et al. 2009, p. 68]. As an example, the statement `wd:Q1040 rdfs:label "Karlsruhe"@de` indicates that `"Karlsruhe"` represents a German-language literal value (language code 'de').

2.3.4 Querying Resources

For querying RDF, the World Wide Web Consortium (W3C) introduced the SPARQL Protocol and RDF Query Language. Its first draft was published by W3C in 2004 where it was described as 'Simple Protocol and RDF Query Language' [Prud'hommeaux and Seaborne 2004] and the latest version under the name 'SPARQL 1.1 Query Language' in 2013 [Harris and Seaborne 2013a]. SPARQL uses simple graphs as fundamental query patters and query variables [Hitzler et al. 2010, p. 262], defined with leading question mark as *?nameOfVariable*. These query graphs again make use of the triple-pattern subject-predicate-object as introduced in Section 2.3.3. For example, a query for `wd:Q1040 rdfs:label ?label` returns the value `"Karlsruhe"@de` for the query variable `?label` using the previously introduced statement. The SPARQL syntax does also allow to abbreviate the namespaces as introduced in Section 2.3.2 when stating the namespace abbreviation as prefix. When using multiple triples within one single SPARQL query, these triples have to be separated by full stops [Hitzler et al. 2010, p. 263]. SPARQL queries may also contain literals as object of the query triple. The type of the literal is stated with *^^type* and the language with *@lang*. Another use of variables in SPARQL is the assigning of values with the SPARQL keyword *VALUES*, which is available since SPARQL version 1.1 [Harris and Seaborne 2013b]. To get each unique URI that matches the query pattern only once, the keyword *DISTINCT* can be assigned after *SELECT*. A list of values as variable in SPARQL is especially useful, when multiple predicates have the same meaning. All predicates with the same meaning can then be assigned to a variable such as *?predicate* and SPARQL will find all triples with any of these predicates.

2.4 Organizing the Semantic Web

In order to organize knowledge in the semantic web and other semantic systems, different layers of the semantic web technology stack as shown in Figure 2.3 have to

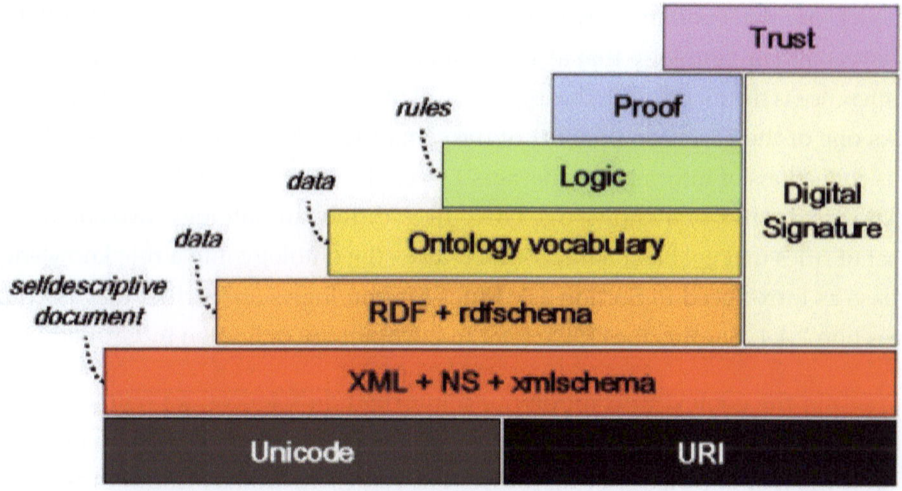

Figure 2.3: Layers of the semantic web technology stack [Koivunen and Miller 2001]: Ontologies are built on top of RDF that supports logic for proofing statements. Trust can be implemented on top of proofs and digital signatures.

be addressed[2]. This section therefore introduces ontologies, LOD, and definitions for completeness, rules, and trust.

2.4.1 Ontologies

Model	Structure
Glossary	Terms with explanation
Folksonomy	Result of social tagging
Taxonomy	Hierarchy of concepts
Thesaurus	Extension of the taxonomy to similarity and synonym relation
Topic Map	XML with topics, Associations and scope
Ontology	Relation between terms, enables inference

Table 2.3: Semantic Data Description Models.

Various models with varying semantic expressiveness have been developed for the electronic representation of knowledge. Table 2.3 shows an overview of some common data models in ascending sequence of their semantic richness, where

[2]See http://www.w3.org/2007/03/layerCake.png for the W3C version of the semantic web technology stack. A more recent interpretation can be accessed at: https://smiy.wordpress.com/2011/01/10/the-common-layered-semantic-web-technology-stack

a glossary that contains only terms with their explanation is the model with the lowest and an ontology that also contains relations between terms and enables inference is the model with the highest level of semantics [Pellegrini 2006, p. 9-27]. As one of the basic components of the semantic web, ontologies are employed as collections of information [Berners-Lee et al. 2001]. An ontology contains the TBox and ABox of a knowledge base. In addition, an ontology also contains a set of rules that enable inference which turns the ontology into a rule knowledge base as introduced in Section 2.2. Rules for ontologies are further discussed in Section 2.4.4. For this thesis, we refer to the ontology definition by Gruber:

> 'In the context of computer and information sciences, an ontology defines a set of representational primitives with which to model a domain of knowledge or discourse. The representational primitives are typically classes (or sets), attributes (or properties), and relationships (or relations among class members). The definitions of the representational primitives include information about their meaning and constraints on their logically consistent application. In the context of database systems, ontology can be viewed as a level of abstraction of data models, analogous to hierarchical and relational models, but intended for modeling knowledge about individuals, their attributes, and their relationships to other individuals. Ontologies are typically specified in languages that allow abstraction away from data structures and implementation strategies; in practice, the languages of ontologies are closer in expressive power to first-order logic than languages used to model databases. For this reason, ontologies are said to be at the semantic level, whereas database schema are models of data at the logical or physical level. Due to their independence from lower level data models, ontologies are used for integrating heterogeneous databases, enabling interoperability among disparate systems, and specifying interfaces to independent, knowledge-based services. In the technology stack of the semantic web standards, ontologies are called out as an explicit layer. There are now standard languages and a variety of commercial and open source tools for creating and working with ontologies.' [Gruber 2009]

Ontologies are furthermore distinguished in ontologies describing general knowledge called *upper-level ontologies* and ontologies to model expert knowledge of a given knowledge domain, called *domain ontologies*.

2.4.2 Linked Open Data

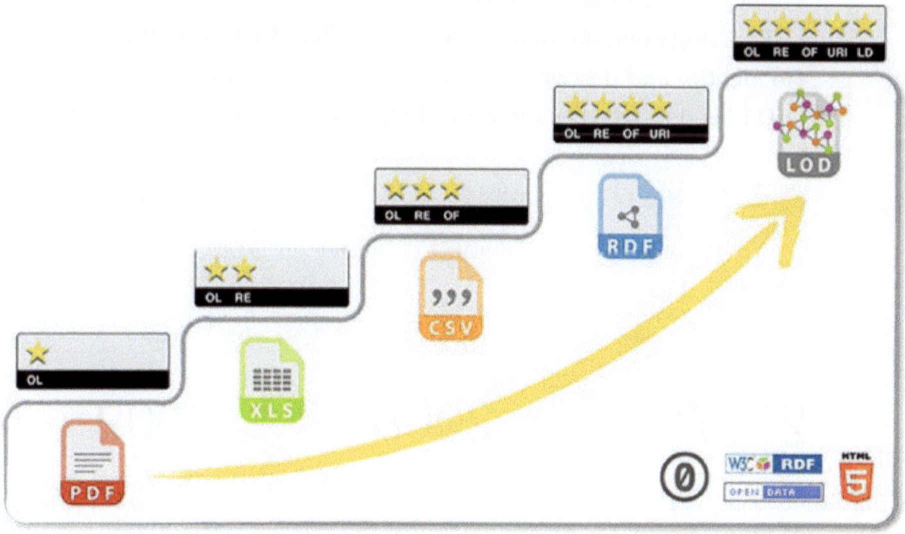

Figure 2.4: Levels of open data [Berners-Lee 2009]: 5-star data has to be machine processable and interlinked with other resources.

The advantage of formalizing knowledge is not only to derive a common understanding of managed concepts within organizations, but to build a global 'web of data', which is described and interlinked in meaningful and machine-processable ways and follows well-defined grammar and language constructs [Hebeler 2009, p. 5]. All data that is published on the web in accordance with the LOD principles becomes also part of a GGG [Heath and Bizer 2011, p. 98]. The first idea of a GGG was introduced in 2007 [Berners-Lee 2007] and became concrete by the definition of LOD in 2009 [Berners-Lee 2009]. Figure 2.4 illustrates the different levels of open data according to Berners-Lee. These levels are summarized as follows, where each level augments all previous levels:

1. **OL** Available on the web (whatever format) but with an open licence which does not restrain the reuse of the data for free, such as one of the Creative Commons (CC) licenses.
2. **RE** Available as machine-readable structured data (e.g. excel instead of image scan of a table).
3. **OF** Available as non-proprietary format (e.g. comma-separated values (CSV) instead of excel).
4. **URI** Using open standards from W3C (URIs, RDF and SPARQL) to identify and describe things in order to allow for references.
5. **LD** Link data to other sources of LOD in order to provide context.

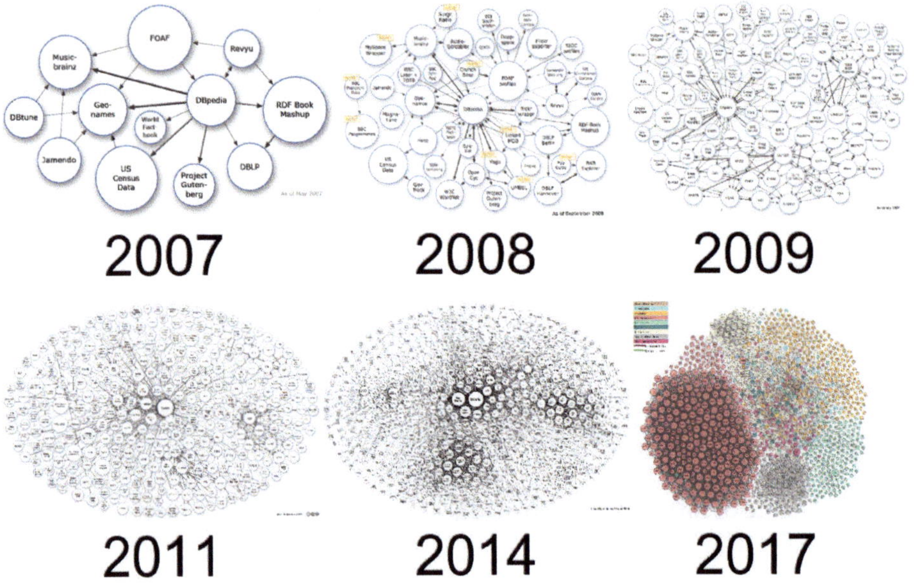

Figure 2.5: Growth of Linked Open Data since 2007 [Abele et al. 2017]: The amount of data sets published as Linked Open Data has increased from twelve in 2007 to more than a thousand in 2017.

The availability of LOD is continuously and rapidly growing (see [Bizer et al. 2009; Hausenblas 2009; Heath and Bizer 2011]). The growth of openly available data sets and their interlinkage within LOD is visualized by the LOD cloud diagram [Abele et al. 2017]. The evolution of this diagram within the first ten years is visualized in Figure 2.5. The figure shows the graph of available datasets published as LOD in the years 2007, 2008, 2009, 2011, 2014 and 2017. The size of the nodes of each graph corresponds to the number of triples in each dataset [Cyganiak and Jentzsch 2014]. Datasets that are interlinked with at least 50 RDF triples are indicated by an arrow, the thickness of that arrow corresponds to the number of links [Cyganiak and Jentzsch 2014]. Figure 2.5 shows that the amount of data sets published as LOD has increased within ten years from twelve data sets in 2007 to more than a thousand in 2017. Among the first LOD data sets since 2007 is also the crowd-sourced community project DBpedia[3] that provides general knowledge extracted from structured content of the information created in various Wikimedia projects and is still a major part of the LOD cloud. Rather than extracting a data scheme *from* heterogeneous Wikimedia projects, Wikidata provides a homogeneous and collaborative data scheme that can be applied *to* those projects [Vrandecic and Krötzsch 2014]. DBpedia and Wikidata still coexist as two major resources of general knowledge of the LOD cloud, besides hundreds of domain-specific LOD data sets that are deeply interlinked within the LOD cloud.

However, although the web infrastructure has proven successful in being able to host the massive publishing initiative of LOD, the challenges faced when consuming LOD and exploiting its content for the purposes of building applications are only now becoming clear. In particular, querying LOD requires new techniques and new ways of thinking forged upon the expertise collected in related areas such as databases, distributed computing, and information retrieval [Harth et al. 2014, p. 47]. As data and documents of LOD are distributed over many sites, the GGG has to be consumed similar to the WWW. This means that GGG search engines can index RDF links and infer relationships. By employing the follow-your-nose method of discovery (manual traverse), it is possible to start with any web resource that contains links and navigate from site to site and aggregate all related data that is retrieved along the way. This kind of information retrieval can also be supported by tools that follow the crawling pattern such as Sindice, SameAs.org or Data Hub [Wood et al. 2014, pp. 62-66]. Applications that implement that crawling pattern, but also applications that rely on other patterns, typically implement modules for data access, data integration and local data storage [Heath and Bizer 2011, p. 98].

[3] https://wiki.dbpedia.org/about

2.4.3 Assumption of Truth

For the interpretation of sensor observations, we have to determine the level of completeness of observation data, including assumptions about the truth value of a statement. The assumption of truth is categorized in different levels [Baader et al. 2003; Doherty et al. 2000]. The following levels are relevant for this thesis:

- The open-world assumption is the assumption that the truth value of a statement may be true irrespective of whether or not it is known to be true.
- The closed-world assumption is the assumption that the truth value of a statement is only true if it is known to be true, otherwise it is considered as false.
- A locally closed environment refers to a knowledge base that is treated under closed-world semantics, although the underlying concepts are derived from an open domain under an open-world assumption. This allows for completeness assertions as required for our approach.

Open-World and Closed-World Assumptions: For this thesis, we refer to the definitions of closed-world assumption and open-world assumption by Baader et al.:

> 'While a database instance represents exactly one interpretation, namely the one where classes and relations in the schema are interpreted by the objects and tuples in the instance, an ABox represents many different interpretations, namely all its models. As a consequence, absence of information in a database instance is interpreted as negative information, while absence of information in an ABox only indicates lack of knowledge. [...] This means that, while information in a database is always understood to be complete, the information in an ABox is in general viewed as being incomplete. The semantics of ABoxes is therefore sometimes characterized as an "open-world" semantics, while the traditional semantics of databases is characterized as a "closed-world" semantics.' [Baader et al. 2003, pp. 74-75]

Locally Closed Environment: The Open-world assumption applies especially to LOD, as LOD due to its RDF-based nature aims to be extendable by anyone at anytime and it is not assumed that complete information about any resource is available [Klyne and Carroll 2004]. It is therefore not possible to verify the truth value of statements that are not known to be true. However, the verification of truth as it is provided under the closed-world assumption is a basic requirement for the automated processing of sensor observations. In order to address both, the open nature of LOD and the requirement of verifiable truth, we employ the concept of a locally closed environment [Doherty et al. 2000] for our approach. This allows to verify the truth of statements, even if the locally closed environment includes statements that are retrieved from LOD. The locally closed environment can be considered as the closed part of a partial-closed world assumption [Razniewski and Nutt 2014; Razniewski et al. 2016].

Corporate Knowledge Graph: Within the scope of this thesis, the concept of a locally closed environment is implemented as a *corporate knowledge graph* [Bellomarini et al. 2017]. As the term *knowledge graph* is used to describe different knowledge representation applications [Ehrlinger and Wöß 2016], we refer a knowledge graph according to the definition of Färber et al. as an RDF graph [Färber et al. 2018] as introduced in Section 2.3.3. We further define a corporate knowledge graph as a knowledge graph which is completely under control of a single organization. Such an organization could be an enterprise, NGO, civil service, or any other kind of organization that pursues knowledge managed. Similar concepts are also known as enterprise knowledge graph [Masuch 2014; Aasman 2017; Hogan et al. 2020], industrial knowledge graph [Hubauer et al. 2018], or proprietary knowledge graph [Fensel et al. 2020].

2.4.4 Semantic Rule Languages

Depending on the intended assumption of truth discussed in Section 2.4.3, we have to apply a set of rules that enable inference and allow for automated processing of sensor observations for a knowledge-driven harmonization. These rules turn the knowledge base into a rule knowledge base as introduced in Section 2.2. Rules, reasoning and constraint checking on RDF data are supported by different rule languages which all have their strengths and weaknesses as discussed in the following:

OWL Rules: Although the Web Ontology Language (OWL)[4] is primarily an ontology language that provides classes, properties, individuals, and data values for RDF documents, it also includes basic mechanisms for validation and inference such as co-reference resolution respectively distinguishing and property restrictions for values and cardinality that can be executed by OWL reasoners.

SWRL Rules: As OWL allows only for basic reasoning, the Semantic Web Rule Language (SWRL)[5] has been introduced as an extension for the OWL terminology which makes use of the Rule Markup Language for more advanced rules, for example derived properties and assertions. SWRL does also provide a set of build-in functions for comparisons, math operations, and XML Schema Definition (XSD) data type specific manipulation functions.

SPIN Rules: However, SWRL does not provide templates for shape constraints or a notion for user-defined functions. These limitations are addressed by the SPARQL Inferencing Notation (SPIN)[6], which aims to provide general business rules expressed in SPARQL. SPIN therefore allows for a more flexible implementation of user-defined models and constraints as they are required for our work.

SHACL Rules: Knublauch and Kontokostas have introduced the Shapes Constraint Language [Knublauch and Kontokostas 2017] which can be regarded as the legitimate successor of SPIN[7]. It aims to describe and constraint especially the contents of RDF graphs by defining shapes that specify conditions that apply to a given RDF node using a high-level vocabulary. Shapes Constraint Language (SHACL) was firstly introduced as W3C public working[8] draft in October 2015 and is now available as W3C recommendation for validation mechanisms of RDF graphs, lastly updated on 20 July 2017. The definition of required attributes, cardinality of relations or datatype restrictions in the form of shapes is an important aspect to ensure data quality for any productive system. The creation of SHACL shapes is supported by various tools, e.g. a dedicated SHACL plugin[9] for the Protégé editor or as part of TopBraid Composer[10]. As SHACL shapes are also

[4] https://www.w3.org/TR/owl2-overview/
[5] https://www.w3.org/Submission/SWRL/
[6] http://spinRDF.org/
[7] http://spinRDF.org/spin-shacl.html
[8] https://www.w3.org/TR/2015/WD-shacl-20151008/
[9] https://github.com/fekaputra/shacl-plugin
[10] https://www.topquadrant.com/products/topbraid-composer/

defined in RDF, they share the same format as the validated data, in contrast to e.g. SWRL rules. This eases the required technology stack and reduces the amount of used libraries.

Due to the discussed advantages of SHACL as a lightweight and well supported semantic rule language that allows for defining homogenous shapes that can be applied to heterogeneous RDF data, we pursue the application of SHACL as a suitable framework to address heterogeneity in RDF models of sensor observations. In addition to the validation of shapes, we aim to employ SHACL for defining inclusion axioms that enable inference on heterogenous sensor observations.

2.4.5 Provenance and Trust

When exploiting LOD for corporate knowledge graphs, it is crucial to be able to assert the trustworthiness, reputation, and reliability of retrieved triples [Theoharis et al. 2011]. Although trust in the form of trusted agents and services or digital signatures is a fundamental component of the semantic web since its first draft [Berners-Lee et al. 2001], the implementation of trust for the semantic web is still work in progress [Iancu and Sandu 2016] and a unique standard for trust in LOD is missing. Current approaches implement trust by either modeling trust explicitly, deriving trust from provenance information, building trust based on cryptography or deriving trust from statistical analytics. These four techniques are discussed in the following:

Model Trust Explicitly: Trust can be modelled explicitly either as boolean trust assessment in order to find which statements are trusted or not, or as a ranked trust assessment where every statement is associated with a rank that indicates the most statements and statements that are completely untrusted [Theoharis et al. 2011]. The asserted trust values are materialized as explicit properties that specify one level of trust on an implementation specific scale [Golbeck et al. 2003]. Trust assessment can be provided centralized by a trusted authority or distributed [Shirgahi et al. 2017]. A popular approach for distributed trust assessment is creating or employing a so-called *web of trust* as a trust network on the semantic web, in which each user maintains trust in a small number of other users [Caronni 2000; Golbeck et al. 2003; Richardson et al. 2003]. Having users specify which others they trust leverages this web of trust to estimate a user's belief in statements supplied by any other user [Richardson et al. 2003]. Trust can also be evaluated using explicit reputations of agents who used resources or the trust of the creators of a resource [Bok et al. 2019]. In addition to trust of the creators, there are also techniques emerging to explicitly express trust of detailed reasoning processes when statements are being inferred by reasoners [Moreau 2010]. However, explicitly modeled trust depends on a person's subjective belief at a certain point in time [Sacco and Breslin 2014] and distributed trust assessment depends on receiving enough introductions from agents that are member of a trust federation and have some degree of trust in a source and its policies [Chadwick and Hibbert 2013].

Derive Trust from Provenance: Besides modeling trust explicitly, the provenance of statements can also be tracked, recorded, and made available to its users in order to ensure that statements from different sources can be trusted and used appropriately [Ram and Liu 2012]. Provenance of a statement can be considered as metadata that expresses source and history of that statement, therefore the trust of a statement can be estimated by tracing the according provenance information [Bok et al. 2019]. In order to make the provenance of statements explicit, we have to be able to make statements about statements. A description of a statement using the built-in vocabulary of RDF, namely the type *rdf:Statement*, and the properties *rdf:subject*, *rdf:predicate*, and *rdf:object*, is known as *reification* of statements [Manola and Miller 2004]. However, adding a reification quad for every triple causes at least a five fold increase in the total number of triples and adding a statement about such reified triples requires minimally one extra triple which then also has to be duplicated for every reified triple that it describes [Carroll and Stickler 2004]. The RDF semantics does also explicitly not interpret reification as a form of quotation [Hayes 2004]. To avoid these problems several authors propose quads, consisting of an RDF triple in conjunction with a URI, bnode or ID, which could be used to refer to information sources that provide context knowledge or to uniquely identify the triple for further statements about that triple. A reformulation of quads in which the fourth element's distinct syntactic and semantic properties are clearly distinguished is provided with the concept of named graphs. A named graph is therefore defined as an RDF graph which is uniquely identified by a URI that could be referred either in the graph itself, in other graphs, or not at all [Carroll et al. 2005]. Using the previously introduced example, we can add an URI with the QName `ex:ckg` to identify the graph that contains the triple, turning it into the quadruple `ex:ckg {wd:Q1040 rdfs:label "Karlsruhe"@de}`. In order to make a statement about this graph, we can refer to it using its URI. As an example, we may state that the graph origins from wikidata, identified by QName `wd:Q2013`. A named graph stating that provenance could then be serialized as `ex:ps {ex:ckg ex:origin wd:Q2013}`. By defining a named graph per statement it is also possible to annotate each statement separately and abstractly describe the provenance of a statement as a set of appropriate, unique, abstract labels (so-called *provenance tokens* in relational modeling terms) [Theoharis et al. 2011]. Provenance of statements should be tracked immediately at source and also for each manipulating event, as post hoc tracking of provenance is a very difficult task and almost impossible to achieve [Ram and Liu 2012]. However, none of the previously discussed approaches specifies how provenance itself should be represented, they rather offer a placeholder for its representation [Moreau 2010]. A specific representation of provenance information does therefore require additional provenance modeling, such as it is provided by the PROV Ontology [Lebo et al. 2013] or the Web Annotation Data Model [Sanderson et al. 2017]. A more serious limitation of deriving trust from provenance information originates in the fact that existing provenance information cannot provide objective trust evaluation, because trust in provenance still depends on users input of their subjective trust information [Bok et al. 2019]. This issue has therefore to be addressed individually when deriving trust from provenance information. In addition, there is often a trade-off between the expressiveness of provenance models and the system utilization for processing the corresponding provenance expressions. It is therefore reasonable to rely on less-informative abstract provenance models for systems that only need to support a subset of the provenance expressions in order to provide improved performance [Theoharis et al. 2011].

Trust by Cryptography: Objective trust for LOD could be provided by employing cryptographic systems that technically proof the authenticity of a statement and prevent malicious manipulation. An approach to achieve this are digital signatures for statements, which are encrypted blocks of data that computers and agents can use to verify that the statement has been provided by a specific trusted source [Berners-Lee et al. 2001]. However, even digitally signed statements can only achieve that level of trust which is associated with the key that was used to sign it. To provide a public and trusted infrastructure for keys, either a hierarchical key infrastructure based on certification authorities or a decentralized infrastructure based on asymmetric cryptography (e.g. RSA or Diffie-Hellman based) that provides peer authentication could be employed [Caronni 2000]. Although digital signatures are widely used to proof the *authenticity of sources* of web content providing X.509 certificates signed by a trusted authority, including sources of LOD such as Wikidata or DBpedia, digital signatures are still hardly used to proof the *authenticity of statements*. Approaches to sign RDF statements digitally in order to proof the authenticity of statements are discussed by several authors [Carroll 2003; Carroll et al. 2005; Tummarello et al. 2005; Bizer 2006; Kasten 2016], however, they are not widely adopted to LOD yet. Iancu and Sandu therefore propose the usage of blockchain systems for providing a trust layer for the semantic web [Iancu and Sandu 2016].

Trust by Statistical Probability: An alternative to model trust explicitly, derive it from provenance or gain it by cryptography are approaches that employ statistical probability in order to estimate the trustworthiness of statements. For example, the approach of Nolle et al. is based on the assumption that the more data sources are integrated, the higher is the probability that correct assertions occur redundantly. Applying this approach to four LOD sources within the domain of library science has shown that 39.5% of the detected conflicts could be solved with a precision up to 97% [Nolle et al. 2017]. Shirgahi et al. propose to estimate the value of websites reputation by communication parameters of web networks such as the number of links to these pages and evaluate the trust based on estimated reputation [Shirgahi et al. 2017]. A similar approach is pursued by Diefenbach and Thalhammer who propose to calculate page rank scores on RDF graphs [Diefenbach and Thalhammer 2018].

The discussion of the introduced techniques reveals the unresolved issues for implementing trust for the semantic web and especially LOD. We therefore argue for handling trust locally within the corporate knowledge graph itself in order to build a practicable solution, rather than relying on techniques that are neither fully standardized nor fully implemented for LOD.

2.5 Summary of Chapter 2

In Chapter 2, we have introduced the formal representation of knowledge according to Ogden and Richards as it is used for this thesis. This concept is technically implemented consistent with Klyne and Carroll by modeling the resources using RDF. An important fact is that resources are identified globally unique using URIs which allows us to clearly relate to a concept, regardless of the specific conditions of implementation. We have also introduced endeavors to publish a shared understanding of concepts identified by stable URIs published as LOD. Due to the heterogeneity in modelling and semantics of LOD, we introduced and discussed semantic rule languages that enable reasoning and validation on an abstracted semantic level that is independent of the information source. As outcome of our discussion, we have identified SHACL as a suitable framework to address heterogeneity in RDF models. We also have discussed techniques to assert trustworthiness of retrieved triples and revealed the unresolved issues for implementing trust for the semantic web. Based on these foundations, we propose an architecture for meaningful interpretation of heterogenous sensor observations by exploiting LOD for this thesis. Before we investigate how to exploit LOD specifically in the context of environmental sensor observations, we discuss how to exploit LOD in general within a corporate knowledge graph in Chapter 3.

3

Leveraging Knowledge Graphs with Linked Open Data

In Chapter 3, we present our findings for answering the research question of identifying and sufficiently addressing the challenges in exploiting Linked Open Data as a lever for the knowledge contained in corporate knowledge graphs (RQ1). This involves testing the hypothesis of whether the comprehensive knowledge which is provided as Linked Open Data can be exploited to leverage the knowledge represented in a corporate knowledge graph (H1). Contents of this chapter have been published in [Frank and Zander 2017b], [Frank and Zander 2017c] and [Frank and Zander 2017a].

3.1 Introduction to Chapter 3

Section 3.1 provides the motivation for research question RQ1 in Section 3.1.1, outlines the addressed challenges in Section 3.1.2, and lists the contributions to these challenges in Section 3.1.3.

3.1.1 Motivation for exploiting LOD

Building meaningful corporate knowledge graphs for organizations such as enterprises, NGOs, or civil services is a complex and labour intensive task [Ehrlinger and Wöß 2016; Hubauer et al. 2018; Hogan et al. 2020]. Complex because of modeling decisions that have to be made in terms of granularity, structure, and referencing within the corporate knowledge graph. Labour intensive because of all the statements that have to be formalized in order to describe each concept, including classes, properties, and instances. Also, not all concepts of real-world subjects which are relevant to an organization do exclusively belong to the intellectual property of that organization. It is rather the case that many concepts such as regions, persons, technical, legal bases or even products are universally valid, irrespective of their definition within a corporate knowledge graph. It is therefore likely that someone else has formalized and published statements about that subject before. Modeling those concepts individually for each corporate knowledge graph therefore causes several issues: multiple definitions of the same concepts lead to expensive *redundant* work, also the varying definitions are potentially *inconsistent* which could cause conflicts for inclusion axioms and lead to different conclusions in various corporate knowledge graphs. Statements about a real-world subject within an isolated corporate knowledge graph may also be *incomplete* or *not trusted* as mechanisms to verify these statements are missing.

As explained in Section 2.4.3, we aim to employ a corporate knowledge graph as a locally closed environment to enable verifiable truth values of statements for the automated processing of sensor observations. Therefore, we have to pay special attention when including data from sources other than the curated corporate knowledge graph, such as it is the case for LOD. As a consequence, Chapter 3 addresses the following research question:

RQ1: How can Linked Open Data be exploited as a lever for the knowledge contained in corporate knowledge graphs?

From research questions RQ1 we derive the following hypothesis:

H1: The comprehensive knowledge which is provided as Linked Open Data can be exploited to leverage the knowledge represented in a corporate knowledge graph.

If the benefit of such an approach is greater than its implementation effort, we consider hypothesis H1 to be confirmed. Keeping in mind that each concept refers to the set of statements that every human associates with a real-world subject (see Section 2.1), we would also conclude that leveraging a corporate knowledge graph with LOD leads to better founded knowledge representation. The reason for this better founded knowledge representation is the inclusion of statements and context knowledge that humans outside of the organizational context associate with the respective real-world subjects. A well-curated corporate knowledge graph that includes trusted statements of LOD would therefore increase its information value. In addition, the costs of corporate knowledge management could be reduced by avoiding redundant definitions of concepts within a corporate knowledge graph, if these concepts are already defined and published as LOD. However, if the implementation effort exceeds the benefits, we consider hypothesis H1 to be refuted. We test hypothesis H1 in Section 3.5.

As we have defined a corporate knowledge graph in Section 2.4.3 to be a corporate specific implementation of an RDF graph, it could be implemented as an RDF store that is maintained by semantic web experts who curate the content using SPARQL queries. However, this approach would limit the group of potential contributors to those of semantic web experts. In order to allow a larger group of domain experts, who are not necessarily semantic web experts, to curate the content of the corporate knowledge graph, Krötzsch et al. have introduced an approach that allows users of a collaborative wiki platform to create, curate, and query semantic statements using established wiki markup [Krötzsch et al. 2006]. The semantic statements of such semantic wiki systems do also resemble a collaboratively created corporate knowledge graph in accordance with the definition in Section 2.4.3.

Although existing semantic wiki approaches (relevant examples are discussed in Section 3.2.2) are built upon established semantic web technologies, their utilization is primarily bound to a syntactic level. Support for wiki users in reusing established vocabularies for a common terminology, the TBox in description logics as introduced in Section 2.2, and exploiting public available properties of entities that are published as LOD in the ABox are still neglected, as those systems rather focus on building organization-specific domain ontologies as introduced in Section 2.4.1. In order to reduce complexity for wiki users, these ontologies aim to be lightweight and therefore do not incorporate a generalized schema knowledge and its semantics per default (cf. [Janowicz et al. 2014]) which hinders retrieving knowledge from external sources such as other organizations or LOD. As a consequence, current semantic wiki systems are also not able to exploit and benefit from the growing availability of LOD. Moreover, the exploitation of additional knowledge from external sources hosted by other organizations or LOD as well as sharing knowledge in a meaningful way across organizational boundaries is difficult due to the lack of a common vocabulary among these approaches.

In Section 3.1.2 we discuss the challenges that have to be addressed in order to leverage the statements of semantic wiki systems with LOD.

3.1.2 Challenges Addressed in Chapter 3

The challenges that arise when exploiting LOD within a corporate knowledge graph in general are identified as follows:

As discussed in Section 2.1, concepts of real-world subjects which are published as LOD could be defined independently by varying authors, and multiple URIs may refer to the same subject. A basic requirement for exploiting LOD within a corporate knowledge graph is therefore the *identification of equal concepts* among multiple sources of formalized knowledge representations such as LOD, even if these concepts are referred by different URIs.

Once similar concepts are identified and interlinked, *redundant* and *inconsistent* statements can be identified. Redundant statements could support the trustworthiness of a statement, providing that the provenance of each statement is independent of each other and not a mirrored information which may also mirror a statement that conflicts to a statement which is known to be true. For inconsistent statements, it has to be determined which statement should be regarded as the most appropriate one and therefore considered as fact within a corporate knowledge graph.

Besides redundant and inconsistent statements, we also have to identify and handle *incomplete concepts*. Due to the open-world assumption of LOD as discussed in Section 2.4.3, a mechanism is required that evaluates the completeness of a concepts w.r.t. to a specified schema when including the concepts to a corporate knowledge graph. If no explicit schema is provided for a specific concept , there still could be an implicit schema that applies to all relevant concepts of classes, properties and individuals of the same category. When deriving that schema, e.g. from related concepts, it can be employed in order to identify statements that are likely missing. For example, if 80% of all concepts of relevant weather stations provide statements about their geographic coordinates, it is likely that these statements are missing for the other 20% of concepts.

Our approach addresses these challenges in the context of semantic wiki software in order to leverage the semantic statements of a wiki that assemble a corporate knowledge graph. We detail the contributions to address these challenges in Section 3.1.3.

3.1.3 Contributions

In order to contribute to the domain of semantic wiki software, we propose a generic extension for wiki systems that allows to leverage the semantic statements of a wiki with statements from LOD (C1).

The proposed approach aims to overcome the limitation of ambiguous schema definitions in various corporate knowledge graphs as identified in Section 3.1.2 and provides an alignment to a common schema definition by supporting the annotation of organization-specific schema knowledge with the common and well-established terminology of LOV [Janowicz et al. 2014] within semantic wiki systems.

Based on the resulting extended and interlinked schema knowledge, the TBox of ontologies, additional statements about a concept in the TBox can be queried directly from LOD and integrated within a semantic wiki system, and customized to the corporate context.

In addition, the interlinked TBox helps to integrate concepts of individuals for the ABox of a corporate knowledge graph and to interlink these concepts with representations of an equal concept which is available as LOD. Statements retrieved from LOD about both, concepts of classes and properties in the TBox and also concepts of individuals in the ABox, help users in maintaining properties of concepts described in the corporate knowledge graph. The correctness and validity of concepts can be evaluated on the basis of acquired externally hosted statements where a common and shared agreement is prevalent.

The inclusion of potentially not trusted, inconsistent or redundant statements and potentially incompletely defined concepts within a corporate knowledge graph poses the additional challenge of how such statements can be evaluated automatically and correctly within the respective context. We address this challenge by *maintaining provenance information* for each statement that allows algorithms to maintain a corporate knowledge graph by applying domain-specific rules that evaluate statements based on their provenance. The trust value of each statement is quantified based on the tracked provenance information with a value in the range of 0.0 to 1.0. A trust value of 0.0 means that the statement was proven to be false, 0.5 that the statement could be neither proved nor disproved and 1.0 that the statement was proven to be true. We therefore summarize our contributions to the domain of semantic wiki software as follows:

C1.1: Provide a mechanism to suggest and curate LOD resources that match the organization-specific concepts described in a wiki system. In order to derive a preferable complete overview of a concept in LOD, we have to prepare a set of URIs which also refer to this concept. We contribute to a solution of this issue by suggesting and curating equality links for semantic wiki systems that leverage organizational specific concepts.

C1.2: Identify *statements that are redundant* within the corporate knowledge graph federated of statements from a semantic wiki and LOD. If statements retrieved from varying sources about the same concepts are identified as equal, this statement is included in the corporate knowledge graph only once. However, in order to quantify the trust value for this statement, the provenance information of all applicable sources is included as well. The trust value of the statement is defined by the maximum trust value among all tracked sources of this statement.

C1.3: Identify *statements that are inconsistent* within the corporate knowledge graph federated of statements from a semantic wiki and LOD. If statements retrieved from varying sources about the same concepts are identified as conflicting, only the statement from the source with the highest trust value is included and the conflicting values are ignored or treated as false.

C1.4: Identify *statements that are likely missing* according to schema knowledge in order to describe concepts within a semantic wiki. When a schema is explicitly defined or implicitly learned for relevant concepts of classes, properties and individuals of the same category, statements that apply to most but not all of these concepts can be identified as missing statements for the concepts that do not provide that statement. Additional sources can be queried automatically for these missing statements. If a missing statement can not be found on any of the known sources, it is marked as missing for manual curation.

C1.5: Estimate *trust for statements* used within a semantic wiki, including statements derived from LOD. If a statement is not supported by a trust value of more than 0.5, additional sources with higher trust values can be queried for that statement. If that statement can still not be supported with a trust value of more than 0.5, it is marked as not trusted for manual curation.

Chapter 3 is organized as follows: In Section 3.2, we discuss current semantic wiki approaches with respect to the implementation of semantic web technology both on a syntactic and semantic level. In Section 3.3, we detail our approach of interlinking corporate knowledge graphs with LOD. The implementation of the approach is described in Section 3.4. In Section 3.5, we discuss the potential of leverage by interlinking user created statements with Wikidata and DBpedia as two major resources for LOD. We conclude Chapter 3 in Section 3.6.

3.2 Related Work

In Section 3.2, we analyze the related work for research question RQ1. First, we define the criteria for the review in Section 3.2.1. Next, we introduce and discuss related work with respect to *semantic wiki software* with special emphasis to their openness towards a semantic technology stack in Section 3.2.2 and *approaches for linked data management* in Section 3.2.3. We summarize the current state and the limitations of all introduced approaches in Section 3.2.4.

3.2.1 Criteria for the Literature Review

We discuss the approaches introduced in Section 3.2.2 and Section 3.2.3 with respect to the following characteristics:

- **Employ LOV:** Does the approach employ and reuse LOV for the TBox in order to support data integration on a schema level?
- **Link LOD:** Does the approach provide a mechanism to link corporate concepts to LOD concepts?
- **Exploit LOD:** Does the approach provide a mechanism to complete corporate facts about an entity with facts that can be retrieved from a linked LOD entity?
- **Track Provenance:** Does the approach keep track of provenance for statements within the corporate knowledge graph, especially if they are retrieved from an external source?
- **Versioning:** Does the approach provide a versioning mechanism for facts about an entity in the corporate knowledge graph?
- **Export RDF:** Does the approach provide a mechanism to export facts about entities captured within the corporate knowledge graph as RDF in order to support reuse in other RDF aware applications?

3.2.2 Semantic Wiki Software

The probably most widely known project for collaboratively combining knowledge and information and also 'the most widely used encyclopedia' [Lehmann et al. 2015] certainly is Wikipedia. While the the MediaWiki engine of Wikipedia supports both, access but also contributions from nearly any human user – with some restrictions regarding content quality –, less than 0.05% of visitors to Wikipedia are also active contributors to the encyclopedia[1]. In addition, many automated bots are currently actively maintaining the Wikipedia sites [Tsvetkova et al. 2017]. Nevertheless, its content is not natively machine-processable as e.g. no meaning is attached to links between wiki sites. Semantic wiki approaches close this gap

[1]https://strategy.wikimedia.org/wiki/Wikimedia_users#Contributors_as_a_percentage_of_all_visitors

and allow more specific, semantically defined annotations and relations. In order to characterize semantic wiki software in contrast to plain wiki systems, Kämpgen et al. have identified functional requirements for semantic wiki software that are specific to enterprises, such as record, share and collaboratively refine relevant enterprise knowledge structures, ensure data quality, keep track of changes, and distinguish incorrect from relevant information, while preserving flexibility of what to put into the wiki [Kämpgen et al. 2011]. In addition, the authors also identified the non-functional requirements that the wiki should be intuitive to use, also by users without technical background, minimally invasive to established workflows and the enterprise IT landscape and also run sufficiently fast with loading times similar to external webpages. The adoption of such semantic wiki approaches in enterprise contexts and other corporate environments has recently begun and is continuously growing [Ghidini et al. 2008; Kleiner and Abecker 2010; Aveiro and Pinto 2013]. In the following part, we introduce various approaches for corporate knowledge management that implement semantic wiki software.

Semantic MediaWiki: A prominent representative of semantic wiki software is Semantic MediaWiki (SMW) [Krötzsch et al. 2006], an extension for the popular MediaWiki engine of Wikipedia, that aims to provide a 'semantic Wikipedia' [Krötzsch et al. 2007]. SMW introduces elements of the W3C's semantic web technology stack (see Section 2.4) such as the RDF's triple model [Klyne and Carroll 2004], semantic properties (so-called *roles* in DL terms) as well as *SMW-concepts*, i.e., dynamic categories that resemble the notion of domains in the RDF Schema language [Brickley and Guha 2014]. Those semantic features in conjunction with its collaborative knowledge engineering capabilities make SMW based systems even more attractive for a deployment in professional environments (cf. listing '*Wiki of the Month*'[2] and 'WikiApiary'[3]). SMW provides enhanced query construction capabilities with respect to organization-specific vocabularies and their specific contexts and allows to treat query results as first-class citizens and present them dynamically within wiki pages. Organizations such as enterprises, NGOs or civil services can benefit from such features, which enable query construction, query expansion, and filtering using a lightweight set of ontological semantics [Vrandecic and Krötzsch 2006; Zander et al. 2016b]. SMW was firstly released in

[2]https://www.semantic-mediawiki.org/wiki/Wiki_of_the_Month
[3]https://wikiapiary.com/wiki/Semantic_statistics

2005 and is still enhanced and maintained by an active community[4]. The latest release[5] of SMW supports the development of organization-specific knowledge bases and enables the querying of contained data (so-called facts) within the wiki in structured and well-defined ways. It is also possible to export semantically described facts to an external RDF store, which allows to use the W3C standardized query language SPARQL for extended query capabilities. Other extensions for SMW provide better syntactical linkage of data modelled in SMW and RDF data such as the SparqlExtension[6], the RDFIO[7] extension, or a triple store connector based on RDF2Go [Schied et al. 2010]. All these approaches for exporting facts of SMW have in common that they provide semantic web technology merely on a syntactical layer rather than a full-fledged integration on a semantic layer. Therefore, there is no dedicated support for integrating facts about the same entity described in various sources and it is not possible to leverage the resulting corporate knowledge graph with concepts of LOD.

Although SMW provides mechanisms to employ externally defined vocabulary terms from e.g. LOV, this kind of vocabulary import is still cumbersome and therefore hardly used. Further, it is possible to link entities of the corporate knowledge graph to LOD, but these links are not exploited by SMW. Tracking of versioning is well backed by the underlying MediaWiki engine. In contrast to the provenance of a change within the MediaWiki syntax (the editor), the provenance of query results is not clearly presented.

WikiBase: In contrast to SMW, where data is managed and presented within the same application, Wikibase[8] splits the semantic wiki application into a repository and an independent client [De Dauw 2014]. Both parts are implemented as extensions for the MediaWiki engine. The central repository provides capabilities to collaboratively store and manage structured non-relational data. One ore more clients can retrieve and embed structured data from the central repository into the respective organizational wiki system. Although this approach provides a dedicated management structure for the corporate knowledge graph, the state-

[4]https://www.semantic-mediawiki.org
[5]https://github.com/SemanticMediaWiki/SemanticMediaWiki/releases
[6]https://www.mediawiki.org/wiki/Extension:SparqlExtension
[7]https://www.mediawiki.org/wiki/Extension:RDFIO
[8]http://wikiba.se/

ments within the central repository still have to be curated manually and are not interlinked with concepts of LOD.

Wikibase strongly depends on the MediaWiki data model, but provides additional features for querying and serializing facts of a knowledge base. The data schema is contained within the knowledge base and not generally defined as LOV. Although linking of corporate entities to LOD entities is supported, facts about the linked entities are not retrieved. Rather, the Wikibase approach depends on facts that are provided by an Wikibase repository for a Wikibase client.

Cargo: Koren presents the MediaWiki extension Cargo [Koren 2015]. The author argues that the usage of most semantic wiki applications is limited to structure and query data within an organizational wiki rather than integrating data on a semantic level or providing facilities of addressing semantic heterogeneity. To address this use case, the Cargo extension provides functionality for structuring and querying data by implementing a wrapper around relational databases and exploiting the well-established functionality of SQL. Cargo does not employ any semantic web technology, therefore the creation of rules for conclusions is hardly possible. Due to the proposed architecture, the Cargo approach is limited to concepts that are known within an organization and does not aim for including shared concepts as they are provided by LOD.

The Cargo approach aims to simplify the usage of structured data within tables, rather than graphs, within a corporate knowledge graph. The focus is on efficient storage and querying mechanisms for such data structures, including rendering of query results. Tracking of versioning is well backed by the underlying MediaWiki engine. However, Cargo can not reproduce the benefits of semantic approaches such as interlinking external RDF resources.

OntoWiki: One example for a non-MediaWiki based semantic wiki applications is OntoWiki [Auer et al. 2007][Frischmuth et al. 2015]. OntoWiki focuses on modelling a machine readable knowledge base without providing a knowledge presentation for human readers such as natural language provided as unstructured text. Although the introduced semantic wiki software applications support semantic web technology such as RDF or even SPARQL on a syntactic level, the data integration across multiple data sources still requires a lot of manual effort due to the establishment of a common data scheme on a semantic level. OntoWiki follows a different approach by providing an authoring, publication and visualization interface for the web of data. OntoWiki supports navigation through RDF knowledge bases using SPARQL-generated lists, tables and trees. However, the authors do not mention the support for creating new links as they focus on accessing existing links only. The implemented RDFauthor approach builds on RDF in Attributes (RDFa) [Herman et al. 2015] by preserving provenance information in RDFa representations following the named graph paradigm as introduced in Section 2.4.5. The approach also establishes a mapping of the representations from the RDFa view to the author widgets. A number of tools in addition to OntoWiki are discussed that focus on data linking, quality improvement, enrichment, evolution and visualization. The advantage of the OntoWiki approach is the comprehensive user interface for arbitrary RDF knowledge graphs. However, there is a risk of overloading the user interface with more features which may decrease the usability. Also, the approach does not cover the exploitation of LOD for corporate knowledge graphs.

OntoWiki is an approach for modeling corporate entities on the base of RDF concepts, rather than wiki pages. Due to its generic RDF architecture, external vocabularies such as LOV can be employed, although this is not further specified by the authors. Only a limited subset such as Friend of a Friend (FOAF) or RDF data cube is addressed more in detail. Versioning and provenance tracking of RDF statements is provided by the underlying Erfurt API[9].

The literature overview of Section 3.2.2 points out that the introduced semantic wiki systems do either lack in native support of RDF knowledge management as it is the case for SMW, Cargo, or WikiBase, or managing unstructured content as it is the case for OntoWiki. Furthermore, the introduced semantic wiki systems do not support linkage from concepts within an organizational knowledge base to LOD, e.g. by providing adequate recommendations, nor do they track provenance information of derived statements. Therefore, we provide further literature review with a special focus on managing linked data in Section 3.2.3.

[9]http://aksw.org/Projects/Erfurt

3.2.3 Linked Data Management

In this part, we introduce different approaches for managing linked data.

Wikidata: Although the semantic wiki software applications introduced in Section 3.2.2 support semantic web technology such as RDF or even SPARQL on a syntactical level, the data integration across multiple data sources is still hard due to a common data scheme on a semantical level. Vrandecic and Krötzsch describe the collaborative data scheme in Wikidata [Vrandecic and Krötzsch 2014] as one possible solution for a common data scheme in order to extend schema knowledge in other wikis, especially Wikipedia. However, this approach does also define a data schema which is independent from LOV. Wikidata employs WikiBase as the underlying semantic data management system.

Wikidata can be considered as one of the core providers of LOD and also a major source for data in various national Wikipedia projects, technically built on Wikibase. Wikidata relies on a highly structured and language-independent data schema and supports open editing by any user. However, due to its plurality on a global scale, Wikidata allows conflicting data to coexist. This issue is addressed by references that can be added to each claim in order to track the provenance of statements.

SemVersion: Völkel and Groza have introduced a generic versioning methodology that can be applied to various ontology languages. Their SemVersion approach [Völkel and Groza 2006] is based on several layers for versioning of data management, structural differences, and storage. The basic RDF versioning layer supports an overlying ontology versioning layer in order to version RDF-encoded ontology languages, including semantic differences that take the semantics of the specific language into account, and provides merging with semantic conflict detection as language specific conflicts can not be detected at the RDF level. In addition to handle syntactical differences between URI resources and literals among two ontology versions, the SemVersion approach also addresses the issue of bnodes that may have different IDs in various versions as introduced in Section 2.3.3. The required bnodes extension is provided by enriching all bnodes with an inverse functional property that has a globally unique URI as its value, such as a UUID as introduced in Section 2.3.2. Similar versioning frameworks for RDF are also provided by the framework for ontology evolution as discussed by Klein who provides a dedicated meta ontology of change operations [Klein 2004] and the ontology evolution system discussed by Stojanovic that enables handling of ontology changes, ensures consistency of the underlying ontology and all dependent artifacts, supports the user to manage changes more easily, and offers advice to the user for continual ontology reengineering [Stojanovic 2004].

SemVersion provides a generic versioning approach for ontologies and also addresses bnodes. As this approach is based on RDF ontologies, facts about entities can easily be reused in other RDF aware applications. However, this approach does neither explicitly address LOV, LOD, nor the provenance of statements.

Versioning and Evolution Framework: The Versioning and Evolution Framework for RDF Knowledge Bases [Auer and Herre 2007] provides a compatibility concept between ontologies and an assistant for changes which involves the user in the decision whether or not to accept a change. The authors use ontology versioning to keep track of different versions of an ontology and provide the possibility to allow branching and merging operations. The approach is based on atomic changes, for example additions or deletions of statements to or from an RDF graph, which are aggregated to a hierarchy of changes and facilitate the human reviewing process on various levels of detail. The changes can be annotated with meta-information and classified as ontology evolution patterns. The advantage of this approach is that it is similar to well-known versioning approaches as they are widely used in software development, for example the popular GIT-system. However, the work on this framework has been discontinued in favour of OntoWiki.

The idea behind the Versioning and Evolution Framework is to model hierarchies of atomic changes within an RDF based knowledge management system. Although linking and exploiting LOD in the context of corporate knowledge is not addressed by this approach, the detailed modeling of changes, including provenance for each change in RDF, are related to the issue of incorporating LOD in knowledge management systems.

SoftWiki: The SoftWiki approach [Auer et al. 2007] provides semantic wiki representations for building an enterprise knowledge base. SoftWiki enables users to create, enrich, and manage defined requirements. It provides web-based accessibility for ease of use. No installation is required on the user side and collaborators can be invited through a hyperlink. Provenance information are not implemented in SoftWiki. The approach provides traceability of changes and optional comments and discussions for every single part of the requirements engineering knowledge base. The advantage of the SoftWiki approach is that is has already been applied to a real business context. However, the approach is still on an early stage and further evaluation is needed. Especially the cloud based approach may not fit the security policies of organizations.

The SoftWiki approach employs OntoWiki as its underlying knowledge base. In addition, SoftWiki supports the linking of relevant information which is accessible on the web or Intranet. However, the authors do not state how these links can be exploited in order to retrieve additional facts about entities or how users can be supported in establishing such links based on e.g. semantic similarities.

Linked Data Washing Machine: The Linked Data Washing Machine approach [Auer 2011] aims on creating knowledge out of interlinked data. Adaptive user interfaces and interaction paradigms empower users to formulate expressive queries for exploiting the rich structure of linked data. Users are able to give feedback on the automatically obtained suggestions in order to improve them. User interaction has to preserve privacy, ensure provenance, and be regulated using access control. Authoring tools should hide technicalities of the RDF, RDF-Schema (RDFS), or OWL data models and assist the user through what-you-see-is-what-you-get (WYSIWYG). Different information structures need to be seamlessly combinable in a provenance preserving way in a single visualization or authoring environment even if the information to be visualized or authored is obtained or stored in various linked data sources. The authors investigate unsupervised and supervised machine learning techniques to enable knowledge base maintainers to produce high quality mappings. They also use a semi-automatic repair method to increase the quality of Linked Data. Users have to be enabled to effortlessly give feedback to improve quality of Linked Data. Tools and services should be deployed to classify and interlink datasets automatically, to assess their information quality, and suggest enrichments and repairs to the published datasets. The advantage of the Linked Data Washing Machine is the integrative approach which combines the individual challenges rather than regarding them isolated. However, this approach still lacks on practicality of the discussed solution and remains on a theoretical stage.

The LD Washing Machine approach is build on the assumption that web data sources often mix terms from different vocabularies. Therefore, the employment of LOV is not addressed explicitly, but as part of improving the structure of LOD. The proposed LOD improvement cycle includes interlinking, fusing, classification, enrichment, repair and also manual revision of LOD. Whereas linking and provence of LOD are addressed, exploiting it is limited by manual revisioning due to the generalized nature of the approach.

What-you-see-is-what-you-mean (WYSIWYM): Khalili and Auer introduce the WYSIWYM approach, which aims at authoring structured content based on Schema.org [Khalili and Auer 2013]. The authors describe the manual composition process aiming at the creation of documents which use semantic knowledge representation formalisms. The manual composition is supported by a graphical user interface. The work does not focus on provenance, origin or source of LOD. The approach provides a set of quality attributes for semantic content authoring (SCA) systems with corresponding user interfaces for their realization. Those include usability, automation, generalizability, collaboration, customizability, and evaluability. The paper provides a consolidated literature review of existing approaches including in-depth review of four SCA systems.

The WYSIWYM approach employs annotations based on Schema.org[10], which also covers LOV to a large extend. This allows authors of structured content to interlink entities with LOD. However, the focus of the authors is graphical user interfaces (GUIs) for authoring and annotation (unstructured) content in a structured way. Tracking of provenance and versioning is not addressed explicitly.

Wikidata Concepts for the DBpedia Data Stack: The approach of Ismayilov et al. aims at exploiting the potential of both Wikidata and DBpedia. For this purpose, the authors use concepts defined in Wikidata and apply them to the DBpedia data stack [Ismayilov et al. 2015]. The approach uses the human-readable Wikipedia article identifiers to create IRIs for concepts in each Wikipedia language edition, uses RDF and Named Graphs as its original data model, and provides

[10]https://schema.org/

http://wikidata.dbpedia.org/ as a Linked Data interface and SPARQL endpoint. Wikidata uses language-independent numeric identifiers and developed its own data model, which provides better means for capturing provenance information. Wikidata has a smaller dataset than DBpedia but higher quality and provenance information due to manual curation. Provenance extractors can be used to export as much knowledge as possible. Extractors can get labels, aliases, descriptions, different types of sitelinks, references, statements, and qualifiers.

Mapping Wikidata properties to ontologies as discussed in Wikidata concepts for the DBpedia data stack is a valuable example for employing terms of LOV within a corporate knowledge graph, although it is limited to the TBox of only one platform in this scenario. However, the authors demonstrate that even a small integration of LOV leads to impressive leverage effects of more than one billion RDF triples on the ABox level. In order to track the provenance of triples, meta information such as revision IDs or redirects are extracted as well.

LODFlow: Rautenberg et al. discuss a workflow management system for linked data processing called LODFlow [Rautenberg et al. 2015]. They use LODFlow to create and manage the execution of workflows which interact with workflow participants. In addition, they provide visual programming frontends to enable users to construct their applications as a visual graph by connecting nodes together. LODFlow can help to preserve provenance by adding comprehensive metadata such as the version, invocation, and configuration of the tool execution in a concrete workflow instantiation. The authors plan workflows for Linked Data datasets maintenance to enable provenance extraction and reproducibility over time. LODFlow engine supports the interpretation of resources from the Linked Data Workflow Project Ontology and the invocation of additional tools, e.g. for extraction, mapping, linking, and quality analysis. The advantage of LODFlow is that it is tested and applied to a large-scale real-world use case. However, the complexity of a full workflow management system for linked data aims to data scientists and cannot be used without special training. Therefore it does not fit to our intended use as an organizational wiki system which can easily be used by any employee.

The LODFlow approach aims to provide reproducible LOD querying results, thus maintaining provenance information for each retrieved fact is one of the underlying core principles. Rather than employing LOV, the authors propose the Linked Data Workflow Knowledge Model. LODFlow preserves provenance information and adds comprehensive metadata, such as the version, invocation, and configuration of the tool execution in a concrete workflow instantiation, however, not in particular for any derived fact.

OpenAnno: In contrast to the Wikidata approach, the OpenAnno approach [Frank and Zander 2016a] focuses on mapping individually created ontologies to LOV in order to support the interlinkage of local knowledge bases with existing LOD sources in a semi-automated fashion.

The OpenAnno approach aims to exploit LOD for a specific application domain by mapping both, the TBox and ABox of a corporate knowledge management system to LOV and LOD respectively. Provenance and versioning of annotations are tracked by employing the Open Annotation Data Model (OADM). Although statements can be exported as RDF, the approach does not cover to which extend new facts retrieved from interlinked LOD entities are included in the model.

X-Link: Fafalios et al. introduce X-Link [Fafalios et al. 2015] to support the exploitation of LOD for open and configurable Named Entity Extraction (NEE). This approach aims on identifying entities in texts and linking them to related (web) resources. The authors also propose an extension of OADM for relating the output of the NEE process. X-Link allows users to define categories of entities and exploiting one or more semantic knowledge bases. However, the approach does not consider any other statement about a concepts within an organizational context besides the label of this entity.

X-Link proposes a method for exploiting LOD to configure NEE systems. Rather then employing terms of LOV, the approach implements the Open NEE Configuration Model to exchange configuration requirements. This implies that any service that has to exploit the configuration has to be capable of the model.

3.2.4 Summarization of Current State and Limitations

A summarization of the characteristics defined in Section 3.2.1 applied to the introduced approaches for leveraging corporate knowledge with LOD is presented in Table 3.1. The symbols used within the concept matrix are explained in Table 1.1 of Section 2.

Approach	Observed Criteria					
	Employ LOV	Link LOD	Exploit LOD	Track Prov.	Versioning	Export RDF
Semantic MediaWiki [Krötzsch et al. 2007]	(✓)	✓	–	(✓)	✓	✓
Wikibase [De Dauw 2014]	–	✓	–	(✓)	✓	✓
Cargo [Koren 2015]	–	–	–	(✓)	✓	–
OntoWiki [Frischmuth et al. 2015]	(✓)	✓	–	✓	✓	✓
Wikidata [Vrandecic and Krötzsch 2014]	–	✓	–	✓	✓	✓
SemVersion [Völkel and Groza 2006]	–	–	–	–	✓	✓
Versioning and Evolution [Auer and Herre 2007]	–	–	–	✓	✓	✓
SoftWiki [Auer et al. 2007]	–	✓	–	–	✓	–
LD Washing Machine [Auer 2011]	(✓)	✓	(✓)	✓	–	–
WYSIWYM [Khalili and Auer 2013]	✓	✓	–	–	–	(✓)
Wikidata Con. for DBpedia [Ismayilov et al. 2015]	(✓)	✓	(✓)	✓	–	✓
LODFlow [Rautenberg et al. 2015]	–	–	✓	✓	(✓)	✓
OpenAnno [Frank and Zander 2016a]	✓	✓	(✓)	✓	✓	✓
X-Link [Fafalios et al. 2015]	–	✓	–	–	–	–

Table 3.1: Concept matrix of leveraging corporate knowledge with LOD.

In Section 3.2.2 we have shown that current semantic wiki applications provide technical integration of semantic web technology on a syntactic level. In Section 3.2.3 we have outlined first approaches for enriching corporate knowledge graphs with addition information from LOD. However, the introduced corporate knowledge management approaches do not support the annotation and interlinkage of corporate knowledge with LOD on a semantic level while considering the formal, model-theoretic semantics of the underlying ontology language, i.e., a vocabulary's formal semantics. An exemplary recommendation system is provided by OpenAnno, but it is not integrated in any of the introduced semantic wiki applications. The statements maintained by one of these semantic wiki applications cannot be updated by external services as the statements contained within a wiki are always considered as master data. When importing statements from external sources into an organizational wiki, none of the introduced semantic wiki applications consider the context or the linkage of the data. Both is important in order to evaluate given statements, especially when they are inconsistent, redundant or ambiguous. To overcome these limitations, we introduce our Linked Data Wiki approach in Section 3.3.

3.3 The LD-Wiki Approach

In Section 3.3, we introduce the LD-Wiki, an approach that aims to leverage a corporate knowledge graph composed of statements from a semantic wiki with LOD. The approach is separated in three parts: In Section 3.3.1, we sketch the initial state of a semantic wiki system in accordance with Section 3.2.2 and also define the target state we want to reach with the LD-Wiki approach. The requirements that have to be addressed by the approach in order to reach that target state are discussed in Section 3.3.2. In Section 3.3.3, we propose the architecture for the LD-Wiki approach.

3.3.1 Initial and Target State

In order to identify the requirements for the LD-Wiki approach, we sketch the initial state of a semantic wiki system based on the findings of Section 3.2.2, and the state of formalized knowledge that is available outside of the corporate knowledge graph such as LOD. Further we describe the intended target state of the resulting corporate knowledge graph.

Initial Corporate Knowledge Graph: For the initial state, we assume a semantic wiki system in accordance with Section 3.2.2 that holds a set of organization-specific semantic statements. These statements represent a corporate knowledge graph as discussed in Section 2.4.3. However, these statements are not linked to any concept definition outside the corporate knowledge graph. Therefore, let corporate knowledge graph $CKG = \{(s, p, o, c)\}$ be the set of RDF statements modelled as quads with subject s, predicate p, object o and context c (see Section 2.4.5). In addition to this definition, we assume that context c of each statement is associated with a subgraph that has an explicit trust value in the range of 0.0 to 1.0 to quantify the trustworthiness of statements as introduced in Section 3.1. Subgraphs that are proven to be true, e.g. by dedicated knowledge workers of that organization, gain a trust value of 1.0 and are therefore characterized as reliable in the sense that they are maintained by the organization and controlled in well-defined ways, which also allows for more specialized statements dedicated to the knowledge demand of the organization. We therefore regard this subset of statements in CKG as trusted. However, this reliability and specialization requires high maintenance effort and can only be applied to a limited subset of statements within the corporate knowledge graph, depending on the resource constraints of the organization.

Initial Knowledge Outside of the Corporate Knowledge Graph: In addition to the statements defined in CKG which have an explicitly modeled value of trust, there is a large body of formalized public knowledge represented as statements in LOD where a trust value in the range of 0.0 to 1.0 has to be determined. Let $LOD = \{(s, p, o) \in \mathbb{RDF}\}$ be the set of RDF statements in LOD. In terms of an organization, statements in LOD are characterized in contrast to the knowledge maintained by knowledge workers as freely available, extensive but general description of common concepts that are eligible to leverage the concept definitions of CKG. Besides LOD, there could be further sources of formalized knowledge inside or outside an organization with undetermined trust value that could be treated in the same way. The provenance of statements retrieved from outside of CKG is therefore varying and potentially *not trusted* in case of a completely unknown source. As statements about the same concept could be retrieved from different sources, these statements could be *redundant* or even *inconsistent*. This has to be evaluated by testing the concepts for subject, predicate and object of each statement for equality. Due to the open-world assumption of LOD, a mechanism has to be applied that determines the *completeness* of retrieved concepts. This mechanism has to ensure that each concept covers all statements that are relevant for the respective concept class. For example, it could be expected that each concept of a city covers at least one statement about the name(s) of the city, the country in which the city is located, and about the number of residents.

Target Leveraged Organizational Knowledge: The target state represents a corporate knowledge graph CKG' that contains all statements of CKG, but enriched with sets of RDF statements that leverage the description of concepts defined within CKG. For this enrichment, we propose three additional sets of statements and their contexts for the corporate knowledge graph:

- The first set contains statements that *link* concepts of CKG to concepts in LOD by a semantic relationship. These links are required in order to identify URI resources in LOD that represent the same concept and potentially provide additional statements for that concept or confirms statements that are available within CKG but without trusted provenance information. This set of statements ist therefore defined as $LS = \{(s, p, o, c)\}$
- The second set contains statements that are *derived* from LOD concepts which are linked to CKG by LS. This set of statements ist therefore defined as $DS = \{(s, p, o, c)\}$.
- The third set contains statements about the *provenance* of statements in LS and DS, referenced by their context ID c. The provenance information is required in order to determine a trust value for each statement. This set of statements ist therefore defined as $PS = \{(s, p, o, c)\}$.

The target state that contains all statements of CKG enriched with links to external concepts, derived statements and statements of their provenance is defined as $CKG' = CKG \cup LS \cup DS \cup PS$.

Based on the initial and target state of CKG, we identify and formalize the requirements for our approach in Section 3.3.2.

3.3.2 Requirements to Meet the Addressed Challenges

In contrast to providing statements about a concepts within a semantic wiki system exclusively from CKG as single source of truth, we aim to leverage the statements of CKG by deriving statements about equal concepts from external sources, including sources of LOD. These external statements are linked to CKG by statements in LS. However, the inclusion of external statements in DS causes issues when the same concept is described in multiple sources. Therefore, the approach has to address the challenges that arise in general when exploiting LOD within a corporate knowledge graph as identified in Section 3.1.2:

R1.1: Identify equal URIs. In order to derive a preferable complete overview of a concept in LOD, we have to prepare a set LS of URIs that refer to equal concepts.

R1.2: Identify redundant statements. As of the nature of LOD outlined in Section 3.1, redundant statements may exist among different sources of LOD. Redundant statements may appear between statements in CKG and DS but also within DS. Although redundant statements do not lead to a knowledge gain, these statements could influence trust of statements in CKG'. Provided that a redundant statement has a trusted provenance, this redundancy can be seen as confirmation of the statement and increase the trust value. However, the provenance of redundant statements has to be independent in order to prevent improper trust due to error propagation. The aspect of error propagation requires additional supervision and is not addressed in detail within this work. On the other hand, if a redundant statement is known to be false, this redundancy can be seen as an indication to refute the statement and decrease the trust value.

R1.3: Identify inconsistent statements. Similar to redundant statements, inconsistent statements might appear within statements in CKG and DS and also within DS. Inconsistency could result from statements that are known to be disjoint. For example, a statement indicating that a subject is an instance of the human class could be declared as disjoint to a statement indicating the operating voltage of a subject, since it is not (yet) known that humans are electrically operated. Similarly, incorrect cardinality can also be declared as inconsistency. For example, if statements about a functional property such as a person's birthplace have different values (in contrast to different identifiers that refer to the same subject), this could indicate an inconsistency as well. Such inconsistent statements can decrease the trust of statements in DS. To decide which statement of DS should be included in CKG', threshold values for trust in provenance in conjunction with the time of the last update of a statement can be defined and evaluated to decide for the most appropriate statement. If this decision can not be made by formalized provenance information, it should to be made by curators of CKG'.

R1.4: Identify missing statements. We also have to address the issue of formalized concept representations that can never cover all statements that are associated with a real-world subject as outlined in Section 3.1. Statements in CKG or different sources of LOD may therefore cover different aspects of a subject and it can be assumed that some statements are always missing. To highlight at least the most relevant missing statements commonly associated with that subject, common statements of similar concepts in LOD can be exploited. If most of the concepts within a specific class of concepts contain statements using the same predicate, a statement using that predicate is likely missing for the rest of the concepts within that class. For example, if most concepts within the class of 'cities' contain statements using the predicate 'has major', statements using this predicate are potentially missing for the other concepts within the class of 'cities' and can be suggested for supervision in order to derive a more complete definition of that concept.

The previously discussed requirements cover potentially redundant or inconsistent statements. In order to address these issues, the proposed approach has to provide a mechanism to estimate trust of statements as discussed in Section 2.4.5. Trust of statements in LOD is not explicitly modeled on a global scale, nor provided by cryptography. Trust by statistical probability could be a solution, however, this would also mean that an organization has no explicit control about the statements that should be included in the corporate knowledge graph. We therefore argue that deriving trust from provenance is the most suited way for organizations to estimate trust of statements derived from outside corporate knowledge graph. This implies that the approach has to track the provenance information of derived statements and estimate trust of these statements based on the according provenance statements. Therefore, in addition to the requirements that arise in general when exploiting LOD within a corporate knowledge graph, we also aim to implement a set of statements PS that contains meta information about provenance and estimate trust of the derived statements in DS in order to support the automated evaluation of statements within semantic wiki systems. For this new approach, the following additional requirements have to be addressed:

R1.5: Provenance of statements. When including statements from LOD with an unknown trust value to statements in CKG, we have to keep track of the provenance of each statement and make it transparent to consumers of CKG' in order to gain trust. Tracking the provenance information is particularity essential for statements in LS and DS, as these statements contain resources that are not under control of the semantic wiki system. For LS, relevant information includes at first the author of the statement and the role the author embodies within the organization. Authors of statements in LS can be software agents that assume a link of a concept in CKG to LOD based on similarity algorithms as discussed in Section 2.4.5 or members of the organization that curate CKG. Taking into account the trustworthiness of an author, it can be estimated whether to include statements about the linked concept in LOD to CKG' or not. As concepts in CKG as well as in LOD may change over time, it is also important to track the point in time when a statement was added to LS or DS. All statements about the provenance in LS and DS are included in PS. Although the provenance information in PS is necessary in order to evaluate the trustworthiness of statements in DS, it would be confusing for the users of a wiki system to show all available provenance information in PS for each statement in DS. We therefore have to evaluate the provenance information in the background and show only the most likely statement to the user with an option to expand the underlying provenance-based derivation of the statement.

R1.6: Trustworthiness of statements. As discussed before, the provenance information of each statement retrieved from interlinked concepts is tracked in PS in order to estimate the trustworthiness of these statements. The selection of statements based on trustworthiness could be done manually by dedicated curators. However, due to the hugh amount of statements in LOD, this approach would not scale very well. The evaluation of provenance information has therefore to be performed automatically based on explicitly modeled or automatically learned rules. For example, if at least one trustable source provides the geographic coordinates of a fixed weather station, these coordinates can be adopted for a corporate knowledge graph, including the provenance information. Redundant statements within other sources can support these coordinates. However, if the coordinates of the weather station are already known and verified to be true within a corporate knowledge graph and the longitude and latitude properties of the geographic coordinates are known to be functional[11], it can be inferred that a statement that conflicts to one of these functional properties has to be considered as false and must not be included in the corporate knowledge graph, regardless of how many other sources share a different value that may have been mirrored among those sources. Subject to the level of trust of a statement in DS, each statement is regarded as trusted or not within the organizational context. Although statements that are

[11] A functional property can have only one (unique) value for each instance.

not explicitly trusted could help for a better understanding of a concept, they can not be used as proof for other statements. To increase trust of statements in DS, these statements could be verified by an author trusted by the organization.

In Section 3.3.3 we propose an architecture for semantic wiki systems that exploits statements from outside the corporate knowledge graph in order to leverage the statements in CKG. How this architecture covers the discussed requirements is detailed in Section 3.4.1.

3.3.3 Architecture of the LD-Wiki Approach

As discussed in Section 3.2.2, related semantic wiki systems such as SMW rely on a single data source for both, *semantic statements* for CKG and also the *non-semantic part* of the wiki which includes unstructured text, placeholders for statements of CKG, and wiki markup syntax. As a reference, the system structure of SMW is shown in Figure 3.1.

In order to manage semantic statements independently of the wiki system, statements of CKG have to be mirrored to an optional RDF store. However, this approach causes the issue that exported statements have to be synced from the wiki system to the RDF store whenever there is a change within the wiki system and back from the RDF store to the wiki system whenever there is a change by an external reasoning or updating service that effects the RDF store. Therefore, any change within the wiki or by an external service could cause inconsistency between the data base of the wiki and the RDF store. In contrast to that approach, we propose an architecture that strictly separates statements of CKG from the non-semantic part of the wiki. This separation of semantic and non-semantic data allows to manage the statements of CKG independently of the wiki software and is therefore a prerequisite for providing efficient reasoning and including statements other than statements from CKG.

Overview: The technical architecture for the LD-Wiki approach consists of two layers as illustrated in Figure 3.2: the *semantic layer* maintains the semantic statements of the wiki system, and the *wiki layer* covers the non-semantic part of the wiki, including unstructured text, wiki markup syntax, and also placeholders

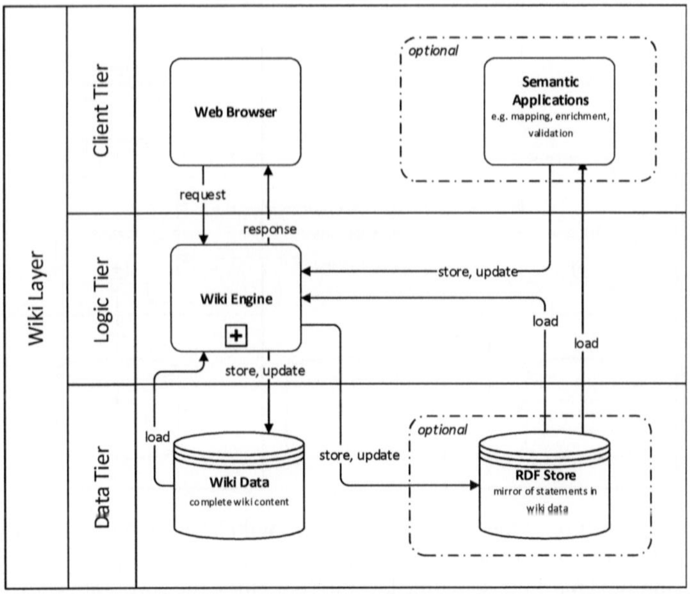

Figure 3.1: Architecture of SMW (own illustration based on [Krötzsch et al. 2006]): the wiki layer covers all aspects of both, semantic data management and also user friendly representation of the resulting corporate knowledge graph by including unstructured content and wiki markup. Although semantic applications may read data from an optional RDF store that mirrors statements of the wiki, updates still have to be performed using the wiki engine as the single source of data authority.

for statements of the semantic layer. By separating the semantic layer from the wiki layer, we avoid the issue of syncing statements between the data base of the wiki engine and an external RDF store. Additionally, we are able to include an independent software module to maintain and curate the semantic statements of an external RDF store without causing inconsistent data within the wiki system. While the wiki layer can be well addressed by common wiki software, we propose an additional software module that handles all relevant aspects of the semantic layer. The main contribution is thus not on a technical layer for the wiki itself, but aims at supporting the schema integration on the semantic layer. For this integration, we provide a set of established LOV to encourage the reuse of these vocabularies in organizational wikis. A prototypical implementation of the LD-Wiki approach is introduced in Section 3.4.

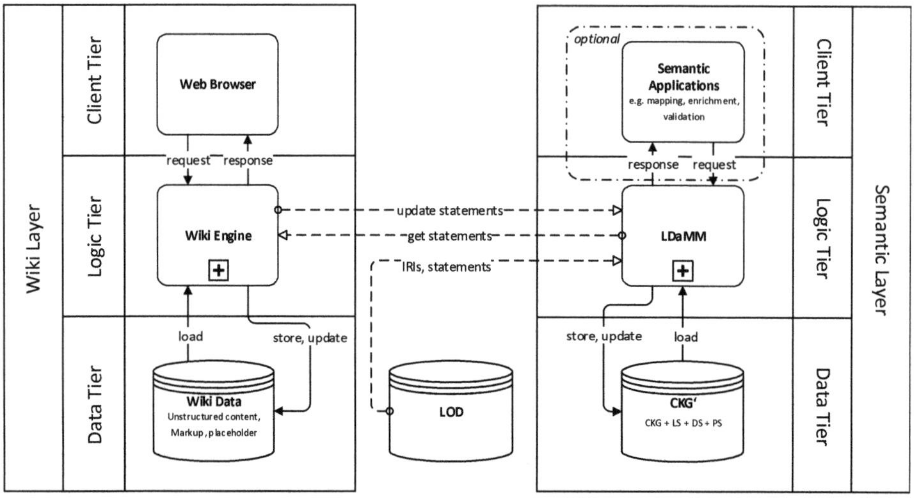

Figure 3.2: Architecture of the LD-Wiki-approach: wiki layer for a user friendly representation of the corporate knowledge graph by including unstructured content and wiki markup, semantic layer for enriching the corporate knowledge graph with Linked Open Data and curating it.

Wiki Layer: As business logic module for the wiki layer, the LD-Wiki approach involves a wiki engine to collaboratively modify unstructured content, statements in CKG by invoking the semantic layer, and also the structure of the wiki pages using a simplified markup language. For the knowledge representation, the wiki engine relies on the statements of CKG' provided by the semantic layer, rather than relying on statements of CKG managed by the wiki engine itself as it is done by e.g. SMW. By avoiding redundant management of statements, we ensure that the corporate knowledge graph is always in a consistent state. However, the wiki engine still has to provide additional unstructured content for a human friendly presentation such as unstructured text and markup information which is stored separately in a wiki data storage.

Semantic Layer: As the core element of the semantic layer, we propose the Linked Data Management Module (LDaMM) as the stand-alone business logic module which queries LOD on demand, updates the corporate knowledge graph in CKG' and serves the non-semantic layer with curated statements. The LDaMM is also responsible for reasoning and rule execution, which help to curate the corporate knowledge graph. The resulting corporate knowledge graph CKG' using LOV is the foundation for further recommendations of annotations in LS from CKG to LOD. These annotations allow to enrich the corporate knowledge graph with additional information in DS derived from LOD. In order to distinguish organization-specific statements originated from CKG and statements gathered from DS within CKG', the LDaMM tracks the provenance information of each statement in PS. The provenance information is stored using named graphs in the RDF-store, which extend the default triple model consisting of subject s, predicate p and object o to quadruples, containing an ID c that refers to the context of each statement. The context ID c allows us to attach provenance information to each single statement for statements with a unique context ID, but also to a group of statements that share the same context ID. Using the provenance information in PS, we can also handle inconsistent statements in DS or statements that have an insufficient explicit trust value, and provide consumers of CKG' with the latest and most suitable information. This process is detailed in Section 3.4.1.

3.4 Implementation of the LD-Wiki Approach

For a prototypical implementation of the LD-Wiki approach as introduced in Section 3.3, we build on the open source framework of MediaWiki[12] for the wiki layer. In contrast to other MediaWiki-based approaches discussed in Section 3.2.2, we implement the semantic layer with LDaMM as a stand-alone module that controls storing, querying, updating, reasoning, and rule execution of RDF statements, rather than integrating the semantic layer in MediaWiki itself. This allows for a lightweight MediaWiki extension that triggers LDaMM for modifying, creating and rendering wiki pages. We introduce the use cases of the LD-Wiki implementation in Section 3.4.1 and provide a showcase in Section 3.4.2. The implementation of the LD-Wiki approach is evaluated in Section 3.5.

[12]https://www.mediawiki.org/wiki/Download

3.4.1 Use Cases of Linked Data Management

In order to leverage the statements of CKG with LOD, LDaMM as the core component of the semantic layer has to address the requirements discussed in Section 3.3.2.

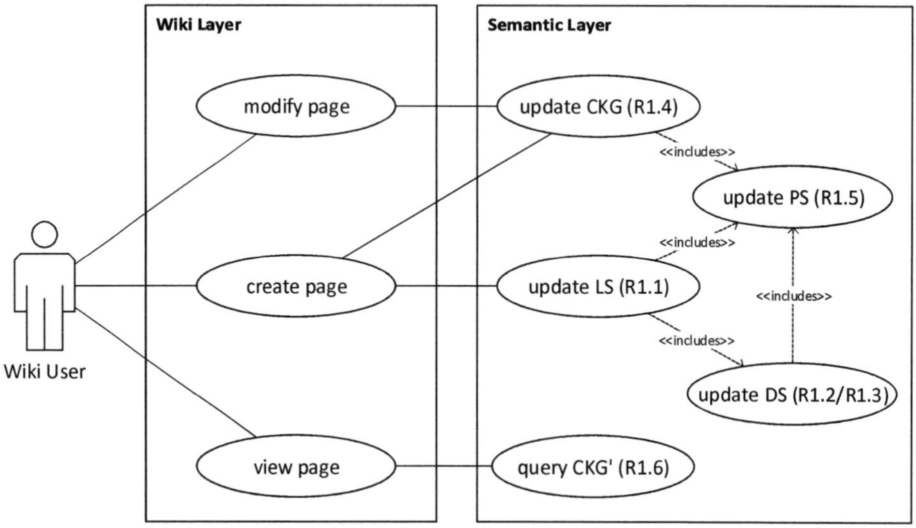

Figure 3.3: Use cases of the LD-Wiki: modifying existing pages in the wiki layer is associated with updating CKG with statements and schema knowledge (R1.4) in the semantic layer, which in turn includes updating PS (R1.5). Creating pages in the wiki layer is additionally associated with updating equal IRIs within Linked Open Data in LS (R1.1) in the semantic layer, which in turn includes updating DS (R1.2 and R1.3) and also PS (R1.5). To view a page, the wiki layer renders the most trusted statements of CKG' provided by the semantic layer (R1.6).

Use Cases: The use cases of the LD-Wiki are shown in Figure 3.3. As the wiki layer provides the user interface of LD-Wiki, the users of the wiki are involved in basically three use cases contained in that layer: *modifying* the content of a page, *creating* new pages, and *viewing* the content of a page. However, each use case of the wiki layer is associated with at least one other use case within the semantic layer. Modifying existing pages in the wiki layer is associated with updating CKG in the semantic layer with statements provided with that edit. Updating statements in CKG also includes updating the provenance information for these statements in PS as defined in requirement R1.5. To meet requirement R1.4, the new set of statements has to be compared to the according schema knowledge in order to identify missing statements. Creating pages in the wiki layer is associated with updating CKG in the semantic layer as well, however, it is additionally associated with updating IRIs of LOD that refer the same real-world subject in LS of the semantic layer as required by R1.1. Updating statements in LS includes updating statements that are derived from the linked concepts in DS, which includes identifying redundant statements as required by R1.2 and also inconsistent statements as required by R1.3. For each affected statement in LS and DS the semantic layer has also to include the according provenance information in PS as required by R1.5. The use case of viewing pages in the wiki layer is associated with querying the related statements of CKG' in the semantic layer. In order to fulfil requirement R1.6, the semantic layer provides the most trusted statements for each rendered page.

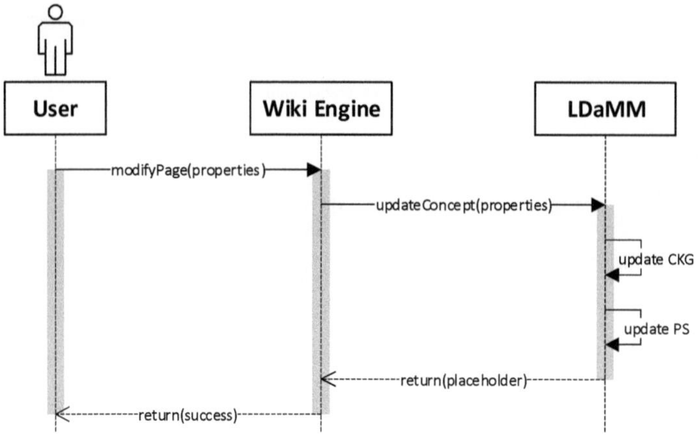

Figure 3.4: Modifying a page in LD-Wiki.

Modify Pages: The sequence for the use case of modifying existing pages is depicted in Figure 3.4. Users of LD-Wiki send a message containing the new content of the affected page to the wiki engine via their web browsers. The wiki engine in turn sends a message that contains new and altered statements of the modified page to the semantic layer. The LDaMM updates the affected statements in CKG, adds user information and time stamp as the provenance of this edit to PS, and returns a list of IDs for the statements to the wiki engine which uses these IDs as placeholder for the values associated with a wiki page. Updating statements in CKG does also include the provenance of statements in PS as defined by requirement R1.5. In order to identify missing statements as required by R1.4, the set of statements about the new page are compared to the schema that applies to that page.

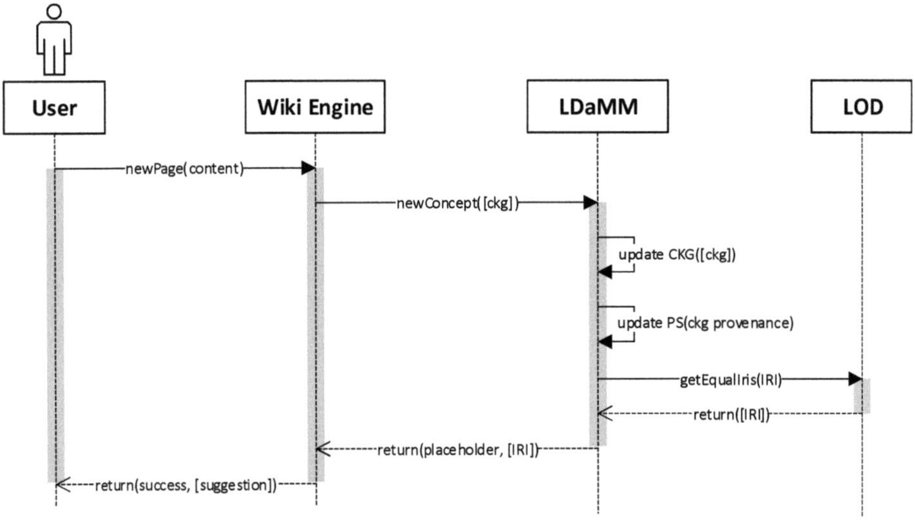

Figure 3.5: Creating a new page in LD-Wiki.

Create Pages: The sequence for the use case of creating new pages is depicted in Figure 3.5. To create a new page in LD-Wiki, users of the wiki send content of a new page to the wiki engine via their web browsers. The wiki engine in turn sends a message that contains the set of statements of the new page to the semantic layer, which also includes an identifier for that page. This identifier could be an instance of an IRI or of any subset of it as discussed in Section 2.3.2. The LDaMM updates CKG using the provided statements and also updates PS with user information and time stamp in order to track the provenance of statements as required by R1.5. Creating new pages in LD-Wiki is additionally associated with updating IRIs of concepts in LOD that refer the same real-world subject as required by R1.1. Therefore, the provided statements about a new concept are also used to query similar concepts on LOD. The retrieved concepts are returned to the wiki engine, together with a list of IDs for the statements to the wiki engine

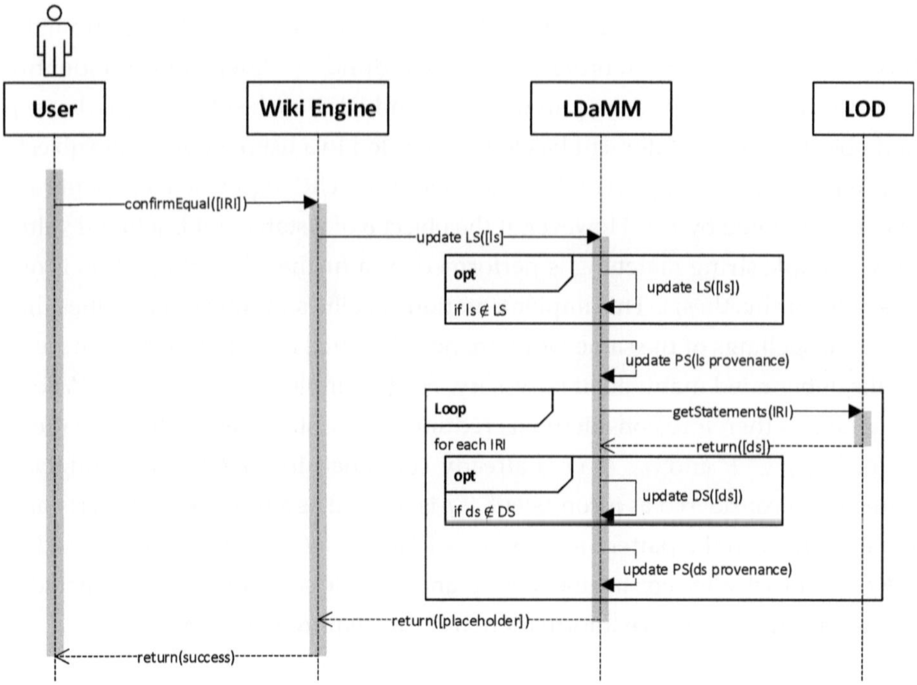

Figure 3.6: Deriving new statements from Linked Open Data.

which uses these IDs as placeholder for the values associated with a wiki page. However, linking the wiki concepts to LOD concepts requires one additional step to confirm the equality of those concepts. In order to ensure that all statements in LS are reviewed by an authorized wiki user, the retrieved list of similar concepts in LOD is returned as suggestions to the wiki user by the wiki engine. The user has then to select the appropriate suggestions and send the confirmation back to the wiki engine as depicted in Figure 3.6. The necessary effort required for this manual review of statements that link wiki concepts to LOD concepts is justified in the further use of these statements as the basis for leveraging those concepts. The wiki engine forwards the confirmed statements to LDaMM where each statement is tested if it is already included in LS or otherwise updates LS with the new statement. Regardless whether the statement has been in LS before or not, the provenance information of the linking statement is included in PS in order to ensure traceability of each statement in LS at any time. Updating statements in LS does also include updating statements that are derived from the linked concepts in DS. In order to identify redundant statements and identify inconsistent statements as required by R1.2 and R1.3, each subject s, predicate p and object o of each statement has to be extended to a list of equivalent subjects S, predicates P and objects O. If the element is an URI, equivalent elements are explicitly defined by LS. However, if the object o of a statement is a literal value, only a simple string matching is performed, as a further disambiguation is out of scope for this thesis. This implementation specific simplification implies that different spellings of the same word are not identified as redundant and have to be disambiguated manually if necessary. For the implementation of LD-Wiki, a statement is therefore considered as redundant if a statement with the pattern $s_n \in S$, $p_n \in P$ and $o_n \in O$ is already contained in CKG'. Accordingly, a statement is considered as inconsistent, if p is defined as a functional property and a statement with the pattern $s_n \in S, p_n \in P$, and $o_n \notin O$ is already contained in CKG'. For each affected statement in LS and DS, the semantic layer also includes the according provenance information in PS as required by R1.5.

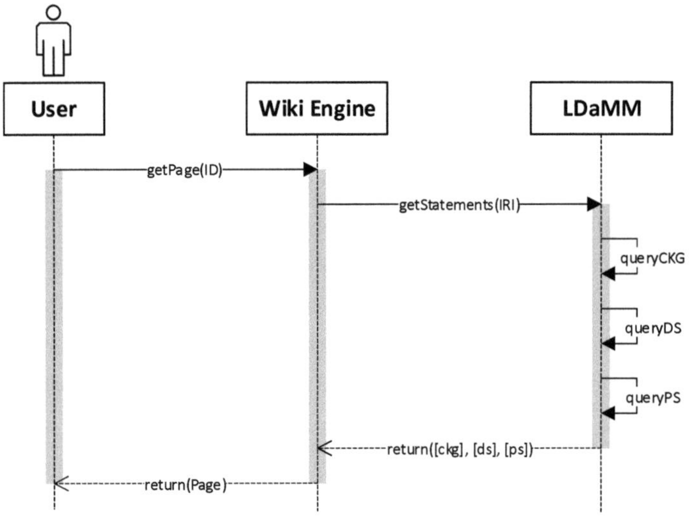

Figure 3.7: View a page in LD-Wiki.

View Pages: The sequence for the use case of viewing existing pages is depicted in Figure 3.7. To view a wiki page, users of the wiki have to send a request for that page via their web browser by using the ID of the intended page. The wiki engine provides the full template for the page, including unstructured content, markup, and placeholder for values provided by the semantic layer. In order to replaces these placeholders with the actual values, the wiki engine sends a request to the LDaMM for the required URIs. The LDaMM in turn queries CKG and DS for all statements about that URI. In order to address trustworthiness of statements as required by R1.6, the semantic layer also queries the according provenance information in PS. The provenance information is used in two ways: first, they are provided as a reference to users of the wiki. Second, they are used to determine which statement to return to the users if statements are inconsistent. In this case, only the value retrieved from the source with the highest explicit trust value is considered.

In order to demonstrate the implementation of LD-Wiki, we provide a showcase in Section 3.4.2.

3.4.2 Showcase

The showcase demonstrates the implementation of LD-Wiki with focus on leveraging statements curated in the wiki layer with statements derived from LOD.

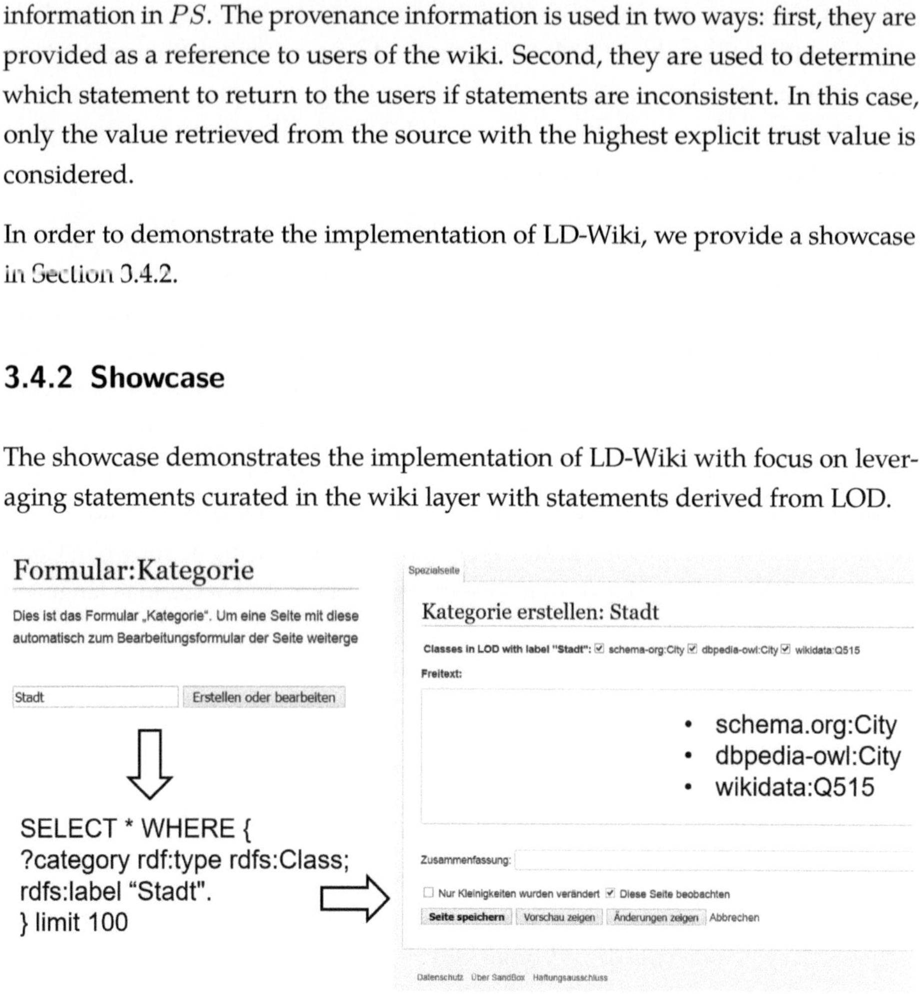

Figure 3.8: Interlink new category in LD-Wiki with existing class in LOV [Frank and Zander 2017b]: Classes of concepts in schema.org, DBpedia and Wikidata are recommended for a new category with the label 'Stadt'.

Link TBox-concepts to LOV: The key factor to making the LD-Wiki implementation work well is to build a TBox that can be interpreted in the context of LOD. It is therefore necessary to link concepts of classes and properties in CKG with the corresponding concepts from LOV. Classes are represented as categories in MediaWiki, the concept of semantic properties is provided by the SMW extension by wiki pages within a dedicated namespace. Figure 3.8 illustrates an exemplary creation of a new category in LD-Wiki. Whenever a new category or property is created within the wiki, LDaMM is triggered to query for existing concepts in LOV with the same label as the label for the new category or property respectively. If one or more classes are found, users of LD-Wiki can select the classes that represent the intended concept at the best.

For creating new classes within the semantic layer and the resulting corporate knowledge graph CKG, the user opens the special page for creating a new category in MediaWiki and provides the string that labels that new class of individuals. When submitting this string, MediaWiki sends it to LDaMM in the semantic layer. LDaMM invokes SPARQL queries to search for concepts of classes in LOD that have a label property with the same string as literal value. If, for example, the user would like to create a new category of cities for a German-language terminology, he or she would probably enter the string 'Stadt' for this category. To find classes related to that string in LOD, LDaMM produces a query string as shown in Code Example 3.1 to discover classes that have the label 'Stadt' with a German language tag.

```
SELECT * WHERE {
  ?category rdf:type rdf:Class;
  rdfs:label "Stadt"@de. }'
```

Code Example 3.1: Query classes with German label 'Stadt'.

This query string is then executed at available public SPARQL endpoints to discover adequate classes of concepts. Expected results would be for example `schema:City`[13], `dbp-ont:City`[14] or `wd:Q515`[15]. LDaMM returns these results to the MediaWiki engine within the wiki layer where the user can select the adequate

[13]http://schema.org/City
[14]http://dbpedia.org/ontology/City
[15]http://www.wikidata.org/entity/Q515

concepts. On creation of the new category in MediaWiki including the interlinked concepts, the information of the new category and the linked concepts are sent back to LDaMM and stored to LS. In addition, the provenance of these statements is added to PS as introduced in Section 3.4.1.

Retrieve statements from LOD: For each category of LD-Wiki which is linked to the according concept of a class in LOV by a statement in LS, we can assist the user on creating new concepts for the ABox in the wiki. Individuals of a class are represented as pages within the category that represents that class in the wiki. Therefore, whenever a page is created, LDaMM is triggered to query for existing concepts in LOD that have a label property with the same string as literal value and the same class as the category of the new wiki page. If one or more concepts are found, users of the wiki can select the concept that represent the intended subject for the new wiki page. The benefit for this kind of interlinkage is that we can query directly for properties of these concepts in LOD or retrieve a summary of entity data using entity summarization tools such as LinkSUM [Thalhammer et al. 2016]. However, entity summarization is not within the scope of our implementation. Figure 3.9 shows how creating new pages for individuals is done in LD-Wiki.

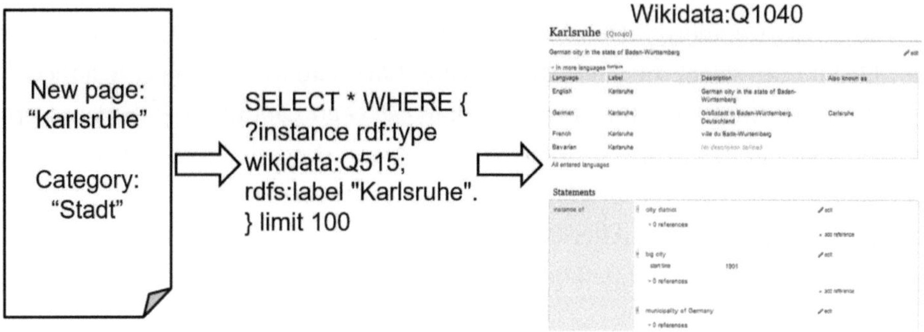

Figure 3.9: Interlink new instance in LD-Wiki with concept from LOD [Frank and Zander 2017b]: Statements about the concept are retrieved from Wikidata.

For creating a new concept of an individual, users of LD-Wiki can open the special page for creating concepts of individuals in LD-Wiki, provide the string that labels that individual and select the category of which the new concept page should be an instance of. When submitting this string, LD-Wiki sends it to LDaMM in the semantic layer together with the identifier of the selected category. LDaMM invokes SPARQL queries to search for concepts in LOD that are labeled with the same string and are instances of any of the classes that the given category is linked to. If, for example, the user would like to create a new instance of the category 'Stadt' for the German-language terminology in our showcase, he or she would enter the name of this city as string, e.g. 'Karlsruhe', and select the category 'Stadt' for it. To find instances related to that string and category in LOD, LDaMM produces the query string as shown in Code Example 3.2 in order to discover any instance that has the German label 'Karlsruhe' and type `wd:Q515`[16], as this is one of the classes which is linked to the category 'Stadt'.

```
SELECT * WHERE {
  ?instance
  rdf:type
  <http://www.wikidata.org/entity/Q515> ;
  rdfs:label "Karlsruhe" . }
```

Code Example 3.2: Query concepts of class 'Stadt' with label 'Karlsruhe'.

This query string is then executed at available public SPARQL endpoints to discover adequate concepts. An expected result would be for example the concept identified by the URI `wd:Q1040`[17] which symbolizes the German city in the state of Baden-Württemberg. LDaMM returns these results to MediaWiki where user of LD-Wiki can select the adequate concept. On creation of the new instance in LD-Wiki, information of the new concept in CKG and about the linked concept are send back to LDaMM and stored to the corporate knowledge graph, including all statements that are retrieved from the linked entity in DS and also their provenance information in PS. After this procedure has finished, all related statements are available in the corporate knowledge graph within CKG'.

Viewing wiki pages: In addition to the statements provided by the semantic layer, the pages of the wiki layer in LD-Wiki consist of unstructured text for a human-readable presentation, placeholder for the semantic statements and MediaWiki syntax as a simplified markup language to format the style of the page. When a page in LD-Wiki is requested by a user, the according parser function[18] of the LD-Wiki extension requests the necessary data from LDaMM and replaces

[16]http://www.wikidata.org/entity/Q515
[17]http://www.wikidata.org/entity/Q1040
[18]https://www.mediawiki.org/wiki/Parser_functions

each placeholder with the according value from the knowledge base CKG' as described in Section 3.4.1.

3.5 Evaluation of the LD-Wiki Approach

In Section 3.5 we evaluate the LD-Wiki approach as detailed in Section 3.3 regarding identifying and sufficiently addressing the challenges in exploiting Linked Open Data as a lever for the knowledge contained in corporate knowledge graphs (RQ1). For the evaluation, we employ the implementation introduced in Section 3.4. We focus on the leverage effect that exploiting LOD provides for semantic wiki systems while considering the requirements proposed in Section 3.3.2. Setup and data used for the evaluation are introduced in Section 3.5.1. In order to demonstrate structure and idea of the evaluation, we apply the the LD-Wiki approach to the showcase of Section 3.4.2 and explain the details in Section 3.5.2. For meaningful results, we test the leverage effect of the LD-Wiki approach applied to an existing semantic wiki of the environmental domain in Section 3.5.3. Finally, we examine the leverage effect of the LD-Wiki approach applied to the continuous example of this thesis in Section 3.5.4. The results of the evaluation are discussed in Section 3.5.5.

3.5.1 Setup and Data

For the evaluation of RQ1, we conduct a field study. The focus of the evaluation is on the leverage effect that exploiting LOD provides for semantic wiki systems. Therefore, the evaluation setup consists of a set of statements that represent a corporate knowledge graph CKG and a subset of LOD that is employed as the set of statements LOD in order to leverage the statements of CKG. In total, we use three different datasets for CKG as introduced in the following paragraph in order to evaluate the LD-Wiki approach in three stages:

Probed corporate knowledge graphs: In order to demonstrate structure and idea of the evaluation in detail, we use the dataset of the showcase introduced in Section 3.4.2 as CKG_1 to perform the first stage of the evaluation in Section 3.5.2.

For the second stage in Section 3.5.3, we employ Biodiversity of India (BoI)[19] which is a public wiki resource for Indian biodiversity and therefore used as representative of a wiki of the environmental domain. The corporate knowledge graph CKG_2 retrieved from BoI contains more than 8,000 statements contributed by 161 registered users since 2010[20]. It also covers concepts of 663 species including their biological classification and geographical region of appearance. We therefore expect promising results for leveraging these domain-specific statements with LOD using the LD-Wiki approach. Finally, we employ the continuous example introduced in Section 1.5.1 as CKG_3 for the third stage of the evaluation.

Probed LOD: In order to retrieve a subset of LOD to employ as the set of statements LOD, we make use of the SPARQL endpoints of DBpedia[21] and Wikidata[22] as two major resources of LOD. Due to the different implementation of these endpoints, the query string has to be mapped to meet the individual characteristics.

Based on the three datasets CKG_1, CKG_2, CKG_3 in conjunction with the subset of LOD in LOD, we perform three stages of evaluation. For each stage, we carry out three steps for the evaluation process:

Step 1: First, we identify equal URIs (R1.1) and create statements in LS_n that link concepts of CKG_n with equal concepts in LOD. For this step, we also calculate the *precision* of suggested equal URIs by dividing the cardinality of URIs that are approved to be equal by a user of the wiki system (true positive only) by the cardinality of total suggestions (true positive and false positive). In addition, we calculate the *recall* of equality statements as the number of concepts where a link to an adequate LOD concept could be established divided by the number of concepts where no adequate LOD concept is found.

Step 2: In the second step of each stage, we derive statements from LOD for DS_n in order to leverage the concepts in CKG_n. To determine the set of new statements about a concept of a subject s in CKG_n, we calculate the difference quantity of $DS_{sn} \subseteq DS_n$ to $CKG_{sn} \subseteq CKG_n$. For this process, we also have to identify redundant statements (R1.2) and identify inconsistent statements (R1.3) in order

[19] http://www.biodiversityofindia.org/index.php
[20] http://www.biodiversityofindia.org/index.php?title=Special:Statistics
[21] http://dbpedia.org/sparql
[22] https://query.Wikidata.org

to determine the difference quantity as the set of truly new statements correctly. The set of statements in DS_{sn} is defined as a subset of statements in DS_n which are about subject s in CKG_n. The set of statements in CKG_{sn} is defined as a subset of statements in CKG_n which are about subject s in CKG_n.

Step 3: In order to quantify the leverage effect of the LD-Wiki approach, we calculate the cardinality of new statements $DS_{sn} \setminus CKG_{sn}$ in relation to the cardinality of linking statements $LS_{sn} \subseteq LS_n$ that are required in addition. The set of statements in LS_{sn} is defined as a subset of statements in LS_n which are about subject s in CKG_n. The quantified leverage effect l_{sn} for a concept of a subject s in CKG_n provided by the LD-Wiki approach is therefore defined as the ratio of the cardinality of the difference quantity of DS_{sn} to CKG_{sn} to the cardinality of LS_{sn}:

$$l_{sn} = \frac{|DS_{sn} \setminus CKG_{sn}|}{|LS_{sn}|}$$

In addition to the quantified leverage effect, we quantify the enrichment e_{sn} for a concept of a subject s in CKG_n provided by the LD-Wiki approach as the ratio of the cardinality of the difference quantity of DS_{sn} to CKG_{sn} to the cardinality of CKG_{sn}:

$$e_{sn} = \frac{|DS_{sn} \setminus CKG_{sn}|}{|CKG_{sn}|}$$

In order to identify missing statements (R1.4), we investigate the properties that are used to describe different individual of the same class. For all statements in LS and DS, we track the provenance of statements (R1.5) in PS. This allows to estimate the trustworthiness of statements (R1.6) based on provenance as discussed in Section 2.4.5. However, as trusting a specific provenance for statements within a certain domain is still a subjective component depending on the trust structure of an organization, the evaluation of trust is not covered within this thesis, although the necessary techniques are discussed in Section 3.3.

3.5.2 Stage 1: Leverage Showcase

The evaluation of the showcase introduced in Section 3.4.2 is separated into three steps: first, we link concepts of CKG_1 to equal concepts in LOD with statements in LS_1. Second, we derive new statements from LOD to DS_1 in order to leverage the concept descriptions in CKG_1. Finally, we calculate l_1 and e_1 based on results of the first to steps.

Step 1a - link TBox pages to LOD: For the first step, we run the query described in Code Example 3.1 on endpoints of DBpedia and Wikidata in order to discover relevant concepts of classes as candidates for linking statements in LS_1. Wikidata uses the property `wd-prop:279`[23] (subclass of) to describe subclasses of other classes. We therefore map the property-value pair `rdf:type rdf:Class` to this Wikidata property which results in the query described in Code Example 3.3:

```
SELECT * WHERE {
  ?category
  <http://www.wikidata.org/prop/direct/P279>
  ?class ;
  rdfs:label "Stadt"@de .}
```

Code Example 3.3: Query classes with German label 'Stadt' in Wikidata.

When executing this query at the SPARQL endpoint of Wikidata, we receive references to two classes:

- http://www.wikidata.org/entity/Q515
- http://www.wikidata.org/entity/Q15253706

The first result describes a city as a large and permanent human settlement and the second result is the class for a more specific definition of a city by country that holds the size of cities and towns in Korea, Japan, the USA, China, North Korea and France.

For DBpedia, we map the class of rdfs:Class to owl:Class as DBpedia makes use of OWL and the default configuration of this endpoint does not imply superclasses which would include rdfs:Class as well. The result is the query described in Code Example 3.4:

[23] http://www.wikidata.org/prop/direct/P279

```
SELECT * WHERE {
  ?category rdf:type owl:Class ;
  rdfs:label "Stadt"@de .}
```

Code Example 3.4: Query classes with German label 'Stadt' in DBpedia.

When executing this query at the SPARQL endpoint of DBpedia, we receive again references to two classes:

- http://dbpedia.org/ontology/City
- http://dbpedia.org/ontology/Town

Step 1b - link ABox pages to LOD: Next, we test the retrieval of instance data for a given concept. In our example, we want to execute the query shown in Code Example 3.5 on the SPARQL endpoints of DBpedia and Wikidata.

```
SELECT * WHERE {
  ?instance
  rdf:type
  ex:Stadt;
  rdfs:label "Karlsruhe"@de. }
```

Code Example 3.5: Query structure to find instances of 'Stadt'.

Wikidata uses the property `wd-prop:P31`[24] (instance of) to indicate that an instance belongs to a specific category. We therefore map the property `rdf:type` to the Wikidata-specific term as shown in Code Example 3.6:

```
SELECT * WHERE {
  ?instance
  <http://www.wikidata.org/prop/direct/P31>
  <http://www.wikidata.org/entity/Q515> ;
  rdfs:label "Karlsruhe"@de .}
```

Code Example 3.6: Query concepts of class 'City' with German label 'Karlsruhe' in Wikidata.

For this query, we get two matching instances:

- http://www.wikidata.org/entity/Q1040
- http://www.wikidata.org/entity/Q1026577

[24]http://www.wikidata.org/prop/direct/P31

The first result refers to the German city in the state of Baden-Wuerttemberg, the second result refers to a city in North Dacota. Depending on the instance the user wants to refer to, he or she has to select the appropriate one. This example does also show that a completely automatic information retrieval is difficult to control and therefore human supervision of this process is still reasonable. If we run the query with the more strict definition of a city by country using the query string shown in Code Example 3.7, we do not get any result.

```
SELECT * WHERE {
  ?instance
  <http://www.wikidata.org/prop/direct/P31>
  <http://www.wikidata.org/entity/Q15253706>;
  rdfs:label "Karlsruhe"@de .}
```

Code Example 3.7: Query concepts of class 'like a city' with German label 'Karlsruhe' in Wikidata.

For DBpedia, we run the query for instances of `dbp-ont:City`[25] or `dbp-ont:Town`[26]:

```
SELECT * WHERE {
  ?instance rdf:type <http://dbpedia.org/ontology/Town> ;
  rdfs:label "Karlsruhe"@de .}
```

Code Example 3.8: Query concepts of class 'Town' with German label 'Karlsruhe' in DBpedia.

The single result of this query is the instance of `dbp:Karlsruhe`[27].

In total, we have discovered 7 statements in LOD of which 5 are approved to refer equal concepts. That corresponds to a precision of 0.71. For both concepts of the wiki in the showcase, an adequate concept is revealed in LOD which corresponds to a recall of 1.0.

Step 2 - derive statements for the corporate knowledge graph from LOD: To evaluate the number of subclasses that currently exist in Wikidata as the potential leverage of LOD for corporate knowledge graphs, we query the amount of formalized classes in Wikidata as shown in Code Example 3.9:

[25] http://dbpedia.org/ontology/City
[26] http://dbpedia.org/ontology/Town
[27] http://dbpedia.org/resource/Karlsruhe

```
SELECT * WHERE {
  ?category
  <http://www.wikidata.org/prop/direct/P279>
  ?class .}
```

Code Example 3.9: Number of formally described subclasses in Wikidata.

For the number of instances of a given class (or instances of subclasses of the given class), e.g. the class of cities, we use the query described in Code Example 3.10 which returns a number of 20.867 results:

```
PREFIX wd: <http://www.wikidata.org/entity/>
PREFIX wdt: <http://www.wikidata.org/prop/direct/>
SELECT * WHERE {
  ?instance wdt:P31/wdt:P279* wd:Q515. }
```

Code Example 3.10: Number of formally described instances of class Q515 ('city') in Wikidata.

For the showcase, we could leverage the concept of 'Karlsruhe' in CKG_1 with the statements in DS_1 retrieved from the linked concept in LOD using the query described in Code Example 3.11. This query returns a number of 485 statements that can be included in CKG'_1 to leverage the corporate knowledge graph. For comparison, using the Wikidata concept of 'New York City' (Q60), the query returns 831 statements.

```
SELECT * WHERE {
  <http://www.wikidata.org/entity/Q1040>
  ?p
  ?o .}
```

Code Example 3.11: Number of statements for Q1040 ('Karlsruhe') in Wikidata.

Step 3 - quantify leverage and enrichment: In order to quantify the leverage and enrichment for the concept of subject 'Karlsruhe', we employ the definition of Section 3.5.1 with the results of Wikidata from step 2:

$$l_1 = \frac{|DS_1 \setminus CKG_1|}{|LS_1|} = \frac{485 - 2}{1} = 483$$

According to the definitions in Section 3.4.2, there are exactly two statements about the subject 'Karlsruhe' in CKG_1: the label 'Karlsruhe' and the category 'Stadt'. The cardinality of this set is therefore 2 and the enrichment is quantified as follows:

$$e_1 = \frac{|DS_1 \setminus CKG_1|}{|CKG_1|} = \frac{485 - 2}{2} = 241.5$$

With a quantified leverage of 485 and an enrichment factor of 242.5, we can see that the LD-Wiki approach is suited to leverage corporate knowledge graphs and enrich corporate wikis with additional statements from LOD. In addition to the showcase provided in Section 3.5.2 that illustrates the functionality, we apply the LD-Wiki approach to a large wiki project of the environmental domain for meaningful evaluation results in Section 3.5.3.

3.5.3 Stage 2: Leverage a Semantic MediaWiki Project

For stage 2, we employ CKG_2 derived from BoI as a representative of a wiki in the environmental domain. CKG_2 covers concepts of 663 species including their biological classification and geographical region of appearance. CKG_2 contains $12,577$ statements that describe the concepts of these species, including statements about the context of these statements.

Step 1 - linking concepts to Linked Open Data: In order to create statements for LS_2, we query Wikidata for equivalents of all 663 concepts of species defined in CKG_2. By exploiting the available schema knowledge, we can limit the results to concepts that have a taxon name[28] equal to labels of concepts in CKG_2 and any value for taxon rank[29] which leads to a distinct concept per query and a precision of 1.0. As a result, we retrieve 593 statements that link concepts of CKG_2 to distinct concepts in LOD which corresponds to a recall of 89.4% of the concepts in CKG_2.

[28]https://www.wikidata.org/wiki/Property:P225
[29]https://www.wikidata.org/wiki/Property:P105

Step 2 - derive statements for the corporate knowledge graph from LOD: Based on the statement in LS_2, we derive statements from LOD about concepts that are equal to the concepts in CKG_2. The cardinality of $DS_{s2} \subseteq DS_2$ for all 593 linked concepts in Wikidata ranges from 29 to 740 which results in a total cardinality of $96,725$ for the set of statements in DS_2. The arithmetic mean of statements about each subject LS_2 equates to 161.1 and the median equates to 116.

Step 3 - quantify leverage and enrichment: In order to quantify the leverage effect of statements in LOD based on the equality statements in LS_2 created in step 1, we calculate the ratio of the cardinality of new statements to the cardinality of LS_2:

$$l_2 = \frac{|DS_2 \setminus CKG_2|}{|LS_2|} = \frac{96,725 - 1,186}{593} = 161.1$$

To determine the enrichment factor, we calculate the ratio of the cardinality of new statements to the cardinality of statement that have been in CKG_2 before:

$$e_2 = \frac{|DS_2 \setminus CKG_2|}{|CKG_2|} = \frac{96,725 - 1,186}{12,577} = 7.6$$

In Section 3.5.3 we have shown that the LD-Wiki approach is suited to enrich a well maintained, domain-specific semantic wiki project with additional statements from LOD. In Section 3.5.4 we apply the approach to the continuous example of Section 1.5.1.

3.5.4 Stage 3: Leverage Continuous Example

In stage 3, we evaluate how the LD-Wiki approach is suited to enrich the continuous example introduced in Section 1.5.1 with semantic statements derived from LOD.

Step 1 - linking concepts to Linked Open Data: For all concepts defined in CKG_3, we employ the query structure shown in Code Example 3.12. Within this query, the field `[class]` is replaced by the actual class of individuals that we are looking for, [label] is replaced by the label given by the domain expert and [label_with_replaced_umlauts] is replaced by the same label, however, this times umlauts are replaced by their ASCII equivalent (e.g. ü is replaced by ue) as both variants could be contained within existing labels.

```
SELECT DISTINCT * where {
  ?property rdf:type [class];
  rdfs:label ?label.
  FILTER regex(?label, "(?i)[label]|[label_with_replaced_umlauts]")
}
```

Code Example 3.12: Query structure used for the continuous example.

For an explicit modelling of the concepts covered by Code Example 1.1 and Code Example 1.2, we define quantities and instances within CKG_3 and query Wikidata and DBpedia endpoints for suitable resources. As a concrete example, Code Example 3.13 shows a query on Wikidata that retrieves all Wikidata properties that have at least one label that contains the string "Elevation". The defined properties, the number of results in Wikidata and DBpedia as well as the most suitable resource per source are listed in Table 3.2.

```
SELECT ?instance (count(?label) as ?count) WHERE {
  ?instance wdt:P31/wdt:P279* wd:Q18616576;
    rdfs:label ?label;
    FILTER regex(?label, "(?i)Elevation")
}
GROUP BY ?instance
```

Code Example 3.13: Query Wikidata properties which have labels that include 'Elevation'.

	Wikidata		DBpedia	
Label of Quantity/Property	*count*	*best match*	*count*	*best match*
Elevation	1	wd:P2044	11	dbp:elevation
measures	2	wd:P2575	0	–

Table 3.2: Properties used for the continuous example, number of similar resources in Wikidata and DBpedia most suitable resource per source.

Table 3.3 shows the instances of CKG_3 used for the continuous example and most suitable resource per source in Wikidata and DBpedia as representatives for LOD. For the next step, we add statements to LS_3 that link the concepts of CKG_3 to their identified equivalents in LOD. As a result, we retrieve 21 statements for Wikidata and 20 statements for DBpedia that link concepts of CKG_3 to distinct concepts in LOD. This results correspond to 95.5% of the concepts in CKG_3 for Wikidata and 90.9% for DBpedia. For 21 out of 22 concepts we could identify at least one match in LOD which corresponds to a recall of 95.45%. The 41 approved links out of 52 suggested URIs correspond to a precision of 78.85%.

Label of Quantity/Property	**Wikidata** *best match*	**DBpedia** *best match*
Nitrogen dioxide (NO2)	Q207895	Nitrogen_dioxide
Ozone	Q36933	Ozone
Illuminance	Q194411	Illuminance
Geographic Location	Q2221906	Geographic_coordinate_system
Sulfur dioxide (SO2)	Q5282	Sulfur_dioxide
Particulates (PM10)	Q498957	Particulates
Time	Q11471	Time
Unit of measurement	Q47574	Units_of_measurement
Observation station	Q190107	Weather_station
Thermodynamic temperature	Q264647	Thermodynamic_temperature
parts per billion (ppb)	Q2055118	Parts-per_notation
micrograms per cubic meter (µg/m3)	–	–
Lux (lx)	Q179836	Lux
Longitude (long)	Q36477	Longitude
Latitude (lat)	Q34027	Latitude
Meter (m)	Q11573	Meter
Seconds (s)	Q11574	Second
Unix time (s)	Q14654	Unix_time
ISO 8601 (<date>T<time>)	Q50101	ISO_8601
degree Celsius (°C)	Q25267	Celsius
altitude	P2044	altitude
measures	P2575	measurements

Table 3.3: Instances used for the continuous example and most suitable resource per source in Wikidata and DBpedia.

Step 2 - derive statements for the corporate knowledge graph from LOD: Based on the statement in LS_3, we derive statements from LOD about concepts that are equal to the concepts in CKG_3. The cardinality of DS_{s3} for all 21 linked concepts in Wikidata ranges from 63 to 507 which results in a total cardinality of $5,300$ for the set of statements in DS_3. The arithmetic mean of statements about each subject LS_3 equates to 252.4 and the median equates to 278.

Step 3 - quantify leverage and enrichment: In order to quantify the leverage effect of statements in LOD based on the equality statements in LS_3 created in step 1, we calculate the ratio of the cardinality of new statements to the cardinality of LS_3:

$$l_3 = \frac{|DS_3 \setminus CKG_3|}{|LS_3|} = \frac{5,300 - 42}{21} = 250.4$$

To determine the enrichment factor, we calculate the ratio of the cardinality of new statements to the cardinality of statement that have been in CKG_3 before:

$$e_3 = \frac{|DS_3 \setminus CKG_3|}{|CKG_3|} = \frac{5,300 - 42}{22} = 239.0$$

In Section 3.5.4 we have shown that the LD-Wiki approach is suited to enrich meta data for the continuous example of Section 1.5.1 with additional statements from LOD. These statements are the foundation for mapping observations to explicit semantics as discussed in Chapter 4.

The results of all three stages of the evaluation as introduced in Section 3.5.2, Section 3.5.3, and Section 3.5.4, are discussed in Section 3.5.5.

3.5.5 Discussion of Results

By querying for concepts in LOD that are equal to concepts about real-world subjects in organizational semantic wiki systems, we have shown that adequate LOD records exist to leverage the corporate knowledge graphs CKG_1, CKG_2 and CKG_3 which are maintained by such wiki systems. As shown in Figure 3.10, the suggested concepts in LOD cover the concepts within the probed corporate knowledge graphs with a precision of 83.42% and a recall of 94.97% in average. With the LD-Wiki approach, we have linked concepts maintained by those wiki systems to equal concepts in LOD by linking statements in LS_1, LS_2 and LS_3. Based on these linking statements, we derived hundreds of statements for DS_1, DS_2 and DS_3 that can be employed for a common understanding of concepts across the boundaries of an organization. The results are summarized as follows:

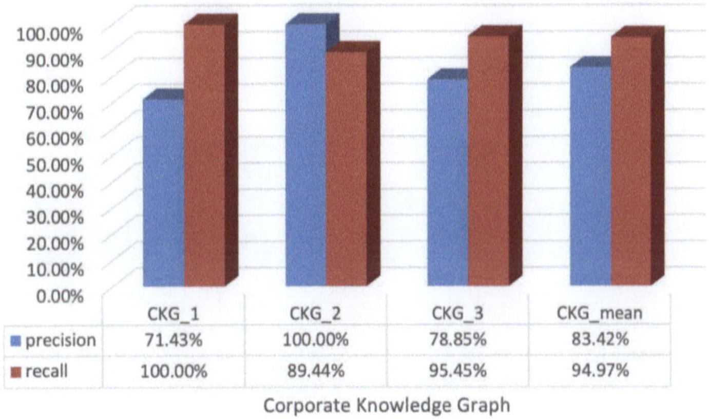

Figure 3.10: Precision and recall for suggested entities in LOD.

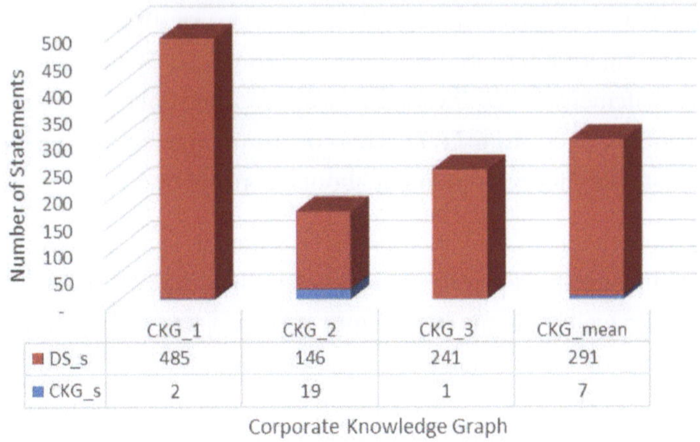

Figure 3.11: Number of statements in DS and CKG per subject.

Derived statements per subject: The numbers of derived statements per subjects are quantified by the average cardinality of sets DS_{s1}, DS_{s2} and DS_{s3} as shown in Figure 3.11. The average number of derived statements per subject for CKG_1, CKG_2 and CKG_3 is 291, compared to 7 statements about each subject that are provided in average by the corporate knowledge graphs.

Leverage and enrichment per subject: The set of derived statements DS_n could also contain statements that are redundant or inconsistent to statements in CKG_n. In order to quantify leverage and enrichment of statements about a concept, we

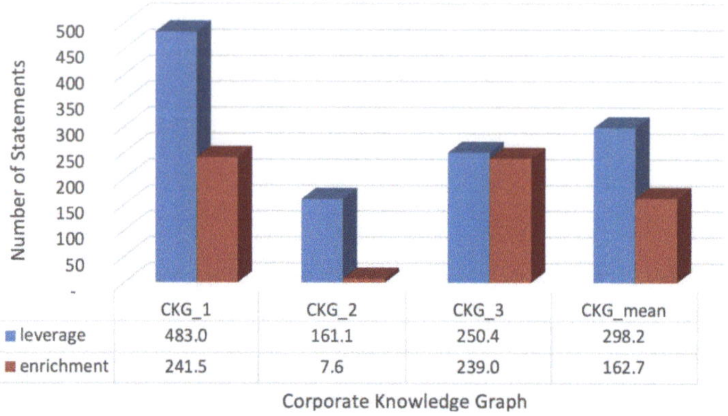

Figure 3.12: Quantified leverage and enrichment per subject.

therefore consider the difference set $DS_{sn} \setminus CKG_{sn}$ of distinct new statements only. The resulting numbers are presented in Figure 3.12. The results show that in average each statement in LS_n leverages the appropriate linked concept with 299.5 new statements derived from LOD. This corresponds to an average enrichment of 163.3 new statements per statement about a concept in CKG_{sn}.

The results show that the LD-Wiki approach is suited to leverage concepts defined within a domain-specific semantic wiki system with additional statements derived from LOD. Even well maintained semantic wiki projects such as BoI can benefit from the approach, as the expense of creating one new linking statement in LS_2 is rewarded by 161.1 distinct new statements in average per subject in CKG_2 and enriches the present number of statements per concept by a factor of 7.6 in average. To conclude Chapter 3, we summarize this chapter in Section 3.6.

3.6 Conclusion of Chapter 3

In Chapter 3, we have evaluated the research question of identifying and sufficiently addressing the challenges in exploiting Linked Open Data as a lever for the knowledge contained in corporate knowledge graphs (RQ1). To answer this research question, we have proposed the LD-Wiki approach, a semantic wiki system that encourages and exploits the integration of LOD in corporate knowledge graphs (C1). We employ the approach to provide a mechanism to suggest and curate LOD resources that match the organization-specific concepts described in a wiki system (C1.1), identify *statements that are redundant* within the corporate knowledge graph federated of statements from a semantic wiki and LOD (C1.2), identify *statements that are inconsistent* within the corporate knowledge graph federated of statements from a semantic wiki and LOD (C1.3), identify *statements that are likely missing* according to schema knowledge in order to describe concepts within a semantic wiki (C1.4), and estimate *trust for statements* used within a semantic wiki, including statements derived from LOD (C1.5). The LD-Wiki approach assists users of organizational semantic wikis in establishing and curating meaningful relations to LOD concepts by executing adequate SPARQL queries based on the user's input and the given context.

LD-Wiki foundations: In Section 3.1, we have motivated our research with the demand of building meaningful corporate knowledge graphs for organizations while avoiding expensive redundant work for each new context. We have discussed related work in Section 3.2 and pointed out the missing support for leveraging organizational corporate knowledge graphs with LOD. To overcome this limitation, we introduced the LD-Wiki approach in Section 3.3 which aims to separate the wiki layer from the semantic layer of the wiki system in order to gain a consistent corporate knowledge graph that also covers statements from LOD while keeping track of the provenance of each statement.

LD-Wiki implementation: The implementation of the LD-Wiki approach using primarily open source frameworks is described in Section 3.4. In Section 3.5, we have shown how present semantic wiki systems can be enriched with additional statements derived from LOD by executing adequate SPARQL queries adopted to the data structure of Wikidata and DBpedia.

Outcome: With the implementation of the LD-Wiki approach we have shown how to assist users of semantic wiki systems in creating a set LS of meaningful links to equal concepts in LOD. By exploiting the linking statements of LS, we have shown that a large set DS of additional statements can be derived from LOD, even for well maintained semantic wiki projects. To track the provenance of statements in DS derived from LOD, we have introduced the additional set of statements PS. Statements in LS therefore leverage a corporate knowledge graph CKG to CKG'

without the need to modify existing statements. By evaluating the provenance information in PS, software agents can take the provenance of statements into account to estimate the trustworthiness of statements in CKG' in order to increase the informative value of a corporate knowledge graph. Therefore, we consider the hypothesis that the comprehensive knowledge which is provided as Linked Open Data can be exploited to leverage the knowledge represented in a corporate knowledge graph (H1) as confirmed. In the following Chapter 4, we discuss how the concepts modelled within a CKG can be applied to IoT data streams.

4

Knowledge for IoT Data Streams

In Chapter 4, we present our findings for answering the research question of how a stream of continuous environmental observations can be mapped, validated, and enriched on-the-fly based on contextual knowledge from a corporate knowledge graph (RQ2). This involves testing the hypothesis of whether a well-curated corporate knowledge graph enables automated mapping, validation, and enrichment of ambiguous sensor observations based on explicit semantics (H2). Contents of Chapter 4 have been published in [Frank and Simko 2018] and [Frank et al. 2018].

4.1 Introduction to Chapter 4

Section 4.1 provides the motivation for research question RQ2 in Section 4.1.1, outlines the addressed challenges in Section 4.1.2, and lists the contributions to these challenges in Section 4.1.3.

4.1.1 Motivation for Knowledge-based IoT Data Streams

Publicly available IoT data streams are continually growing in popularity and pervasiveness [Cao and Wachowicz 2019; Elsaleh et al. 2020; Tu et al. 2020]. This also applies to publicly accessible data streams from environmental observation stations such as weather or traffic observations. Examples are public observation stations for traffic noise[1] or air pollution[2], but also private observation stations such as senseBoxes[3] or other weather stations which post their observations in a machine readable format on the internet. Preferentially, these observations are also available as web APIs and not just as historical data dumps. The increasing availability of such data streams leads to opportunities and challenges: domain experts in the field of environmental observations are provided with extensive observations covering large areas with high density of environmental sensors which could hardly ever be provided by a single organization.

However, most of these APIs are offered with ambiguous key-value pairs which do not contain any explicit semantics and are therefore hard to be processed without further data understanding and transformation. These values can therefore not be evaluated on-the-fly. A developer has to read and understand the human-readable documentation of the data structure and build a tailored solution that fits the implicit semantics in order to process the messages of environmental observations correctly. In some cases, where the documentation is unclear, incomplete, deprecated or even not present, a developer of a consuming application has to consult the data provider to fully understand and correctly implement the semantics of the data. Also, further enrichment and transformation of the data could be required in order to interpret the values correctly. Whenever the data provider changes syntax or semantics of the data stream, the developer has to adapt the code of the consuming application manually. This challenge was also identified by Wiener et al [Wiener et al. 2016] when integrating heterogeneous spatio-temporal data.

In addition to the identified issue of ambiguous data models, also the trustworthiness of observations in publicly available data streams is varying due to lacking provenance information, missing values or unreliable providers. Comparing values observed by heterogeneous sensors is hard due to different formats, undocumented syntax and ambiguous semantics of observation messages emitted by such sensors. In practice, we assume that usually groups of people work together to develop innovative applications based on those streams, rather than individual persons. We therefore aim at enabling domain experts to take the opportunity of the high amount of environmental sensor data included in publicly available

[1] http://www4.lubw.baden-wuerttemberg.de/servlet/is/224275/
[2] http://mnz.lubw.baden-wuerttemberg.de/messwerte/aktuell/statDEBW080.htm
[3] https://sensebox.de/

data streams by addressing the associated challenges and assisting them to properly annotate the streams. As a consequence, Chapter 4 addresses the following research question:

> *RQ2: How can continuous environmental observations contained in IoT data streams be mapped, validated, and enriched on-the-fly based on contextual knowledge from a corporate knowledge graph?*

From research questions RQ2 we derive the following hypothesis:

> *H2: A well-curated corporate knowledge graph enables automated mapping, validation, and enrichment of ambiguous sensor observations based on explicit semantics.*

For knowledge-driven harmonization of continuous sensor observations contained in IoT data streams, we have to ensure that the knowledge provided by a corporate knowledge graph enables meaningful mapping, validation, and enrichment of ambiguous sensor observations on-the-fly. If the knowledge provided by a corporate knowledge graph can be employed in this way, we consider hypothesis H2 to be confirmed. If the harmonization without additional inputs is not possible or the total processing time increases to more than a cycle duration of the IoT data stream, we consider hypothesis H2 as disproved. We test hypothesis H2 in Section 4.5.

In the following Section 4.1.2, we discuss the challenges that have to be addressed in order to answer RQ2.

4.1.2 Challenges Addressed in Chapter 4

The challenges that arise when processing observation messages emitted by heterogenous sensors and observation stations are identified as follows:

Lacking semantics: Ambiguous schema and semantics of messages in different observation data streams hinders a meaningful interpretation of the observations. Without explicit semantics, further data understanding and manual data transformation is required in order to process and interpret this data correctly.

Demand for validation: To ensure comparability and eligibility of observation messages provided by heterogeneous sensors and observation stations, a minimum standard for observation messages has to be defined and applied. Depending on the requirements of a specific use case, suitable observation messages have to be validated and filtered.

Missing statements: Heterogeneous observation messages may implicitly cover equivalent or comparable statements about an observed quantity. For automated processing of the observation data, these implicit relations have to be made explicit based on well-defined rules and appropriate reasoning.

Our approach addresses the challenges of semantic *mapping*, *validating*, and *enriching* of sensor observations based on collaboratively created annotations. We detail the contributions to these challenges in Section 4.1.3.

4.1.3 Contributions

In order to contribute to the domain of semantic sensor observations, we propose a semantic stream processing framework that maps observation messages to explicit semantics, validates each message, and enriches them with further statements based on collaboratively created annotations provided by domain experts (C2).

The Linked Stream Annotation Engine for collaboratively annotating streams of sensor observations combines the LD-Wiki approach of Chapter 3 with state-of-the-art technologies of data stream processing and the semantic web stack in order to process observation messages in a meaningful and efficient way. We show how groups of experts can work together to lift existing streams of observation messages to RDF streams by using an intuitive configuration mechanism. The semantic information for the mapping process is derived from collaboratively created semantic annotations of the non-semantic data streams within a semantic wiki platform. In addition, we enable domain experts to define shape constraints for API messages which are validated during runtime. These shape constraints allow for generic preprocessing of data streams without further coding. Our prototypical implementation shows the feasibility of LSane. For the evaluation of the LSane approach, we map data streams of public and private observation stations on-the-fly to explicit semantics for each observation and validate the result based on shape constraints retrieved from semantic annotations. We therefore summarize our contributions to the domain of semantic sensor observations as follows:

C2.1: Map sensor observations on-the-fly to explicit semantics. In order to address ambiguous schema and semantics of observation data streams, we map sensor observations on-the-fly to explicit semantics. The semantic information of observations is derived from collaboratively created semantic annotations for the non-semantic data streams. We provide these annotations with a semantic wiki platform based on the foundation we laid in Chapter 3.

C2.2: Validate sensor observations on-the-fly based on explicit semantics. We enable domain experts to define different message types including shape constraints for sensor observations within a semantic wiki system. These shapes are validated during runtime in order ensure common standards for observations and make values observed by heterogeneous sensors comparable.

C2.3: Enrich sensor observations on-the-fly based on explicit semantics. Our proposed approach enriches sensor observations based on collaboratively created annotations. Depending on the use case and the required information, the enrichment of observations could include provenance information of observations, prediction of missing values, or filtering of unreliable providers in order to increase trustworthiness of observations in publicly available data streams. Enrichment of observations could also address different formats and syntaxes according to format and syntax required by a data consumer.

Chapter 4 is organized as follows: In Section 4.2, we provide and discuss the literature review in the fields of *i*) *mapping and processing of continuous sensor observations*, *ii*) *semantic validation* and *iii*) *semantic enrichment of mapped observations*. Based on the related work, we introduce our approach for semantic annotations for data streams of observation data, semantic mapping of non-semantic data streams and constraint checking based on user created annotations in Section 4.3. We detail the LSane approach with respect to validating and enriching observation messages based on collaboratively created annotations. The implementation of the LSane approach is illustrated in Section 4.4. In Section 4.5, we show how our implementation performs on exemplary data streams of a public observation station and a private observation station. Finally, the results are discussed in Section 4.6.

4.2 Related Work

In Section 4.2, we analyze the related work for research question RQ2. First, we define the criteria for the review in Section 4.2.1. Next, we introduce and discuss related work with respect to *mapping* in Section 4.2.2 and *validation* in Section 4.2.3. We summarize the current state and the limitations of all introduced approaches in Section 4.2.4.

4.2.1 Criteria for the Literature Review

We discuss the approaches introduced in Section 4.2.2 and Section 4.2.3 with respect to the following characteristics:

- **Semantic Annotation:** Does the approach consider the semantic annotation of observations?
- **Semantic Sensor Data:** Does the approach exploit semantic sensor data?
- **Collaborative:** Does the approach support collaboratively created annotations for observations?
- **Semantic Mapping:** Does the approach introduce a mapping technique for key-value observations to explicit semantics?
- **Semantic Validation:** Does the approach introduce a technique to validate observations on a semantic level?
- **Semantic Enrichment:** Does the approach employ a reasoning technique to infer additional information for a processed observation?

4.2.2 Mapping of Observation Messages to Explicit Semantics

In Section 4.2.2, we discuss related work in the fields of mapping observation messages to explicit semantics and semantic stream processing.

Mapping with RML and R2RML: Dimou et al. have outlined limitations of current mapping approaches such as the need of manual alignment on a per-source, per-format or even per-case basis. The authors claim that incorporating data from multiple sources and different formats to LOD remains complicated, although a significant number of tools exist for that purpose and introduce the RDF Mapping Language (RML) [Dimou et al. 2014] as a generic language for integrated RDF mappings of heterogeneous data. In contrast to their work, we aim on processing continuous streams of observation messages, rather than mapping gradually shaped data sets. Although our primary aim is not to incorporate the data of observation stations to LOD, but to enable consuming applications to correctly process observation data of heterogeneous data sources based on explicit semantics, we benefit from adopting the basic principle of uniform and interoperable mapping definitions. Mappings of relational or otherwise formatted data to RDF is possible with the relational database (RDB) to RDF Mapping Language R2RML [Das et al. 2012] (or the broader applicable RML as introduced before which also enables mappings from JSON, Extensible Markup Language (XML) or CSV to RDF). The desired transformations are formulated in RDF by defining the output graph structure by so called Maps and the desired resources. Their URIs can also be specified by URI templates, translating keys or values to valid RDF resources. While R2RML strictly relies on tables and uses column names as resource and attribute identifiers of row-based data objects, RML also transforms the more flexible JSON and XML data by identifying objects according to their keys. Even though some tools have been introduced in order to support the creation of mappings for both approaches, the possibility to collaboratively work on mappings was not part of the design requirements and is still missing.

R2RML and RML aim to map relational data to RDF. Semantic enrichment of data is partly addresses by enabling computed properties. However, semantic annotations and validation are not addressed.

RSPLab: Several ways on how to process data streams are possible, especially when explicit semantic annotations have to be evaluated. As an example, the stream processing could be implemented from scratch using any suitable programming language. This would enable the highest flexibility and minimize the complexity of the infrastructure needed. However, building the whole stream processing framework from scratch for every project would cause a lot of unnecessary workload which would make the development process inefficient. For this reason, distributed systems such as Apache Spark[4] or Apache Flink[5] focus specifically on stream processing. Spark relies on micro batching which adds latency at the value of the batch interval, whereas Flink is designed as a real-time stream processing engine. However, this difference is only relevant if observation messages have to be processed with high frequency in a latency critical setting, which is not the case in our scenario. For processing of RDF streams, Tommasini et al. have introduced RSPLab [Tommasini et al. 2017], a cloud-ready and open-source framework for designing and executing tests that can be used to compare different implementations.

As RSPLab is primarily a benchmarking approach for semantic stream processing, no other observed criteria besides the semantic annotation is addressed by the authors.

4.2.3 Harmonization of Observation Messages

In Section 4.2.3, we discuss related work in the fields of heterogeneity and semantics of sensor streams and semantic annotations for sensor streams to support the harmonization of observation messages in IoT data streams. Markovic et al. have pointed out that streams of low level observation messages from heterogeneous sensors are meaningless without higher level context knowledge that adds explicit semantics to the sensor data [Markovic et al. 2016]. With their work, the authors have shown that controlled semantic vocabularies such as Semantic Sensor Network (SSN) or PROV-O can be exploited to explicitly model the provenance of sensor data. Further, the authors have shown how the vocabulary can be used

[4]https://spark.apache.org/
[5]https://flink.apache.org/

for a semantic stream-based data processing framework [Markovic and Edwards 2016]. Although they have deployed their approach to a relevant use case within the food safety domain, the authors have not stated how experts of this domain are enabled to exploit the expressiveness of the developed ontology or collaboratively annotate data streams of existing sensors. We therefore take a closer look at the following approaches:

SSN and SAREF: The SSN ontology [Compton et al. 2012] defines basic concepts for observations and sensors, in particular applicable in the IoT domain. In recent years, the SSN ontology became more and more the de facto standard vocabulary for describing sensors and sensing events [Haller et al. 2019]. Together with the SAREF ontology [Daniele et al. 2015] these two vocabularies are the most commonly used ones for the semantic description of sensing and actuation [Moreira et al. 2017].

The SSN ontology provides shared vocabularies for an explicit description of sensors and observation platforms. This approach is not dedicated to environmental observations, it also addresses manufacturing sensors or personal sensor devices. SAREF aims to provide semantic annotations on a system level, especially for household appliances that implement heterogeneous networked devices. Although these annotations can be employed for unified access to heterogeneous devices, the semantics of sensor data is not discussed. For both, the SSN and the SAREF approach, advanced techniques such as collaborative annotating, semantic mapping, semantic validation or semantic enrichment of observations are not addressed.

BigGIS: Wiener et al. have shown that variety and veracity of spatio-temporal data of heterogeneous sensor observations are still an unsolved issue that has to be addressed in order to generate meaningful knowledge. In their vision paper, they have discussed an approach for continuous refinement of this data supported by semantic web services and domain experts [Wiener et al. 2016]. However, more research has to be carried out in order to proof this approach.

For the BigGIS vision paper, the authors discuss the need for enriching and validating observations on a semantical level without providing a solution that addresses this issues.

Semantic data model and IoT-Lite: The approach of Duy et al. [Duy et al. 2017] focuses – similar to ours – on sensor observations and describes those through the SSN and SWEET ontology. The streaming data is enriched with semantic concepts and provided by a SPARQL API on top of a graph store, linking observations and measurement stations by RDF predicates. Even if they have implemented a transformation in their program code, they have several modules in their framework that do not support configurable mapping for the streams. A cooperation of several experts is therefore not possible. The IoT-Lite ontology [Marúdez-Edo et al. 2017] reuses the core SSN device and sensor definitions for a broader model of IoT resources with a strong focus on lightweight descriptions.

The semantic data model of Duy et al. exploits semantic annotations to map sensor data to SSN observations. The authors do not describe how such annotations can be created collaboratively or how the observations are enriched and validated. IoT-Lite is similar to this approach, but with the aim to process data more efficiently. Both approaches do not address enrichment and validation of observations.

LD4Streams: Barnaghi et al. provide a framework for stream annotations in combination with data from the LOD cloud in order to improve the location attributes [Barnaghi et al. 2013]. They also provide a web client to support the annotation but only on the level of stream elements and do not assist to create mappings for series of elements which typically is essential for any stream. The approach targets the manual annotation of stored streams but not real-time, automated transformation.

LD4Streams introduces a stream annotation mechanism that is optimized for reducing the size of representation of environmental sensor data streams for storage and query processing purposes. The authors also exploit publicly available LOD sources such as DBpedia or GeoName for explicit semantic annotations of environmental sensor data. Although raw observation tuples are not mapped to triples, the authors introduce a generic architecture to access meta data by unique names. Collaborative annotations, semantic validation and semantic enrichment of observations are not addressed.

Stream Annotation Ontology: Kolozali et al. [Kolozali et al. 2014] developed a framework specifically suitable for IoT stream processing. Their Stream Annotation Ontology (SAO) – which is also implemented by IoT-Lite – defines basic stream concepts and allows RDF modeling of streaming events. Additional concepts are also defined for quality of service, quality of information and provenance features. The proposed stream annotation framework supports the transformation of non-RDF to RDF streams and therefore enables the creation of unambiguously defined stream events through the mentioned ontologies. Nevertheless, the framework misses a straightforward configuration module for those mappings, neither does it support collaborative work on the regarded streams.

The SAO approach provides advanced techniques for semantic annotation in order to obtain semantic sensor data without specifying how this can be done on a collaborative base.

Annotations: Amiguet-Vercher et al. [Amiguet-Vercher et al. 2010] have discussed the challenges of creating, propagating and consuming semantic annotations of data streams of observation messages within sensor networks, especially if the intended semantics of data streams changes over time. They have deployed their approach on a network of environmental observation stations in the Alps, where for example snow on a sensor could cause a semantic change of the observed values. However, the authors do not state how these annotations can be maintained by domain experts in a collaboratively way. Although the authors have described the annotation propagation on a local level for single processing elements that also covers significance of semantic annotations, further research has to provide additional insight for annotation propagation on a workflow level.

The Annotations approach of Amiguet-Vercher et al. provides a well-defined annotation and propagation technique for semantic annotation of environmental sensor data. However, the annotations are made locally by domain experts. The issue of propagating such annotations to other groups of researchers is outlined, but not solved. Further, the authors consider observations as tuples and do not provide a mapping to explicit semantics. Due to missing semantics for the observation tuples, neither a semantic mapping, nor semantic enrichment is possible on an observation level.

4.2.4 Summarization of Current State and Limitations

A summarization of the characteristics defined in Section 4.2.1 applied to the introduced approaches for enriching environmental observations is presented in Table 4.1. The symbols used within the concept matrix are explained in Table 1.1 of Section 2.

Approach	Observed Criteria					
	Semantic Annotation	Semantic Sensor Data	Collaborative	Semantic Mapping	Semantic Validation	Semantic Enrichment
RML [Dimou et al. 2014]	–	–	–	✓	–	(✓)
R2RML [Das et al. 2012]	–	–	–	✓	–	(✓)
RSPLab [Tommasini et al. 2017]	✓	–	–	–	–	–
SSN [Compton et al. 2012]	✓	✓	–	–	–	–
SAREF [Daniele et al. 2015]	✓	–	–	–	–	–
BigGIS [Wiener et al. 2016]	✓	✓	–	–	(✓)	(✓)
SDM [Duy et al. 2017]	✓	✓	–	✓	–	–
IoT-Lite [Marúdez-Edo et al. 2017]	✓	✓	–	–	–	–
LD4Streams [Barnaghi et al. 2013]	✓	✓	–	(✓)	–	–
SAO [Kolozali et al. 2014]	✓	✓	–	–	–	–
Annotations [Amiguet-Vercher et al. 2010]	✓	✓	(✓)	–	–	–

Table 4.1: Concept matrix for enriching environmental observations.

From the related work we can learn that there are already tools that allow for RDF mapping, executing, processing and evaluation of RDF streams and also frameworks for modelling RDF constraints using explicit semantics and shared vocabularies. What is still missing is a framework that maps non-semantic data streams of heterogeneous observation stations to an RDF stream with meaningful explicit semantics based on collaboratively gathered annotations, including constraint validation and data provenance. We address this issue with a new approach as introduced in Section 4.3.

4.3 The LSane Approach

To overcome the limitations of current semantic data stream processing frameworks as identified in Section 4.2, we introduce the Linked Stream Annotation Engine (LSane) in Section 4.3. Furthermore, we demonstrate how collaboratively created annotations can be employed both effectively and efficiently to add explicit semantics to non-semantic data streams originating from observation stations on-the-fly. The underlying principle corresponds to a generic framework of loosely coupled and platform independent components that communicate over message brokers or web APIs.

We provide an overview of the LSane approach in Section 4.3.1. The requirements that have to be addressed by the approach are discussed in Section 4.3.2. We propose the architecture for the LSane approach in Section 4.3.3. In Section 4.3.4, we discuss how key-value pairs can be mapped to explicit semantics. The validation of observations with explicit semantics is discussed in Section 4.3.5 and enriching these messages with derived statements in Section 4.3.6. A prototypical implementation of the LSane approach is introduced in Section 4.4.

4.3.1 Overview of the LSane Approach

An overview of this generic framework is shown in Figure 4.1 and detailed in the following. The processing order of the messages is not necessarily static, but depends on the composition of the individual modules.

Sensor observations: Raw data of environmental sensor observations is provided by potentially heterogenous observations stations as key-value tuples with varying syntax and semantics. The data streams of observations produced by observation station 1 to observation station n are published to the according data streams S_1 to S_n.

Corporate Knowledge Graph: The corporate knowledge graph is the primary source for any context knowledge. It provides three types of metadata: Metadata M contains explicit semantics for tuples in observation messages. The semantic mapping process (A) relies on M for any mapping of observed tuples to triples

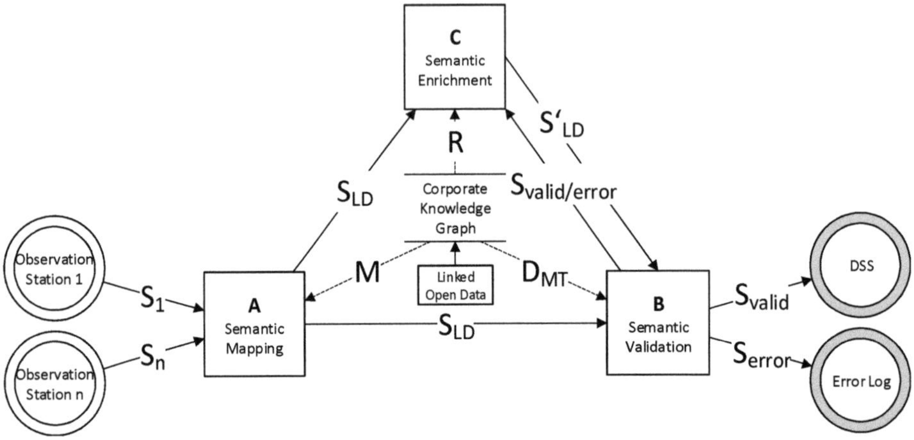

Figure 4.1: Overview of the LSane approach: Messages from environmental observation stations are mapped to explicit semantics (A), validated (B), enriched (C), and passed forward to a DSS. The context of both, sources and sinks, is explicitly modelled in the corporate knowledge graph and influences the mapping, validation and enrichment of messages.

with explicit semantics provided by M. The second type of metadata are definitions of message types D_{MT}. These definitions are used by the semantic validation process (B) in order to classify an observation as valid or not on a semantical level, independently from the originated syntax. The third type of metadata provided by the corporate knowledge graph are semantic rules defined in R. These rules are applied by the semantic enrichment process (C) in order to infer new triples. The corporate knowledge graph can also include LOD as addressed by RQ1 in Chapter 3.

Semantic Mapping (A): The semantic mapping process is subscribed to the streams S_1 to S_n that include observations that consist of key-value tuples produced by various observation stations. The process maps each observation to a new observation message that consists of triples that contain explicit semantics derived from M besides the observed value. The new observation message is published to the data stream S_{LD}. Mapping key-value tuples of sensor observations to triples with explicit semantics is addressed in Section 4.3.4.

Semantic Validation (B): The semantic validation process is subscribed to data streams S_{LD} and S'_{LD} that both contain observation messages with explicit semantics. Based on the definitions of D_{MT}, each message is classified as either valid or invalid. Valid messages are published unchanged to S_{valid}. For invalid messages, a report is attached to the observation message that indicates which part of the definition is violated. An invalid message is published to S_{error}, including the error report. Validation of observation messages is addressed in Section 4.3.5.

Semantic Enrichment (C): The semantic enrichment process is subscribed to data streams S_{LD}, S_{valid} and S_{error} that all contain observation messages with explicit semantics. To infer new triples, the process applies rules defined in R to each message. New messages that also include the inferred triples are published to S'_{LD}. Semantic enrichment based on rules that can be applied as a one-step process is addressed in Section 4.3.6. More complex enrichments that require dynamically composed workflows of varying data transformation services are addressed by RQ3 in Chapter 5.

Decision support: The streams of validated observation messages S_{valid} and S_{error} can be considered as data output of the overall approach. S_{valid} only contains observation messages containing triples with explicit semantics that fulfill the requirements of the data consumer. These observations are the base for a meaningful decision support based on consistent, complete and accurate observations. Messages in S_{error} that do not fulfill the requirements can be logged to an error log for further investigation by the domain experts.

4.3.2 Requirements for the LSane Approach

In order to enable automated processing of heterogeneous sensor observations, we define the following requirements:

R2.1: Map ambiguous schema and semantics in observation data streams to explicit semantics on-the-fly. In order to address the issue of lacking semantics of data streams, we require an adequate description of metadata. Each metadata description has to be represented as a set of key-value pairs that can be used for mapping keys to URIs defined as $M = \{(k, u) : k \in \mathbb{STR}, u \in \mathbb{URI}\}$. The

URIs are required to unambiguously identify the linked concept as introduced in Section 2.1, for example (*temperature, "quantity*[6]*:ThermodynamicTemperature"*).

R2.2: Enable domain experts to define shape constraints for observation messages and validate the shapes during runtime. In addition to adding explicit semantics to observation messages, domain experts have to be able to define demands on observations and filter or transform data as needed for different use cases. We therefore require a set of shape constraints for each message type defined as $D_{MT} = \{(s, p, o, c) \in \mathbb{RDF}\}$.

R2.3: Enable enrichment and transformation of observation messages in order to meet the demand of data consumers based on explicit semantics. Depending on the use case, it could be necessary to enrich the observation message with inferred statements about observed values or transform statements to other representations in order to fulfill the demands defined in D_{MT}. For example, if D_{MT} defines a thermodynamic temperature given as degree Fahrenheit and a sensor only delivers observations of thermodynamic temperature given as degree Celsius, the validation would fail although a simple transformation would fulfill the requirement. We therefore require a set of transformation rules defined as $R = \{(s, p, o, c) \in \mathbb{RDF}\}$.

4.3.3 Architecture of the LSane Approach

To address the requirements identified in Section 4.3.2, we propose a system architecture for the LSane approach as shown in Figure 4.2. We assume that ambiguous observation messages are emitted by various observation stations as motivated in Section 1.1. LSane maps these raw observation messages to explicit semantics based on metadata M provided by a corporate knowledge graph. The corporate knowledge graph is collaboratively maintained by domain experts as detailed in Chapter 3. This corporate knowledge graph further provides shape constraints contained in D_{MT} for validating observation messages and a set of rules R to enrich the semantics of the messages if needed. Finally, observations that conform to the shape constraints of D_{MT} are emitted for the data consumer.

[6] http://qudt.org/schema/quantity#

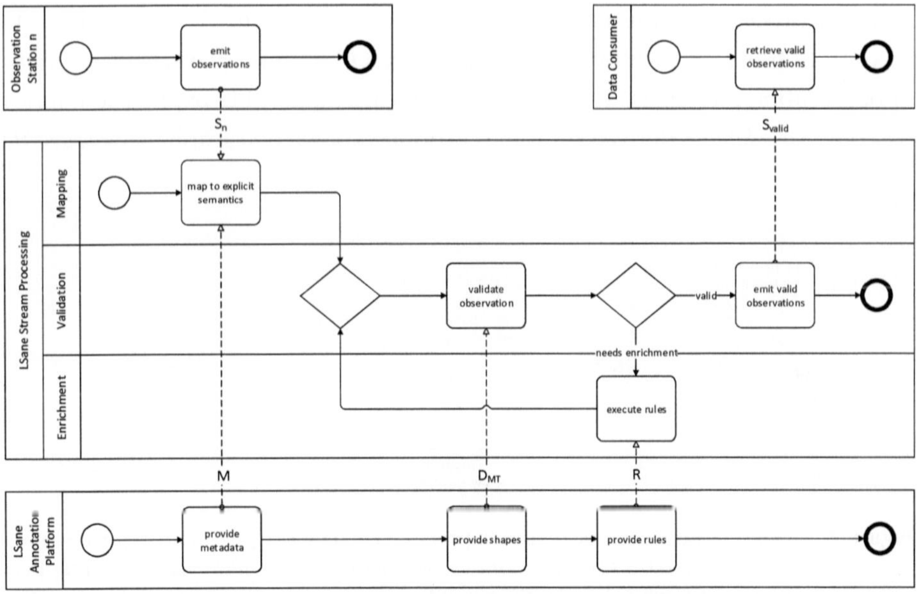

Figure 4.2: Overview of the system architecture of LSane: Ambiguous observation messages emitted by various observation stations are mapped to explicit semantics based on metadata M provided by a corporate knowledge graph, validated using the definitions of D_{MT}, and enriched if needed using rules of R. Finally, observations that conform to the shape constraints contained in D_{MT} are emitted for the data consumer.

The steps for processing an observation message including mapping, validation, and enrichment of observations are detailed in Section 4.3.4, Section 4.3.5, and Section 4.3.6 respectively.

4.3.4 Map Ambiguous Observations to Explicit Semantics

In order to map observation messages (R2.1), we define $\mathbb{STR}$ specifying the set of character combinations for valid keys and $\mathbb{VAL}$ as the set of possible values. Keys are typically interpreted as strings without spaces or special characters, whereas the values typically are strings, numbers, booleans, objects, arrays, or null. Further, we define $\mathbb{URI}$ as the set of valid URIs as introduced in Section 2.3.2. An overview of this semantic mapping process is shown in Figure 4.3. For the mapping process, we assume a number of data streams S_1 to S_N provided by the according observation stations 1 to N that represent exemplary *observation streams* of observation messages. These data streams are mapped to explicit semantics based on *metadata* M derived from the corporate knowledge graph using *semantic mapping* which leads to the outgoing stream S_{LD}.

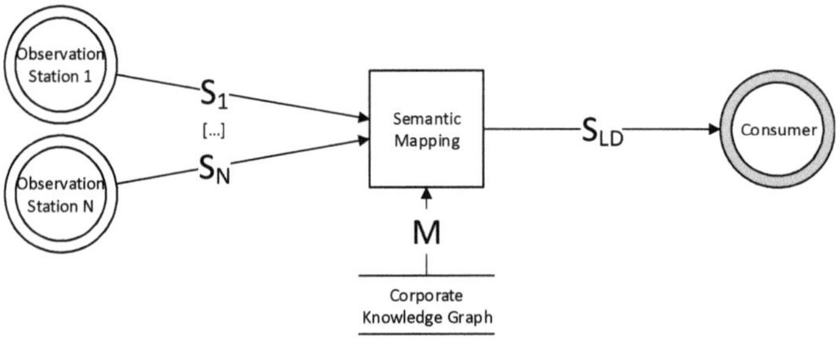

Figure 4.3: Overview of semantic mapping process: Each message without explicit semantics in each data stream S_n of heterogeneous observation stations is mapped to a new stream S_{LD} with explicit semantics based on metadata M of the corporate knowledge graph.

Observation streams: For our approach, we assume that series of observations from multiple observation stations are provided as data streams S_n in the form of continuous observation messages m. Each data stream is defined as $S_n = \{m_1, \ldots m_I\}$ where n specifies the ID of the observation station in a range of 1 to N and i the order of appearance within the data stream in a range of 1 to I. An observation message is defined as $m = \{(k, v) : k \in \mathbb{STR}, v \in \mathbb{VAL}\}$. Observation messages in a stream are represented as sets of key-value pairs such as *"temperature=40"*, which cannot be assumed to contain any explicit and machine-processable semantics per se. In this example, any human with basic knowledge of the English language will correctly interpret the observation as a temperature measurement. Nevertheless, a computer without any additional information only sees a set of characters with no defined relation to the physical quantity. Even a human receiver of that data, depending on the personal background, may interpret the observation as rather cold (if regarded as Fahrenheit) or very hot (if interpreted as Celsius).

Metadata management: To manage the metadata M in the corporate knowledge graph, we propose an annotation platform based on a LD-Wiki as detailed in

Chapter 3. This annotation platform allows for collaboratively created annotations of non-semantic data streams using distinct concepts of LOD. With the annotation platform, we enable domain experts and other users who are not necessarily developers or knowledge workers to intuitively annotate data sources with explicit semantics. Users of the annotation platform are provided with forms, where they can easily select applicable quantities, units and data types from a list of shared vocabularies inside the annotation platform. For context specific vocabularies, where no shared vocabularies can be reused, additional concepts of classes, properties, and individuals can be added and maintained manually. The benefit of having one collaborative platform for all annotations – in contrast to annotations per-source, per-format or per-case – is the logical abstraction of the underlying formats, data structures and serialization, and the possibility to reuse semantic annotations for similar data sources. The output of the proposed annotation platform is a metadata description M of observation streams S_n within the corporate knowledge graph using the annotations of domain experts.

Semantic mapping: To combine messages of observation streams with semantic annotations in a meaningful way, we define the semantic mapping process $SemMap$. For this process, we assume input streams S_n of observation messages provided by heterogenous and independent observation stations. In addition, we assume the existence of a corporate knowledge graph as defined in Section 2.4.3 which contains a machine processable representation of the semantic annotations and a mechanism that sends update notifications whenever there is a change in the corporate knowledge graph. The mapping of each observation message m based on metadata M is defined as $SemMap(m, M) = \{(u, v) : (k, v) \in m, (k, u) \in M\}$. It maps each observation of m which is serialized as a key-value tuple (k, v) to a new URI-value tuple (u, v) according to an adequate key-URI tuple (k, u) of M. The output of the $SemMap$ process is a data stream S_{LD}, which consists of continuous messages from all input streams mapped to explicit semantics. The semantics specify context, observed quantities, units and provenance of the observation as defined in M. The output stream is therefore defined as $S_{LD} = \{SemMap(m, M_n) : m \in S_n\}$ with n indicating the according observation station. Every single element of S_{LD} is the resulting set of tuples (u, v) computed by $SemMap$ taking any observation message m of any observation stream S_n and the according metadata M_n as input. The additional explicit semantics information enables a consuming application of data stream S_{LD} to interpret each message correctly without the need of any further data understanding or application logic. Moreover, whenever there is a change in the corporate knowledge graph, for example due to a newly added or modified annotation, a data stream S_{LD} immediately includes that new semantics and the consumer is able to interpret it correctly without any adaption of the code.

4.3.5 Validate the Semantics of Observations

The semantic validation is built on the assumption that streams of heterogeneous observation messages are mapped to explicit semantics based on statements provided by a corporate knowledge graph which is maintained by a collaborative metadata management platform as described in Section 4.3.4. An overview of this semantic validation process is shown in Figure 4.4 where messages with explicit semantics in S_{LD} are validated based on the message type definition D_{MT} retrieved from the corporate knowledge graph.

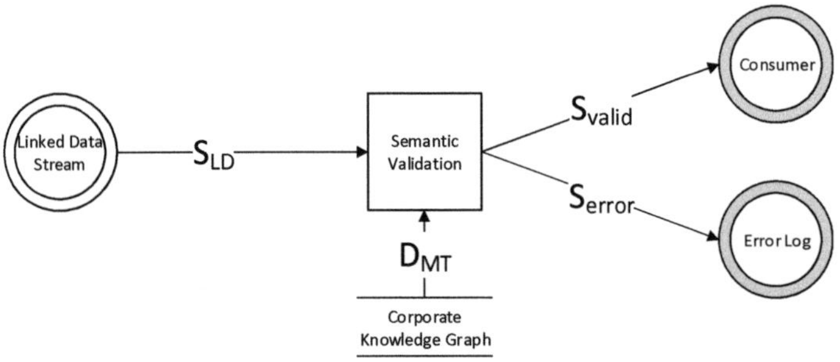

Figure 4.4: Overview of validation process: Messages with explicit semantics in S_{LD} are validated based on the message type definition D_{MT} of the corporate knowledge graph.

Shape constraints: In order to validate observation messages (R2.2), demands of data consumers have to be addressed by defining and evaluating shape constraints. These shape constraints can help to identify and filter invalid observations based on the definition of the message type D_{MT} associated with that class of observations. For example, a message stream with environmental air temperature values can be evaluated on-the-fly to determine whether each message contains a thermodynamic temperature value. These values can be further evaluated with regard to the plausibility of the value in combination with the provided quantity and unit of measurement. If the value is below absolute zero (0.0 K, -273.15 °C, or -459.67 °F respectively [Arora 1998, p.43]), it can in any case be considered invalid. Especially for the case of environmental air temperature, a value below the lowest temperature ever measured (183.95 K, -89.2°C or -128.6°F [7]) or above the highest temperature ever measured (329.85 K, 56.7°C or 134.0°F [8]) could at least be considered suspicious. The proposed generic evaluation of an observation message m based on the shape constraint defined in D_{MT} spares developers to alter the programming code for varying validation demands.

Validation process: For the validation of observation streams, we extend the proposed collaborative annotation platform with shape constraints contained in the definition of message types D_{MT} to distinguish different types of observation messages. Having S_{LD} as the input stream of observation messages mapped to explicit semantics, we validate each observation message m with the shapes for this stream using D_{MT} derived from the corporate knowledge graph. The semantic validation is defined as the split function $SemVal(m, D_{MT})$ that takes an observation message m and the message type definition D_{MT} as input:

$$SemVal(m, D_{MT}) = \begin{cases} m_{valid} = m \cup r_{valid} & \text{if } D_{MT} \subseteq m \\ m_{error} = m \cup r_{error} & \text{if } D_{MT} \supset m \end{cases}$$

If all statements demanded by D_{MT} are serialized in m, the validation function returns the message m_{valid}, even if m contains additional statements which are not demanded by D_{MT}. If one or more statements demanded by D_{MT} are missing in m, the validation function returns the error message m_{error}. The resulting messages m_{valid} and m_{error} are defined as the union of m and the set of statements created as the validation result r_{valid} or r_{error} respectively. The output of the $SemVal$ function applied to data stream S_{LD} are data streams S_{valid} for consumers of validated observation messages and S_{error} which can be used to log validation errors.

[7]https://wmo.asu.edu/content/world-lowest-temperature
[8]https://wmo.asu.edu/content/world-highest-temperature

4.3.6 Semantically Enrich Observations

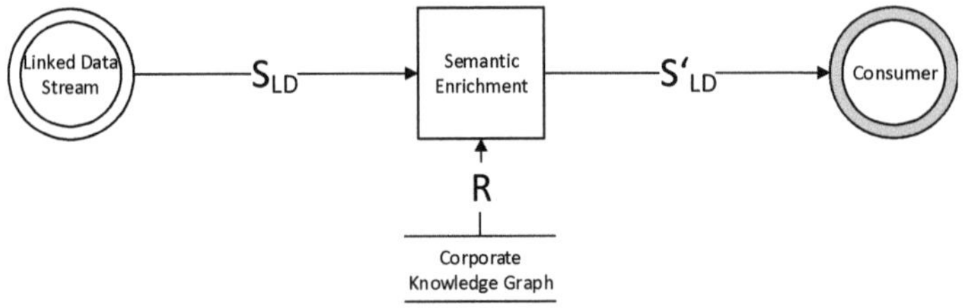

Figure 4.5: Overview of enrichment process: Messages with explicit semantics in S_{LD} are enriched based on rules R of the corporate knowledge graph and published to S'_{LD}.

In order to enrich observation messages (R2.3), we define a semantic validation process as shown in Figure 4.5.

For example, a message stream with values of air pollution can be evaluated on-the-fly whether the legal limit is exceeded or not, based on the definition of the message type D_{MT} associated with that class of observations.

As an example, Table 4.2 shows an observation message m of an observation station that only delivers observations of thermodynamic temperature given as degree Celsius.

ID (c)	Subject (s)	Predicate (p)	Object (o)
$graph_1$	$observation_1$	degreeCelsius	28.76324
$graph_2$	$graph_1$	hasProvenance	$sensor_1$

Table 4.2: Observed properties of observation message m.

Observation message m included in data stream S_{LD} is modeled with explicit semantics as introduced in Section 4.3.4 which allows to process this message without additional information. In order to provide explicit meta statements about each single statement contained within observation message m, we define a named graph per statement that includes a context ID c for each triple (s, p, o) as discussed in Section 2.4.5. Context ID c is required to refer to these triples when evaluating the provenance of observations. Namespaces of URIs are omitted in this example, however, they have to be considered for the implementation of the approach.

Rules: If a shape constraint contained in D_{MT} demanding a thermodynamic temperature given as degree Fahrenheit is applied to m, the validation would fail although a simple transformation would fulfill the requirement. Therefore, we enrich observation messages m to m' by adding derived statements that make this implicit information explicit based on context knowledge from the corporate knowledge graph. However, this requires a rule R that defines how a value of thermodynamic temperature given as degree Celsius is transformed to a value of thermodynamic temperature as degree Fahrenheit. A domain expert could add such a rule to the collaborative annotation platform as shown in Table 4.3.

ID (c)	Subject (s)	Predicate (p)	Object (o)
$graph_3$	$rule_1$	construct	"BIND($?degC * 1.8 + 32$) as $?degF$"

Table 4.3: Rules R from corporate knowledge graph.

Enrichment: The semantic enrichment function $SemEnr$ of LSane exploits this information to derive a new statement in m' based on rule R and the original observed value, in our example the value in degree Celsius contained in m, as $SemEnr(m, R) = m'$. Table 4.4 shows the resulting set of statements in m'. Using m' for the validation in $SemVal$ leads to the valid result m'_{valid}, regardless whether D_{MT} requires a thermodynamic temperature given as degree Fahrenheit or degree Celsius. Applying the $SemEnr$ function to data stream S_{LD} results in the new data stream S'_{LD} which can again be used as input for $SemVal$. As a consuming application is typically subscribed to S_{valid} only, the previously created result m_{error} is ignored.

ID (c)	Subject (s)	Predicate (p)	Object (o)
$graph_1$	$observation_1$	degreeCelsius	28.76324
$graph_4$	$observation_1$	degreeFahrenheit	83.77383
$graph_2$	$graph_1$	hasProvenance	$sensor_1$
$graph_5$	$graph_4$	hasProvenance	$conclusion_1$
$graph_6$	$conclusion_1$	hasInput	$graph_1$
$graph_7$	$conclusion_1$	hasRule	$rule_1$

Table 4.4: Observed and derived properties of enriched observation message m'.

4.4 Implementation of the LSane Approach

In Section 4.4, we describe the implementation of the LSane approach as introduced in Section 4.3. The implementation is done in two steps: first, we set up an annotation platform for collaborative, semantic annotations about raw observation streams, shape constraints, and enrichment rules in Section 4.4.1. Second, we provide a stream processing engine to map key-value pairs to explicit semantics, validate observation messages, and enrich observation messages with additional statements in Section 4.4.2. We showcase the implementation in Section 4.4.3.

4.4.1 Use Cases of LSane Annotation Platform

The LSane approach as introduced in Section 4.3 relies on semantic statements that explicitly describe metadata of observations M, definitions of message types D_{MT}, and rules for the enrichment of observation messages R. In order to enable domain experts and other users of LSane who are not necessarily developers or knowledge workers to intuitively annotate data sources with explicit semantics, we implement the LSane annotation platform based on semantic wiki software. In order to exploit statements from LOD, we employ LD-Wiki as introduced in Chapter 3 for this purpose. For an easy editing of metadata and shape constraints of data sources, we provide templates and forms for the wiki layer of the LSane annotation platform. In the semantic layer, the terms are linked with shared vocabularies which allows for interchange of these terms on other platforms, including explicit semantics for each term.

Use cases: The use cases of LSane are shown in Figure 4.6. As users of LSane primarily interact with the annotation platform, they are involved in three use cases: adding metadata M_n, definition of message types D_{MT}, and rules R. Each of these use cases contained in the annotation platform triggers an associated use case within the stream processing part of LSane: adding metadata M_n triggers LSane to subscribe to the according stream of observation messages S_n and maps each message to S_{LD} as required by R2.1. Adding shape constraints to D_{MT} triggers LSane to validate each message in S_{LD} using D_{MT} as required by R2.2.

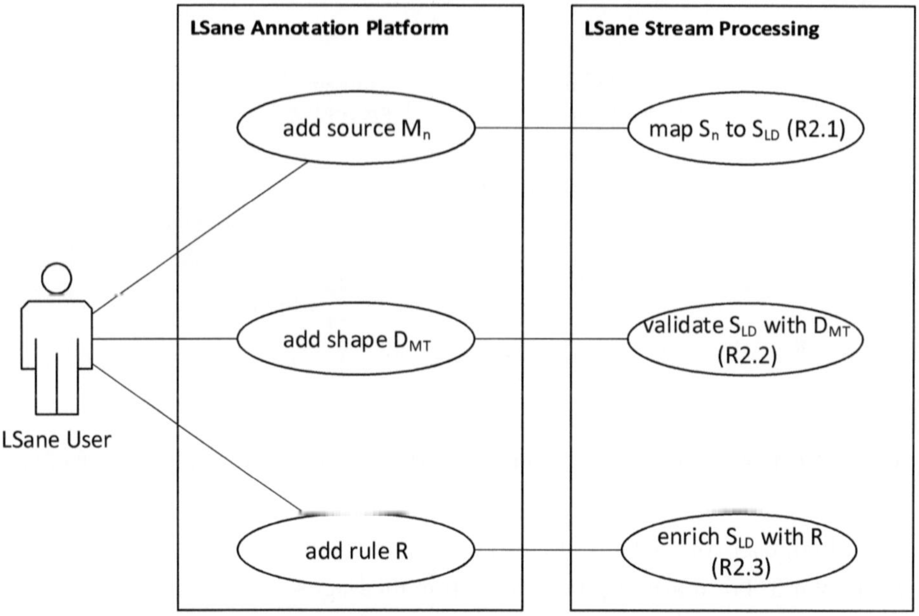

Figure 4.6: Use cases of LSane: adding metadata M_n triggers LSane to subscribe stream S_n and maps each message to S_{LD} (R2.1). Adding a shape constraint to D_{MT} triggers LSane to validate each message in S_{LD} using D_{MT} (R2.2). Adding a rule R triggers LSane to enrich each message in S_{LD} using R (R2.3).

Adding rules R triggers LSane to enrich each message in S_{LD} using R if applicable as required by R2.3.

Add sensor observations: The sequence for the use case of adding metadata M_n of observation station n is shown in Figure 4.7. Whenever a new stream of observation messages is registered to the annotation platform, the stream processing part of LSane is triggered, subscribes itself to the according stream of observation messages S_n, and maps each message to S_{LD} as required by R2.1. For meaningful metadata that can be processed automatically, LSane employs shared vocabularies for sensor observations of observation stations and also describing quantities and units. For this purpose, we provide SSN [Compton et al. 2012] for describing sensors of observation stations, and Quantities, Units, Dimensions and Data Types Ontologies (QUDT)[9] for describing quantities, units and data types.

[9]http://qudt.org/

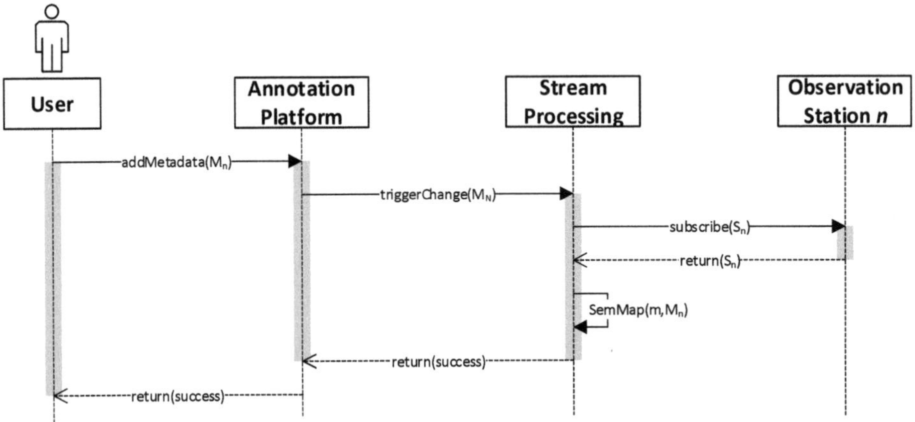

Figure 4.7: Register new stream S_n of sensor observations by providing metadata M_n.

If required, users of LSane could also import additional vocabularies as detailed in Chapter 3. For mapping the observation messages, it has to be ensured that the string value of the key for the new annotations is equal to the string value of the key produced by the annotated observation station in order to ensure that metadata is assigned correctly to the observed values.

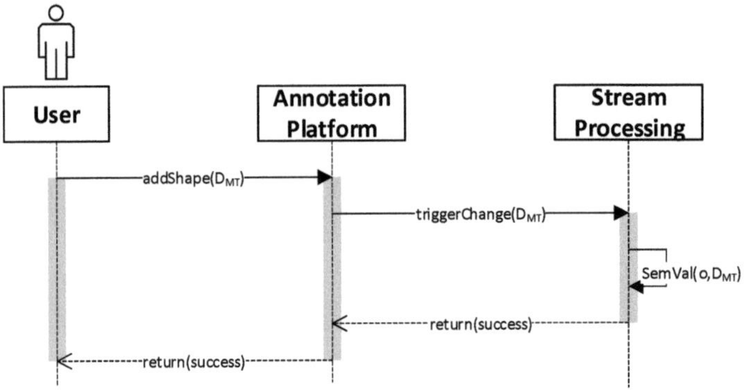

Figure 4.8: Define shape constraints for observation message type D_{MT}.

Add shape constraints: The sequence for the use case of adding a shape constraint to D_{MT} as needed by a certain data consumer is shown in Figure 4.8. Adding shape constraints to D_{MT} to the annotation platform triggers the LSane stream processing to validate each message in S_{LD} using D_{MT} as required by R2.2. In order to define constraints for observation messages, a system of rules has to be included. As discussed in Section 4.2, LSane employs SHACL for this purpose as the basis for shape constraints. This enables domain experts to intuitively define general requirements for observation messages on a semantic abstraction layer, independently from their provenance. Domain experts can select required properties and cardinality constraints using forms of the wiki layer of the LSane annotation platform and apply these constraints to a set of observation streams. In the semantic layer, these constraints are linked to the according SHACL terms for the evaluation.

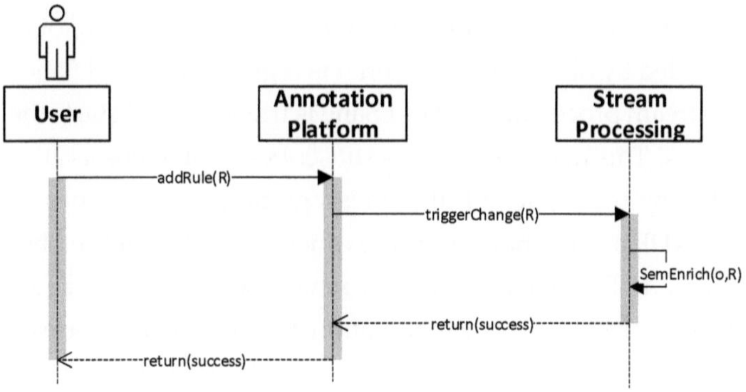

Figure 4.9: Provide rules R for further enrichment of sensor observation messages in S_{LD}.

Add rules for further enrichment: Users of LSane are also able to add a set of rules R as shown in Figure 4.9. Defining rules within the wiki layer of the LSane annotation platform automatically creates the according SHACL terms in the semantic layer. This event triggers the stream processing part of LSane as required by R2.3 to enrich each message in S_{LD} by applying the rules in R if applicable.

The implementation of the stream processing part of LSane is detailed in Section 4.4.2.

4.4.2 Use Cases of LSane Stream Processing

The implementation of the stream processing part of LSane relies on Apache Jena[10] to handle the RDF models and Apache Flink[11] for the actual stream processing. In addition, LSane employs Apache Kafka[12] as the message broker for observation messages. For validation and enrichment of observation messages, LSane employs TopBraid's SHACL API[13] which is based on Apache Jena as well. The use cases of Figure 4.6 that effect the stream processing part of LSane are detailed in the following.

Map observations to explicit semantics: Once a new stream S_n of observation messages provided by observation station n is registered to the LSane annotation platform, the stream processing part of LSane is triggered and starts the according mapping process. This mapping process subscribes itself to observation messages of S_n provided by the Apache Kafka message broker. Each message of S_n is mapped to an RDF model that contains explicit semantics of the observation as demanded by R2.1. The semantics for the new observation message are derived from metadata M provided by the annotation platform. For the stream mapping, LSane implements a consumer for configurable topics based on Apache Flink which also provides the required adapters for Apache Kafka. Whenever a new data source is registered to the annotation platform, the stream processing application receives an update notification and starts a new consumer for the according topic. We assume that messages in each input stream S_n are serialized as JSON. For each JSON object in the stream, the semantic mapping function performs a matching of keys for each member with keys received for metadata M_a from the annotation platform. LSane employs Apache Jena for creating the RDF model. For each message from an observation station, a Flink map function creates a new RDF instance of the class defined in the annotation platform for this station. For this instance, RDF properties are derived from the annotation platform for each match of a JSON member key and a metadata key. The value for the properties are extracted from the JSON object. Members of the message which are not defined in the annotation platform are interpreted as plain literal values and

[10]https://jena.apache.org/
[11]https://flink.apache.org/
[12]https://kafka.apache.org/
[13]https://github.com/TopQuadrant/shacl

added to the RDF model as well. Finally, the RDF model is serialized to JSON-LD and published to S_{LD}. This output stream contains all the explicit semantics provided by the annotation platform and enables data consumers to evaluate each message correctly, including provenance information. Whenever an annotation changes in the annotation platform, another update notification is sent to the stream processing application and immediately affects the semantic mapping process without the need of any code adaption.

Validate observation messages: As demanded by R2.2, LSane validates each message in S_{LD} by applying the shape constraints defined in D_{MT} for the according observation message type as demanded by a certain data consumer. Due to the imported and linked SHACL vocabularies provided by the annotation platform, any application that implements SHACL validation is suitable to perform the message validation. The validation engine of LSane employs the SHACL API provided by TopBraid for this purpose. It holds an Apache Jena RDF model based on the shape constraint defined in D_{MT} provided by the annotation platform. The validation engine validates each observation message m of the observation stream S_{LD} using that shape and includes the validation result to the message.

Enrich observation messages: The semantic stream enrichment of LSane works basically in the same way as the validation engine: rules R that are collaboratively defined in the annotation platform are applied to observation messages m of data stream S_{LD} using the SHACL API. Each observation message m in S_{LD} is enriched with addition statements by applying the rules of R where applicable in accordance with R2.3. However, SHACL distinguishes different kind of rules: whereas the validation engine considers only statements of D_{MT} which contains instances of sh:[14]property, the semantic stream enrichment applies the set of rules R which contains instances of sh:rule. Instances of sh:rule could be further distinguished in rule types such as sh:TripleRule or sh:SPARQLRule. For LSane, we employ rule type sh:SPARQLRule as it allows to encode SPARQL construct queries without the need of further specification.

In order to demonstrate the implementation of LSane, we provide a showcase in Section 4.4.3.

[14]http://www.w3.org/ns/shacl

4.4.3 Showcase

The showcase detailed in Section 4.4.3 demonstrates the implementation of LSane.

Register a new stream of observation messages: An example for a form that allows users of the annotation platform to select the observed quantity and the corresponding unit of measurement from the terms provided by the platform is shown in Figure 4.10. In this example, 'temp' is used as the key $k \in \mathbb{STR}$ to describe a member of an observation message serialized as JSON. This key is explicitly mapped by a domain expert to the URI that identifies the concept of thermodynamic temperature and degree Celsius is assigned as measurement unit for the values $v \in \mathbb{VAL}$.

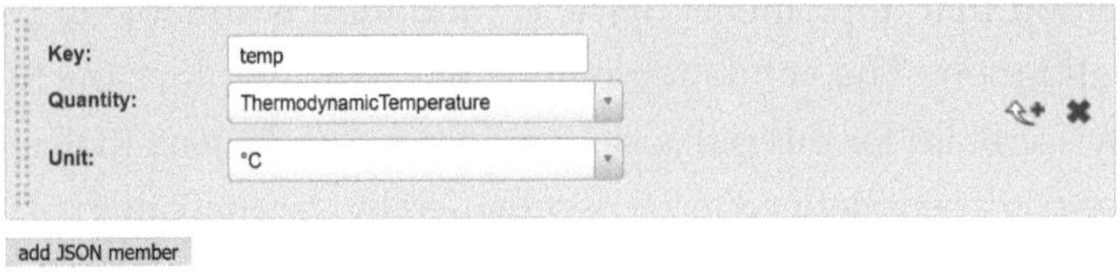

Figure 4.10: Form for collaboratively annotating members of JSON objects in the semantic repository.

Define shape constraints for observation messages: Figure 4.11 shows an example for annotating shape constraints for the messages that are produced by the annotated data source. The resulting RDF encoding that includes the according concepts of SHACL and QUDT is shown in Code Example 4.1. In this example, a domain expert defines a shape constraint for temperature observations. According to this shape, a temperature observation has to include exactly one member which is an instance of thermodynamic temperature and has a value $v \in \mathbb{VAL}$ that can be processed as floating-point number. Due to the employed SHACL vocabulary, the annotation platform delivers an RDF representation of this shape constraint in SHACL that can be interpreted by the validation engine.

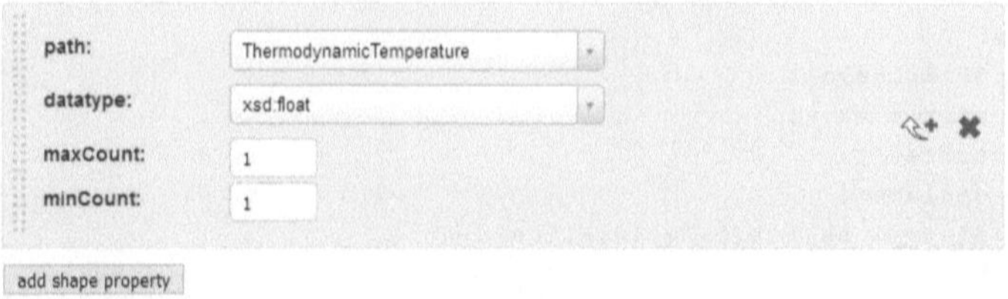

Figure 4.11: Form for collaboratively annotating shape constraints in the semantic repository.

```
ex:shape1
  a sh:NodeShape ;
  sh:property [
    sh:path quantity:ThermodynamicTemperature ;
    sh:datatype xsd:float ;
    sh:maxCount 1 ;
    sh:minCount 1 ;
    ] ;
  .
```

Code Example 4.1: SHACL shape as it results from the annotation process.

Apply shape constraints to observation messages: Figure 4.12 shows an example of a SHACL validation result. This result is created by TopBraid Composer [15], an application that implements SHACL validation in the same way as it is employed by LSane. The validation of the observation message m is based on the definition of the message type D_{MT} provided by the annotation platform. In this example, $SemVal(m, D_{MT})$ returns an error message as the message m used for this example does not contain a thermodynamic temperature and does therefore violate the minimum cardinality constraint of D_{MT}.

Shape	Component	Message
Property quantity:ThermodynamicTemperature: datatype=xsd:integer, minCount=1, maxCount=1, name=temparature	sh:minCount	Property needs to have at least 1 values, but found 0

Figure 4.12: Example for validation result on missing value.

[15]https://www.topquadrant.com/tools/modeling-topbraid-composer-standard-edition/

```
ex:rule1
  a sh:SPARQLRule ;
  sh:prefixes ex: ;
  sh:prefixes [
    sh:declare [
      rdf:type sh:PrefixDeclaration ;
      sh:namespace "http://qudt.org/schema/qudt/"^^xsd:anyURI ;
      sh:prefix "qudt" ;
    ] ;
    sh:declare [
      rdf:type sh:PrefixDeclaration ;
      sh:namespace "http://qudt.org/vocab/unit/"^^xsd:anyURI ;
      sh:prefix "unit" ;
    ] ;
  ] ;
  sh:construct """
    CONSTRUCT {
      $this ex:decC ?decC .
    }
    WHERE {
      $this ex:decF ?decF .
      unit:decC qudt:conversionMultiplier ?decCMultiplier .
      unit:decC qudt:conversionOffset ?decCOffset .
      unit:decF qudt:conversionMultiplier ?decFMultiplier .
      unit:decF qudt:conversionOffset ?decFOffset .
      BIND (?decF * ?decFMultiplier + ?decFOffset AS ?baseUnit) .
      BIND ((?baseUnit - ?decCOffset) / ?decCMultiplier AS ?decC) .
    }"""
  .
```

Code Example 4.2: Conversation rule to transform temperature observations given in degree Fahrenheit to degree Celsius as derived from meta data repository.

Enrich observation messages: An example for the enrichment of an observation message m based on rules in R is given in Code Example 4.2. This example shows a rule for constructing a statement about a temperature value as degree Celsius derived from an observed value as degree Fahrenheit by using the conversion multiplier and the conversion offset of degree Fahrenheit and degree Celsius. In this example, a SPARQL construct query is nested within a rule modeled as SHACL. The nested SPARQL construct query exploits the context knowledge of units as provided by QUDT. For each unit in QUDT, a conversion multiplier and a conversion offset is given. As multiplier and offset correspond to the base unit, the conversion from degree Fahrenheit to degree Celsius has to be carried out in two steps. In line 26, multiplier and offset of degree Fahrenheit are used to derive the quantity value in the base unit. In line 27, this base unit value is converted to degree Celsius by exploiting multiplier and offset of degree Celsius. As a result, this rule converts any degree Fahrenheit value to a corresponding degree Celsius value by exploiting the model only. Further hard coded conversion rules or conversion libraries are not required.

A further evaluation of the LSane approach based on the implementation introduced in Section 4.4 is provided in Section 4.5.

4.5 Evaluation of the LSane Approach

In Section 4.5 we evaluate the LSane approach as detailed in Section 4.3 regarding how a stream of continuous environmental observations can be mapped, validated, and enriched on-the-fly based on contextual knowledge from a corporate knowledge graph (RQ2). For the evaluation, we employ the implementation introduced in Section 4.4. The setup for the evaluation is introduced in Section 4.5.1 and the execution in Section 4.5.2. The results of the evaluation are discussed in Section 4.5.3.

4.5.1 Setup and Data

In order to evaluate the LSane approach, we perform a controlled laboratory evaluation. For this evaluation, we process non-semantic data streams of public and private environmental observation stations, map them to a representation with explicit semantics retrieved from the LSane annotation platform and interpret each message based on shape constraints retrieved from the same annotation platform. The whole framework is executed on a system with Intel®Core™i7-5600U CPU at 2.6 GHz and 12 GB memory.

Source data streams: As the input data stream S_n used for the evaluation, we generate a test set of 10,000 observation messages serialized as JSON based on the message patterns of two concrete environmental observation stations as introduced in Section 1.5.1. The test set is emitted by a Kafka producer that creates non-semantic messages to simulate third-party data streams. The frequency of emitted observations can be configured as needed for the evaluation. Using generated observation messages rather than a live feed allows to adjust the frequency of emitted messages for performance testing and reproducible results. As each observation message of the test set implements the message patterns introduced in Section 1.5.1, we can ensure that the results are compatible with streams of observation messages produced by concrete environmental observation stations.

Metadata: For both types of messages we provide annotations within the LSane annotation platform that fits to the keys of the members of each message type and also the shape information that we assume for a valid message from an observation station.

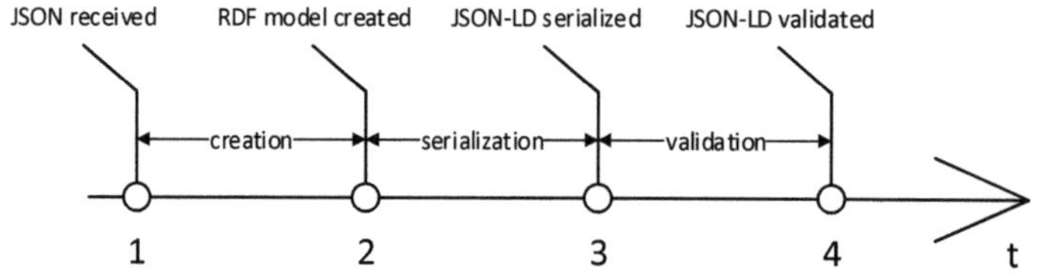

Figure 4.13: Timeline for evaluation of creating, serializing and validating messages.

Stream enrichment and shape constraint checking: To evaluate the processing time, we create a timestamp as shown in Figure 4.13 when 1) a JSON message m from the input stream S_n is loaded into the application, 2) the RDF model of m is created including all metadata from the annotation platform, 3) the RDF model is serialized to JSON-LD and 4) the JSON-LD message is evaluated using the TopBraid SHACL API in conjunction with the according shape constraint from the annotation platform. The test run covers a number of exactly 10,000 messages. As the test runs on a single processing node with limited hardware resources as detailed before, a frequency of about 150 messages per second can be processed at the most.

Observation shapes: For a validation of temperature observations independently from the origin sensor and format, we define an abstracted shape to model the data requirements of an exemplary DSS as shown in Code Example 4.3. This shape constraint defines two requirements: an observation message that fulfills these requirements needs to include exactly one floating-point number that represents the value of an observed thermodynamic temperature and exactly one timestamp that states the time when the value was observed. This shape is applied to all observations after they have been mapped to explicit semantics in order to filter the observations that fulfill the requirements formalized in the shape.

```
{ @prefix ex: <http://example.com/schema#> .
  @prefix rdf: <http://www.w3.org/1999/02/22-rdf-syntax-ns#> .
  @prefix rdfs: <http://www.w3.org/2000/01/rdf-schema#> .
  @prefix sh: <http://www.w3.org/ns/shacl#> .
  @prefix xsd: <http://www.w3.org/2001/XMLSchema#> .
  @prefix quantity: <http://qudt.org/schema/quantity#> .

  ex:TemperatureObservation
    rdf:type rdfs:Class ;
    rdf:type sh:NodeShape ;
    rdfs:subClassOf ex:Message ;
    sh:property [
        sh:path quantity:ThermodynamicTemperature ;
        sh:datatype xsd:float ;
        sh:maxCount 1 ;
        sh:minCount 1 ;
        sh:name "temperature" ; ] ;
    sh:property [
        sh:path :timestamp ;
        sh:datatype xsd:dateTime ;
        sh:maxCount 1 ;
        sh:minCount 1 ;
        sh:name "timestamp" ; ] ; . }
```

Code Example 4.3: Shape constraint for temperature observations messages as derived from meta data repository.

4.5.2 Conducting the Evaluation

We conduct the evaluation in four steps:

1) Generate streams of observations without explicit semantics
2) Map streams to a new stream with explicit semantics
3) Validate each observation with the given shape
4) Evaluate the processing time

Observation Streams: For the execution of LSane, we start two Kafka producers: one for messages in the shapes of a public observation station as detailed in Code Example 1.1 and the other for messages in the shape of a private observation station as detailed in Code Example 1.2 respectively. The resulting data stream S_1 of observations in the shape of the public observation station is visualized in Figure 4.14. In the same way, the resulting data stream S_2 of observations in the shape of the private observation station is visualized in Figure 4.15. Both figures show screen shots of the web based message consumer of LSane.

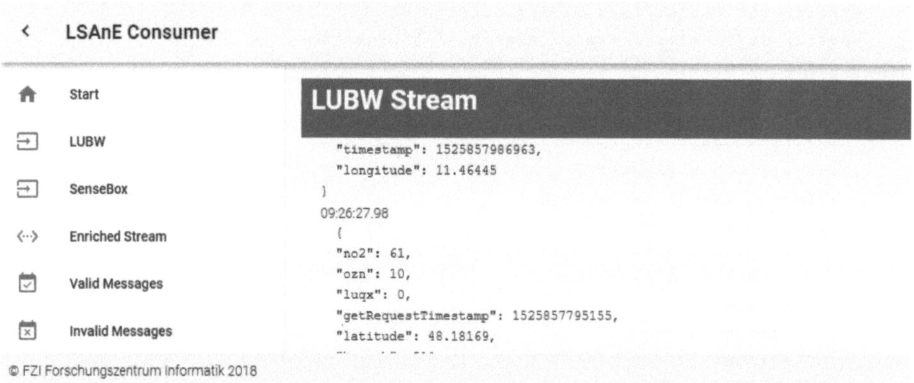

Figure 4.14: Stream S_1 with observation messages from the public environmental observation station.

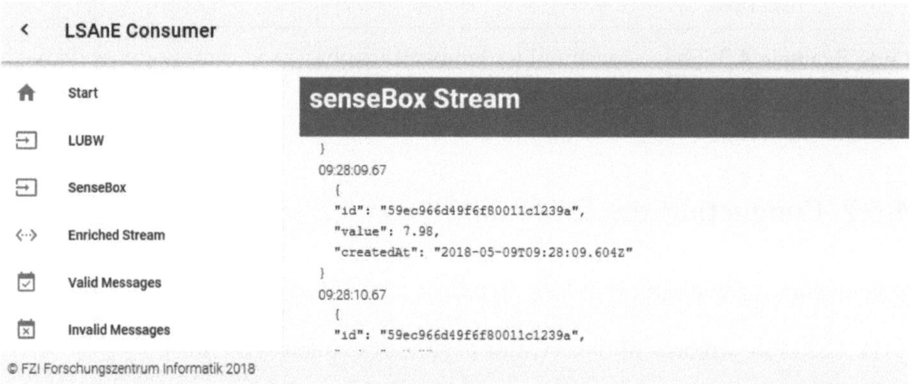

Figure 4.15: Stream S_2 with observation messages from the private environmental observation station.

In Figure 4.14 and Figure 4.15 we can see that the LSane consumer visualizes all messages of the observation streams unchanged in the way as they are produced by the Kafka producer, including the timestamp when they are created. Each observation is serialized as a JSON object that includes the original key-value tuples of the sensor observation.

Map to explicit semantics: To map the streams of observation messages to a new stream S_{LD} with explicit semantics, we start a mapping process that subscribes to both streams of observation messages and maps each single message of S_1 and S_2 to the semantic concepts as defined by M_1 and M_2 provided by the annotation platform. The resulting data stream S_{LD} of combined private and public observation stations including explicit semantics is visualized in Figure 4.16.

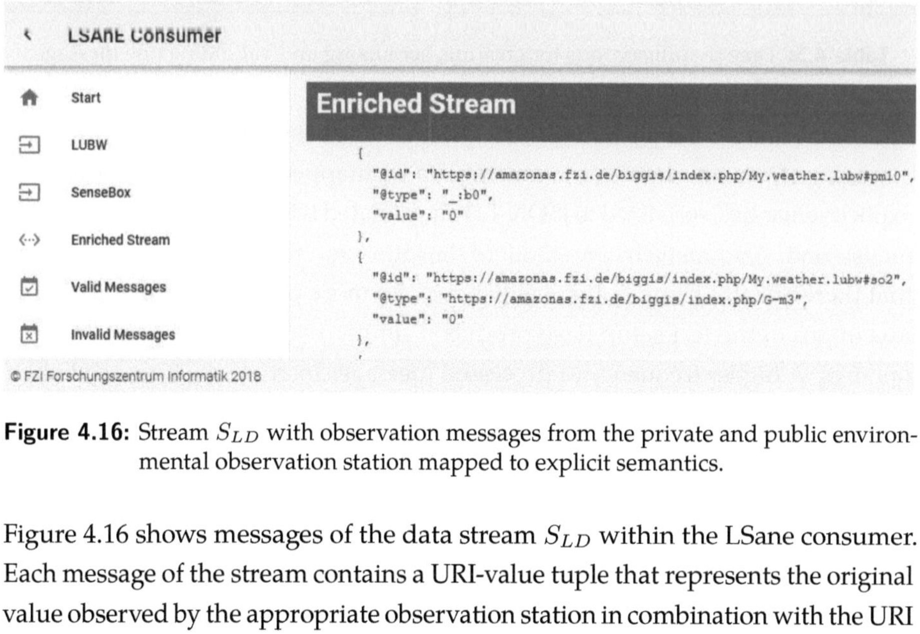

Figure 4.16: Stream S_{LD} with observation messages from the private and public environmental observation station mapped to explicit semantics.

Figure 4.16 shows messages of the data stream S_{LD} within the LSane consumer. Each message of the stream contains a URI-value tuple that represents the original value observed by the appropriate observation station in combination with the URI derived from the annotation platform that refers to the explicit and unambiguous semantic definition of the according concept.

Validate Observations: To validate the observations, we also start a validation process that consumes all messages of S_{LD} and applies the demanded shape as defined in Code Example 4.3 to each observation. Due to the invoked $SemVal$ process, depending on the result of the evaluation, the observations are emitted to either stream S_{valid} in case the requirements of the shape are fulfilled or S_{error} if they are not.

4.5.3 Discussion of Results

The times needed for each processing step as defined in Section 4.5.1 are shown in Table 4.5.

$f \approx 150 \frac{msg}{s}$	Arithmetic Mean	Median Value	Standard Deviation	Min Value	Max Value
Creation	1.460	0.341	3.699	0.196	47.750
Serialization	0.342	0.270	1.372	0.135	130.886
Validation	3.020	0.195	5.684	0.062	129.788
Total	4.822	0.979	6.813	0.468	276.622

Table 4.5: Time in milliseconds for creating, serializing and validating one message.

The minimal and median values show that even with limited hardware resources a message from an observation stream can be mapped to an RDF model with explicit semantics, serialized to JSON-LD an validated with SHACL in less than one millisecond. Arithmetic mean, standard deviation and the maximum values show that there are also some outliers which require more processing time. Multiple executions of the test setup have produced similar results which confirm these findings. A higher frequency of processed messages increase the time needed for processing the serialization and validation of JSON-LD slightly. Both values are still less than one millisecond, even with a frequency of 1,000 messages per second. However, the time interval between receiving the JSON object from the message stream, enriching it with explicit semantic and constructing the RDF model is varying non-linearly from about one millisecond to almost seven milliseconds. As the architecture of the stream processing part of LSane is prepared for distributed systems, a higher message throughput can be realized by adding more nodes to the processing framework.

4.6 Conclusion of Chapter 4

In Chapter 4, we have evaluated the research question of how a stream of continuous environmental observations can be mapped, validated, and enriched on-the-fly based on contextual knowledge from a corporate knowledge graph (RQ2). To answer this research question, we have proposed LSane, a semantic stream processing framework that maps observation messages to explicit semantics, validates each message, and enriches them with further statements based on collaboratively created annotations provided by domain experts (C2). The stream processing part of LSane covers the aspects of map sensor observations on-the-fly to explicit semantics (C2.1), validate sensor observations on-the-fly based on explicit semantics (C2.2), and enrich sensor observations on-the-fly based on explicit semantics (C2.3).

LSane foundations: We have discussed related work in the fields of heterogeneity and semantics of sensor streams, semantic annotations for sensor streams and semantic validation and enrichment of sensor streams and identified the research gap of collaboratively defined rules for mapping, validation and enrichment of observation messages. Based on these findings, we have provided a formal description of the semantic mapping function $SemMap(m, M)$, semantic validation function $SemVal(m, D_{MT})$, and the semantic enrichment function $SemEnr(m, R)$, which exploit collaboratively created semantic annotations of domain experts.

LSane annotation platform: We have introduced the LSane annotation platform based on LD-Wiki for collaborative definitions of rules for mapping, validation and enrichment of observation messages that can be applied to heterogeneous message streams using SHACL. Domain experts are provided with forms and templates where they can easily select applicable quantities, units, data types, and elements for shapes and rules from a list of shared vocabularies.

LSane stream processing: Based on the LSane annotation platform, we have shown how such collaboratively created annotations can be exploited to map non-semantic data streams of public and private observation stations to a representation with explicit semantic information of observations, measured quantities, and measuring units by applying the corresponding context knowledge. Furthermore, we have shown how data shape constraints and rules derived from the annotation platform can be employed for constraint validation and enrichment of observation data streams on-the-fly. For the implementation of LSane, we have implemented stream processing engines for mapping, validation and enrichment of observation messages based on the SHACL API.

Evaluation: For the evaluation of LSane, we have used the shapes of concrete public and private environmental observation stations to generate streams of observation messages and validate these streams with shape constraints from the annotation platform. To evaluate the performance of the LSane stream processing, we have measured the time interval for creation, serialization and validation of messages from a continuous data stream using the message format of exemplary public and private environmental observation stations. The results show that our generic approach for mapping non-semantic streams of observation messages to a meaningful representation with explicit semantic information and validating the shape constraints of messages can be done efficiently on-the-fly without adopting the code to specific data sources.

Outcome: With our work we have shown that heterogeneous messages of environmental observations can be collaboratively validated using semantic annotations of SHACL shapes and also that collaboratively created annotations of rules can be exploited for semantic enrichment of heterogeneous messages of environmental observations. Therefore, we consider the hypothesis that a well-curated corporate knowledge graph enables automated mapping, validation, and enrichment of ambiguous sensor observations based on explicit semantics (H2) as confirmed.

In the following Chapter 5, we present our findings for answering the research question of how preprocessing workflows for environmental observations can be composed automatically based on the contextual knowledge of an observation.

5

Knowledge-driven Automation of Data Harmonization

In Chapter 5, we present our findings for answering the research question of how preprocessing workflows for environmental observations can be composed automatically based on the contextual knowledge of an observation (RQ3). This involves testing the hypothesis of whether contextual knowledge of observations makes it possible to meet the requirements of different data consumers automatically (H3). Contents of Chapter 5 have been published in [Frank 2016] and [Frank and Zander 2016b].

5.1 Introduction to Chapter 5

Section 5.1 provides the motivation for research question RQ2 in Section 5.1.1, outlines the addressed challenges in Section 5.1.2, and lists the contributions to these challenges in Section 5.1.3.

5.1.1 Motivation for Knowledge-driven Automation

GISs are important tools for decision support based on spatio-temporal data. These tools are used in various fields such as civil planning, emergency management, agriculture or environment and nature protection. Due to improved and pervasive sensor technology and data created by mobile devices and users of social web applications, the amount of spatio-temporal data is increasing. At the same time, the reliability of this data may be uncertain and needs to be taken into consideration when used in GIS. In addition, spatio-temporal data from different sources may use different schemas to describe locations, such as addresses, relative spatial relationships or different coordinates reference systems. The quantities measured and units used for data values may also vary across heterogeneous and uncontrolled data sources. Due to these developments, GIS are facing challenges in all four dimensions of big data:

- **Volume**: The prevalence and omnipresence of sensor technology and ubiquitous data sources imposes challenges regarding data volumes to be integrated.
- **Variety**: Unstructured data is a new kind of data for GIS, which requires innovative methods of data interpretation for analyzing, interpolating, predicting and visualizing.
- **Velocity**: In order to permanently integrate acquired sensor data in GIS, the common batch processing of these systems have to be technically and conceptually reorganized in order to enable real-time analysis and activity recommendations.
- **Veracity**: The integration of volunteered geographic information (VGI) and other user-created content as well as integration of remote sensing analyzed image processing data which may be incomplete prevent the assumption that collected data is complete and correct at any given point in time.

By feeding big data into GISs, we have to take these characteristics into consideration with a special focus on the requirements imposed by GISs, including the provenance information of data. The increasing amount of geographic data has the potential to significantly improve the scientific findings of GISs closer to reality. However, the level of improvement strongly depends on a common understanding of concepts across heterogeneous data sources. We therefore argue for applying explicit semantics to environment observations as detailed in Chapter 4. As a consequence, Chapter 5 addresses the following research question:

RQ3: How can harmonization workflows for sensor observations be composed automatically based on the contextual knowledge of an observation?

From research questions RQ3 we derive the following hypothesis:

H3: Contextual knowledge of observations makes it possible to meet the requirements of different data consumers automatically.

Varying DSSs and other data consumers of homogenized observation messages may have different requirements on format and representation of those observations. We hypothesize that a set of semantic transformation rules retrieved from a corporate knowledge graph enables dynamically composed data processing workflows that meet such requirements on demand. If it is possible to compose such workflows automatically based on the knowledge of a corporate knowledge graph, we consider hypothesis H3 to be confirmed. If the composition without additional inputs is not possible, we consider hypothesis H3 as disproved. We test hypothesis H3 in Section 5.5.

In the following Section 5.1.2, we discuss the challenges that have to be addressed in order to answer RQ3.

5.1.2 Challenges Addressed in Chapter 5

The challenges that arise when composing workflows to preprocess observation messages for GISs automatically are identified as follows:

Unknown state of observations: Employing observations for GISs derived by heterogeneous sources includes that states of observations are varying and potentially unknown. The state of each message could therefore differ in schema, semantics, and syntax of describing an observed feature. For employing such messages in GISs, the state of each observation has to be determined and made explicit for further processing.

Varying target states: Depending on the use case or the technical requirements of a DSS used within a GIS, the demanded target state of observations could also vary. We therefore have to ensure that varying message requirements can be met during runtime, even if those requirements are not know at design time of the GIS.

Change state of observations: If the provided state of an observation message does not meet the requirements of the target state, one or more actions have to be applied to the messages in order to change their state. We therefore need a set of actions and an execution environment where these actions can be applied to those messages.

Dynamic adaption of workflows: Due to the varying initial and target states, the preprocessing workflows have to be flexible in order to meet varying requirements on demand. The system has therefore to learn the most efficient sequence of actions to reach a certain target state. This sequence has to be learned for each possible initial state of an observation message.

5.1.3 Contributions

In order to contribute to the domain of automatically composed preprocessing workflows for GISs, we propose a self-learning preprocessing workflow for linked observations that dynamically employs a set of predefined actions in order to meet varying requirements on demand (C3). We detail our contributions to the domain of automatically composed preprocessing workflows for GISs as follows:

C3.1: Explicitly define possible states of observation messages for GIS in a machine interpretable way. We propose to use semantic web technology to *describe data sources and data transformation services* for GIS in a machine interpretable way. For this purpose, we provide explicit definitions of possible states. Based on these definitions, we automatically derive observation states that allow a common understanding of the underlying concepts across heterogeneous data sources.

C3.2: Explicitly define the target state for all observations as required by a data consumer. In order to address varying requirements for format, schema, and semantics demanded by a data consumer, we propose to define the target state for observations explicitly. We exploit the definition of the target state to identify observations which are in a state that already meets the requirements and observations that have to be preprocessed in order to reach the target state as demanded by the data consumer.

C3.3: Explicitly define actions and apply these actions to messages in order to change their state. For observations which are in a state that differs from the target state, actions have to be applied in order to change the state of that observation. Therefore, we provide a set of generic actions that affect schema, syntax and semantic representation of the observation. In addition, we provide an execution environment that is able to preprocess any observation by applying any of the predefined actions.

C3.4: Provide an algorithm to learn the most efficient sequence of actions to reach a certain target state. By describing heterogeneous data sources for GIS together with actions that are employed as transformation services semantically, workflows for processing this data can be composed dynamically in order to fulfill use case specific requirements on demand. For this dynamic composition, we derive a policy that applies the most efficient sequence of actions to observation messages in order to reach a certain target state for any initial state.

Chapter 5 is organized as follows: In Section 5.2, we provide and discuss the literature review in the field of knowledge-driven automation of data harmonization. We introduce our approach for dynamically composed workflows in Section 5.3. The implementation of our approach is illustrated in Section 5.4. In Section 5.5, we show how our implementation can be applied in a self-learning manner to spatio-temporal data. Finally, the results are discussed in Section 5.6.

5.2 Related Work

In Section 5.2, we analyze the related work for research question RQ3. First, we define the criteria for the review in Section 5.2.1. Next, we introduce and discuss related work with respect to *data transformation and interoperability of GIS* in

Section 5.2.2 and *semantic workflow composition* in Section 5.2.3. We summarize the current state and the limitations of all introduced approaches in Section 5.2.4.

5.2.1 Criteria for the Literature Review

We discuss the approaches introduced in Section 5.2.2 and Section 5.2.3 with respect to the following characteristics:

- **Geospatial Data:** Does the approach consider machine-interpretable modeling of geospatial data, including appropriate vocabularies using explicit semantics?
- **Temporal Data:** Does the approach consider machine-interpretable modeling of temporal data, including appropriate vocabularies using explicit semantics?
- **Dynamic Workflows:** Does the approach consider a dynamic composition of services for a flexible fulfillment of data integration tasks during runtime of a system?
- **Linked APIs:** Does the approach employ services, preferable services that are available as linked APIs?
- **Self-learning:** Is the approach self-learning with respect to evaluating unknown services based on results using varying input data?
- **Extendable:** Does the approach describe how additional services can be added during runtime of the system in order to solve a broader range of integration tasks?

5.2.2 Data Transformation and Interoperability of GIS

For the interoperability of spatial data observed by sensors, the W3C Semantic Sensor Network Incubator Group introduced the SSN ontology[1] for describing sensors and observations. For GIS, the Open Geospatial Consortium (OGC)[2] defines standards for interoperability. One of their initiatives is the Sensor Web

[1]http://purl.oclc.org/NET/ssnx/ssn
[2]http://www.opengeospatial.org/

Enablement (SWE)[3] which supports services for web integration of sensors such as the Sensor Observation Service (SOS)[4] which is a web service to query real-time sensor data and sensor data time series. Observations and Measurements (O&M) is the response model used for SOS, for example the Water Model Language (WaterML)[5] for the representation of water observations data. Transforming data from heterogeneous data sources into a unified schema and the interoperability of distributed systems is still an ongoing research topic where web services are commonly used for converting data. As an example, Stolz and Hepp proposed to integrate currency conversion functionality from open web APIs into the LOD cloud in a conceptually clean, scalable way [Stolz and Hepp 2013]. Also the QUDT[6] can be used as a common standard for describing units and their conversion. Kämpgen and Harth presented OLAP4LD, a framework for developers of applications over LOD sources reusing the RDF Data Cube Vocabulary [Kämpgen and Harth 2014]. However, a standardized execution framework to exploit these descriptions is missing. We therefore take a closer look at the following approaches:

Geodata on the Web: In the context of GIS, transformation of spatial data across different coordinates reference systems (CRSs) was addressed by Atemezing et al. which have published a dataset dedicated to the description of CRSs defined and maintained by the French national mapping agency. Similar requirements are also given for the Gauss-Krueger CRS used by national agencies in Germany [Atemezing et al. 2014] .

The 'Geodata on the Web' approach proposes two RDF vocabularies designed for representing structured geometries defined with coordinates expressed in any CRS. Although this allows for a wide range of interpretation tasks of geographic datasets, the dimension of time, which is relevant to sensor streams of environmental observations, is not considered. Further, all data transformation tasks have to be conducted manually.

Geospatial Cyberinfrastructure: Li et al. reported on their efforts to design and develop a geospatial cyberinfrastructure for urban economic analysis and simulation using a service-oriented architecture to allow widespread sharing and

[3]http://www.opengeospatial.org/ogc/markets-technologies/swe
[4]http://www.opengeospatial.org/standards/sos
[5]http://www.opengeospatial.org/standards/waterml
[6]http://www.qudt.org/

seamless integration of distributed geospatial data [Li et al. 2013]. They addressed the uncertainty and positional errors encountered in fusing data from diverse sources and the generation of a chain of web services to tackle such complex problems while capturing and representing provenance of geospatial data.

A service orientated architecture is the foundation of the geospatial cyber infrastructure for urban economic analysis and spatial decision-Making. Data integration of heterogeneous sources of geospatial data is provided by feature matching, mainly based on similarity of feature names. To facilitate sharing, discovery and dynamic binding of geospatial processes, the approach employs a dedicated web processing service. This processing service is not self-learning, but relies on the meta data that is provided along with the processing service. Although this lays the foundation for automated workflow composition and execution, an evaluation for this aim is missing.

Karma: Harth et al. used Karma[7] for a dynamic integration of a reasonable amount of static and dynamic linked data [Harth et al. 2013].

The Karma approach supports rapid integration of new sources of geospatial and temporal data. The system is able to automatically map new sources to a previously defined ontology based on data samples that are compared to sources and services it has already seen to suggest models. As users are required to refine the suggested model manually using a graphical user interface, the self-learning aspect of the approach is fulfilled only partly. The linked API aspect can also be considered partly fulfilled because the approach employs a so-called 'Data-Fu' module that collects data and evaluates queries over it.

GIVA: Cruz et al. have created a semantic framework for geospatial and temporal data integration, visualization, and analytics [Cruz et al. 2013].

The GIVA approach addresses the geospatial and temporal dimensions of environmental sensor data. However, data integration is limited to string matching on column headers and semantic or spatio-temporal matching. Both steps have to be invoked manually by domain experts where applicable. The authors claim that additional services can be added to the framework if needed.

[7] https://usc-isi-i2.github.io/karma/

Linked Sensor Data Cube: Lefort et al. have introduced an approach of how to combine the SSN ontology with the RDF Data Cube vocabulary to a meaningful ontology and applied that ontology on the homogenized daily temperature dataset for the monitoring of climate variability and change in Australia [Lefort et al. 2012].

The Linked Sensor Data Cube considers geospatial and temporal data of heterogeneous environmental sensors. The resulting data cube can easily be queried using established semantic web technologies. On the other hand, the integration of data within the cube requires a lot of manual effort for defining custom mapping rules and Python scripts. The employment of linked APIs, dynamically composed workflows or self-learning algorithms is not considered.

5.2.3 Semantic Workflow Composition

Maleshkova et al. propose the concept of 'Smart Web Services' based on the semantic description of data sources and data transformation services [Maleshkova et al. 2016]. For processing symbolic data, Kämpgen et al. extended the drill-across operation over data modeled in the RDF Data Cube vocabulary[8] to consider implicit overlaps between datasets in linked data, defined convert-cube operation over values from a single dataset and generalized the two operations for arbitrary combinations of multiple datasets with the merge-cubes operation [Kämpgen et al. 2014]. Cherfi et al. proposed and discussed the main constituents of an ontology of quality federating all the aspects of information system components quality [Cherfi et al. 2011]. However, this approach does not address the specific requirements of GIS for geospatial and temporal data. Gil et al. gave an overview of the Organic Data Science framework [Gil et al. 2015], an approach for scientific collaboration that opens the science process and exposes information about shared tasks, participants, and other relevant entities based on SMW. Although the task-centered collaboration approach can be considered as a workflow of distributed services that have temporal and geospatial aspects, this approach does not support dynamic creation of automated data processing workflows. We therefore take a closer look at the following approaches:

[8]http://www.w3.org/TR/vocab-data-cube/

Component catalogues: Gil et al. have formalized an approach how the selection of application components and data sources can be automated in general using semantic web technologies [Gil et al. 2011]. In principle, this approach can also be chosen to address the challenge of how to combine the workflow of data sources and transformation services to meet the requirements of any GIS.

Component catalogues are an important foundation for any kind of dynamic data processing workflow. They include unique references to input data objects, workflows and data products with explicitly modeled properties, relations among properties and inferences about properties. This allows for workflow generation based on generic workflow templates. As the workflow generation relies on workflow templates provided by the request or retrieved from a catalogue, the self-learning aspect can be considered as partly fulfilled.

Lightweight Descriptions: Kopecký et al. presented research in lightweight machine-readable service descriptions and semantic annotations for web APIs, building on the HTML documentation that accompanies the APIs [Kopecký et al. 2011].

Lightweight machine-readable descriptions of services based on WSDL elements can be employed to compose services. Service descriptions are provided following the linked data principles either with the services themselves or within a centralized service registry. The aspect of linked APIs is therefore partly fulfilled. The descriptions are not self-learned but have to be provided manually which is supported by editing and annotation tools.

3G Web APIs: Lanthaler described an approach to build hypermedia-driven web APIs based on linked data technologies and developed Hydra [Lanthaler and Guetl 2013], a small vocabulary to describe web APIs [Lanthaler 2013]. Lanthaler and Gütl also introduced an approach to create machine-readable descriptions for RESTful services and show how these descriptions along with an algorithm to translate SPARQL queries to Hypertext Transfer Protocol (HTTP) requests can be used to integrate RESTful services into a global read-write web of data [Lanthaler and Gütl 2012]. They discussed some of the challenges and choices that need to be made when designing RESTful web APIs and described an alternative, domain-driven approach to design web APIs [Lanthaler and Gütl 2013].

Using the Hydra vocabulary, 3G Web APIs [Lanthaler 2013] can be built for seamless integration into the web of data [Lanthaler and Gütl 2012]. Using this approach, domain experts can focus on the domain model of producer and consumer of web API, rather than struggling with syntax issues of the client-server communication on the web [Lanthaler and Gütl 2013]. In this way, the proposed approach supports the development of and interaction with linked APIs. Exploiting these APIs for dynamic composition of data processing workflows or self-learning of clients is not covered by the authors.

XGSN: Calbimonte et al. proposed the eXtended Global Sensor Networks (XGSN) approach [Calbimonte et al. 2015]. They annotated sensor data and observations using an ontology network based on the SSN ontology and showed how to provide a highly flexible and scalable system for managing the life-cycle of sensor data in the context of the semantic web of things [Calbimonte et al. 2015].

Both, the temporal and geospatial dimensions of environmental sensor observations, are covered by the XGSN approach which allows for higher level abstractions of virtual sensors using explicit semantics. Although the authors describe how observations of heterogeneous sensors can be integrated using a message queue middleware with publish-subscribe architecture, a dynamic integration based on self-learning algorithms for linked APIs is not addressed. Additional services have to be added manually where necessary.

Preprocessing of medical images : Gemmeke et al. have shown that semantic technologies can help to cope with data format heterogeneity, distribution of the data sets and interoperability issues in the medical domain, for example when processing medical images [Gemmeke et al. 2014]. Similar challenges have to be addressed in the domain of GISs when processing raster data created by satellites, drones or surveillance cameras.

Using linked data and web APIs for automating the preprocessing of medical images does employ the concept of linked APIs for a dynamic composition of services for data processing workflows. This composition strongly depends on explicitly described semantics of input and output pattern for each involved API service. Before a service is invoked, a pattern matching is performed in order to verify whether the service is runnable on the available data or not. A self-learning algorithm to match services to data is therefore not required.

Service-oriented architecture for linked data integration: Vettor et al. have shown that a service-oriented architecture can help to solve heterogeneity issues by attaching explicit semantics to data in a company's information system [Vettor et al. 2014].

The service-oriented architecture for linked data integration is implemented as a set of layers according to the different tasks to be performed on data, namely the data source management layer, the semantic annotation layer, the data integration layer, the data filtering layer, and the data consumption layer. Each software component is deployed as a linked data service. This allows for reusable, autonomous components that are abstracted from implementation and location. Therefore, the architecture can be employed for service orchestration. The orchestration itself has to be provided by third party applications or cognitive apps.

Machine-interpretable descriptions: Dimou et al. introduced an approach that takes advantage of widely-accepted vocabularies, originally used to advertise services or datasets, such as Hydra or dcat, to define how to access web-based or other data sources [Dimou et al. 2015].

The machine-interpretable descriptions of Dimou et al. are not dedicated to geospatial or temporal data sources. They rather provide a framework for unified access to heterogeneous data sources and web APIs based on RML and controlled vocabularies such as Hydra. This approach allows to take advantage of widely-accepted vocabularies to define how to access web-based or other data source as linked APIs.

5.2.4 Summarization of Current State and Limitations

A summarization of the characteristics defined in Section 5.2.1 applied to the introduced approaches for dynamic interoperability workflows for GIS is presented in Table 5.1. The symbols used within the concept matrix are explained in Table 1.1 of Section 2.

Approach	Observed Criteria					
	Geospacial Data	Temporal Data	Dynamic Workflows	Linked APIs	Self-learning	Extendable
Geodata on the Web [Atemezing et al. 2014]	✓	–	–	–	–	–
Geospatial Cyberinfrastructure [Li et al. 2013]	✓	✓	(✓)	–	–	✓
Karma [Harth et al. 2013]	✓	✓	–	(✓)	(✓)	✓
GIVA [Cruz et al. 2013]	✓	✓	–	–	–	✓
Linked Sensor Data Cube [Lefort et al. 2012]	✓	✓	–	–	–	–
Component Catalogues [Gil et al. 2011]	–	–	✓	–	(✓)	✓
Lightweight Descriptions [Kopecký et al. 2011]	–	–	✓	(✓)	–	✓
3G Web APIs [Lanthaler 2013]	–	–	–	✓	–	✓
XGSN [Calbimonte et al. 2015]	✓	✓	–	–	–	✓
Pre-proc. of images [Gemmeke et al. 2014]	–	–	✓	✓	–	✓
SOA for LD Integration [Vettor et al. 2014]	–	–	–	✓	(✓)	✓
Machine-Interpretable Descr. [Dimou et al. 2015]	–	–	–	✓	–	✓

Table 5.1: Concept matrix of dynamic interoperability workflows for GIS.

The work presented in this section expresses that exploitation and integration of big data in a way that addresses provenance, veracity, velocity, structural and semantic dissimilarities of spatio-temporal data, especially for GIS, is an ongoing challenge. Based on the related work introduced in this section, we present our collaborative information integration approach for spatio-temporal data in GIS in Section 5.3.

5.3 The Aprolo Approach

In Section 5.3, we introduce automated processing of linked observations (Aprolo), an approach that automatically learns a policy for efficient preprocessing of linked observations and meets the requirements of varying data consumers on demand. The requirements that have to be addressed by the approach in order to enable automated preprocessing of linked observations are discussed in Section 5.3.1. In

Section 5.3.2, we propose the architecture for the Aprolo approach. Two major components of Aprolo are well-defined states and actions as introduced in Section 5.3.3 and Section 5.3.4 respectively. In Section 5.3.5, we detail how Aprolo exploits states and actions in order to learn a policy creating dynamic preprocessing workflows for GISs.

5.3.1 Requirements of the Aprolo Approach

In order to enable automated preprocessing of heterogeneous sensor observations and meet varying requirements of consuming applications on demand, we define the following requirements:

R3.1: Define states and determine state of an observation. For automated preprocessing of heterogeneous sensor observations, the system has to be aware of the state of an observation. For this thesis, the relevant aspects of a state covers explicit syntax and semantics of the observation. The definition of states is further detailed with examples in Section 5.3.3.

R3.2: Define the target state for a set of observations. Besides awareness of states, a target state has to be provided. We define the target state of an observation as the state that is demanded by a data consumer. If the state of an observation is equal to the target state demanded by a data consumer, no further preprocessing is required. The same

R3.3: Define actions and perform actions to states. In order to change the state of an observation, the system has to be able to perform actions on observations of any state. The concept of such actions is detailed with examples in Section 5.3.4.

R3.4: Learn a policy for the most efficient sequence of actions to reach a target state. For composing efficient preprocessing workflows for GISs, a policy has to be learned that indicates which action has to be performed in a certain state in order to reach a target state as demanded by a data consumer. In Section 5.3.5, we detail how these policies are inferred for Aprolo.

5.3.2 Architecture of the Aprolo Approach

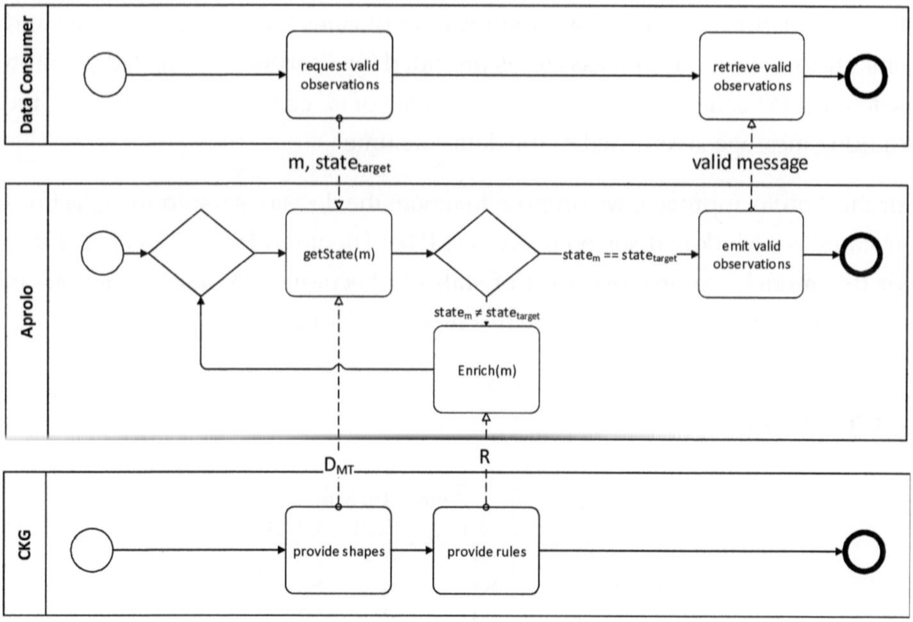

Figure 5.1: Overview of the system architecture of Aprolo: a data consumer processes observation messages m provided by heterogeneous sensors with varying syntax and semantics. For meaningful processing of these observations, the data consumer demands $state_{target}$ for all observations, regardless of their origin. Aprolo determines the state of m based on message type definitions in D_{MT} and performs actions defined in R if required. D_{MT} and R are retrieved from the corporate knowledge graph. Observations that conform to $state_{target}$ are returned to the data consumer.

To address the requirements identified in Section 5.3.1, we propose a system architecture for the Aprolo approach as shown in Figure 5.1. We assume that a data consumer is subscribed to messages m of observations in S_{LD} provided by heterogeneous sensors with varying syntax and semantics as detailed in Chapter 4. For meaningful processing of these observations, the data consumer demands $state_{target}$ for all observations, regardless of their origin. In order to provide the demanded state for all observations, Aprolo determines the current state of m based on message type definitions in D_{MT}. We assume that these definitions are derived from shape constraints provided by a corporate knowledge graph as detailed in Section 4.3.5. If the current state of m is different from the demanded target state, Aprolo performs an action retrieved from R in order to change the state of m. For this purpose, we assume a set of rules that concerns syntax and semantics of observation messages is provided by a corporate knowledge graph as detailed in Section 4.3.6. As soon as the state of m' conforms to $state_{target}$, the resulting message is returned to the data consumer.

For the Aprolo approach, we propose to model the decisions for applying actions on states as a Markov decision process (MDP) [Bellman 1957; Ross et al. 2014]. For this model, we propose a set of states in Section 5.3.3, a set of actions in Section 5.3.4, and methods to solve this model in Section 5.3.5.

5.3.3 States

		Semantic Model		
		String	Float	QUDT
Unit	Target	S6	S7	S8
	Base	S3	S4	S5
	Different	S0	S1	S2

Table 5.2: Classification of states $S0$ to $S8$ with respect to the semantic model of the observed quantity and condition of the associated unit of measurement.

Within the context of this thesis, the state of an observation message is defined as the explicit representation of *semantic model* and *units of measurement* used for this message. Both criteria have to be carefully evaluated in order to enable meaningful and automated preprocessing of heterogeneous sensor observations within GISs. To cover a broad range of available data streams, the intended GIS needs to handle environmental observation data in a various number of potentially unknown states. For the Aprolo approach, we define a set S with a total of nine elements that represent varying states of observations and differ in the way of semantic modeling and also in the units of measurement that are associated with that observations as shown in Table 5.2.

For the dimension of semantic modeling, we consider three variants:

- **String**: Observation values are given as strings that include both, the observed value and a symbol that indicates the applicable unit of measurement. Properties used for this value describe an observed quantity independently from units of measurement that could be used. Each property-value tuple has a shape equal to *quantity* = *"float unit"*.
- **Float**: Observation values could also be given as a float value without any indication of the applicable unit of measurement. Such values can easily be processed for statistical analysis. However, for a valid comparison of values from different sources, properties used for such values needs to imply the applicable unit of measurement. Property-value tuples of this variant therefore have a shape equal to *quantity.unit* = *float*.
- **QUDT**: In contrast to both variants described before, observation values could also be modeled using a more expressive model that includes controlled vocabularies with explicit semantics such as QUDT. Values in this shape can be interpreted and manipulated correctly by exploiting existing third party applications that are aware of QUDT. This enables a model-driven data integration without the need of further programming.

In addition to various ways of semantic modeling, also the unit of measurement that applies to an observation varies for different sources. Depending on the requirements of a DSS that is used for further processing of environmental observations, one of the following three conditions apply:

- **Target**: The unit of measurement that applies to an observation is equal to the unit of measurement that is required as input for the DSS.
- **Base**: The unit of measurement that applies to an observation is not equal to the unit of measurement that is required as input for the DSS, but equal to the base unit of the measured quantity.
- **Different**: The unit of measurement that applies to an observation is neither equal to the unit of measurement that is required as input for the DSS, nor equal to the base unit of the measured quantity.

As a consequence, the states of an observed feature considered for the Aprolo approach, for example a thermodynamic temperature that should be processed by a DSS that requires any thermodynamic temperature to be encoded as °C, are defined as follows:

- **S0**: The observation is a string value that includes a symbol of a unit of measurement that is neither the base unit of its quantity, nor the unit required by the DSS. For example, a value for an observed thermodynamic temperature is equal to *temp = "100 °F"*.
- **S1**: Similar to $S0$, the observed value is neither the base unit of its quantity, nor the unit required by the DSS. However, in this case, the value is given as float together with a property that explicitly indicates the unit of measured, for example *temp.degF = 100.*
- **S2**: Similar to $S0$ and $S1$, the observed value is neither the base unit of its quantity, nor the unit required by the DSS. In contrast to $S0$ and $S1$, observations in $S2$ are modeled explicitly using the controlled vocabulary of QUDT.
- **S3**: Observations in state $S3$ are modeled as string values and given with the appropriate base unit of a quantity, but not with the unit required by the DSS, for example *temp = "310.9 K"*.
- **S4**: The observations are modeled as float values using the base unit of a quantity, but not the target unit of the DSS, for example *temp.K = 310.9*.
- **S5**: Observations modeled explicitly as QUDT values using the base unit of a quantity, but not the target unit of the DSS.
- **S6**: Observations that are defined using the target unit of the DSS and modeled as string values, for example *temp = "37.8 °C"*.
- **S7**: Observations that are defined using the target unit of the DSS and modeled as float values, for example *temp.degC = 37.8*.
- **S8**: Observations that are defined using the target unit of the DSS and modeled as QUDT values.

In addition to the varying units of measurement that could be required by a DSS, also the requirements for the semantic modeling may vary. As these requirements can change during runtime of the GIS, they are unknown at the design time. Therefore, any of state $S6$, $S7$ or $S8$ could be the target state for a DSS. In order to address any possible target state for any of the nine defined initial states, we define a set of actions in Section 5.3.4.

5.3.4 Actions

For the intended GIS, we define a set A whose elements are actions that could be applied to any of the states in S. The actions are defined as follows:

- **A0**: Action $A0$ parses a given graph G and produces a new graph G' that contains the same triples as $A0$. As this action should not change the state of a given graph, it can be used as neutral element to validate the functionality of the workflow execution.
- **A1**: Action $A1$ parses a given graph G and converts all triples that represent observations with float values to string values and produces a new graph G' which contains only the converted triples.
- **A2**: Action $A2$ parses a given graph G and converts all triples that represent observations with float values to values modeled explicitly in QUDT and produces a new graph G' which contains only the converted triples.
- **A3**: Action $A3$ parses a given graph G and converts all triples that represent observations with string values to float values and produces a new graph G' which contains only the converted triples.
- **A4**: Action $A4$ parses a given graph G and converts all triples that represent observations with string values to values modeled explicitly in QUDT and produces a new graph G' which contains only the converted triples.
- **A5**: Action $A5$ parses a given graph G and converts all triples that represent observations modeled explicitly in QUDT to float values and produces a new graph G' which contains only the converted triples.
- **A6**: Action $A6$ parses a given graph G and converts all triples that represent observations modeled explicitly in QUDT to string values and produces a new graph G' which contains only the converted triples.
- **A7**: Action $A7$ parses a given graph G and converts the unit of measurement of all triples that represent observations modeled explicitly in QUDT to the base unit of the observed quantity without changing the semantic modeling itself. The return value of $A7$ is a new graph G' which contains only the converted triples.
- **A8**: Action $A8$ parses a given graph G and converts the unit of measurement of all triples that include observations with the base unit of a quantity and are modeled explicitly in QUDT to the target unit of the observed quantity

without changing the semantic modeling itself. The return value of $A8$ is a new graph G' which contains only the converted triples.

The effect (T) that actions of A have when applied to any state of S is shown in Figure 5.2. Actions that do not produce a valid new state for a certain initial state are not included.

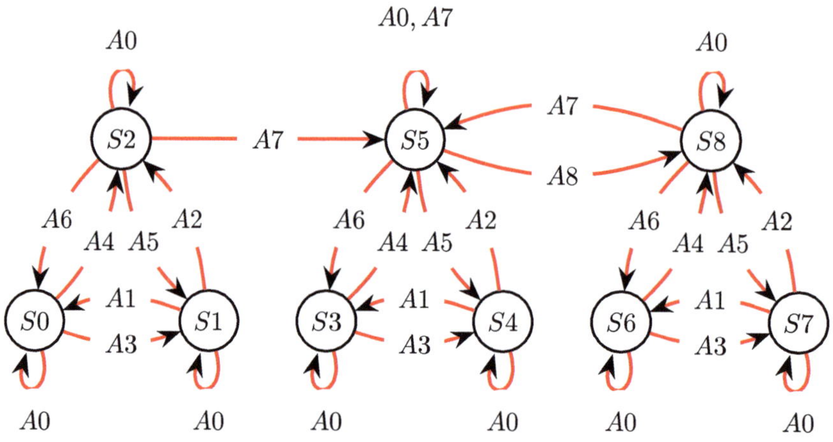

Figure 5.2: Effect (T) of actions A0 to A8 applied to states S0 to S8

5.3.5 Infer Policy

In order to reach $state_{target}$ for each observation message, a workflow has to be composed depending on the respective initial state as defined in Section 5.3.3. Each workflow includes a sequence of actions as defined in Section 5.3.4. This sequence could either be determined by performing random actions on each state until $state_{target}$ is reached, or by learning a policy that specifies the most efficient sequence to reach that state. For learning a policy, we propose to solve the MDP by reinforcement learning using the *Q-learning algorithm* of Watkins as introduced in [Watkins 1989]. Q-learning is a simple way for software agents to learn how to act optimally within a MDP and works by successively improving its evaluations of the quality of particular actions at particular states [Watkins and Dayan 1992]. For creating adequate workflows for varying initial and target states, the agent trains a *quality matrix* based on a *reward matrix* using the set of states S as defined in Section 5.3.3 and the set of actions A as defined in Section 5.3.4. For the initial reward matrix, a reward is granted for each action that results in the target state. Based on this reward matrix, the agent trains the quality of an action for each state that quantifies the expected future reward. From this quality matrix we infer a policy for each possible initial and target state. This policy enables Aprolo to perform a sequence of actions that converts any message into the demanded target state in the most efficient way.

5.4 Implementation of the Aprolo Approach

In Section 5.4, we show an exemplary implementation of the Aprolo approach as introduced in Section 5.3. We introduce the use cases of the Aprolo implementation in Section 5.4.1 and provide a showcase in Section 5.4.2.

5.4.1 Use Cases of Aprolo Execution Environment

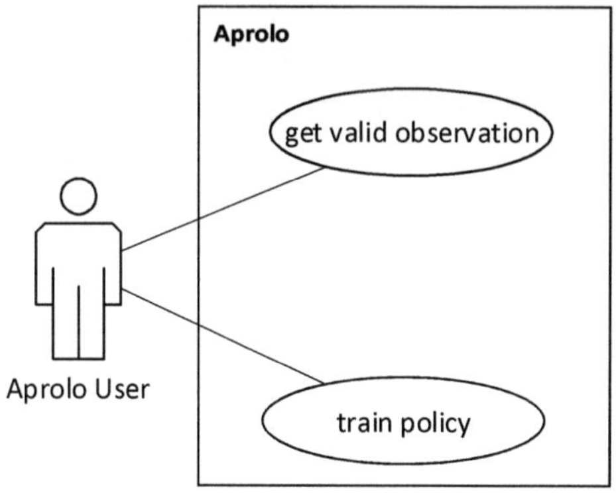

Figure 5.3: Use cases of Aprolo: users of Aprolo demand a certain state for an observation. Aprolo determines the initial state of the observation and applies actions to reach the target state if necessary. Actions could be applied either randomly or by following a policy. This policy has to be trained for each initial and target state in advance.

Use cases: The use cases of Aprolo are shown in Figure 5.3. Users of Aprolo are basically involved in two use cases: retrieve observations that are in a certain target state and train a policy for reaching a certain target state for varying initial states. In order to provide a certain target state, Aprolo determines the initial state of the observation. If necessary, Aprolo applies actions to transform the Aprolo to reach the target state. Actions could be applied either randomly or by following a policy. This policy has to be trained for each initial and target state in advance.

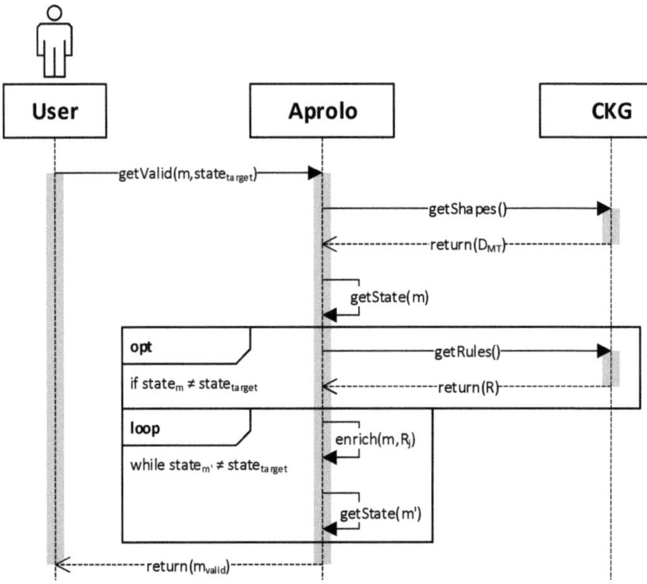

Figure 5.4: Sequence for retrieving observation messages in a certain target state.

Get valid observations: The sequence for the use case of getting valid observations with respect to a certain target state is shown in Figure 5.4. A user of Aprolo requests a valid observation message m with respect to the desired target state $state_{target}$. In order to determine the initial state, Aprolo queries the corporate knowledge graph for shapes D_{MT} of possible states and tests m for a match. If the determined state $state_m$ is equal to $state_{target}$, the observation is regarded as valid and returned to the user. Otherwise, actions that are inferred from rules provided by the corporate knowledge graph are applied to m until the target state is reached. The sequence of actions applied to m could be either random or specified by a policy.

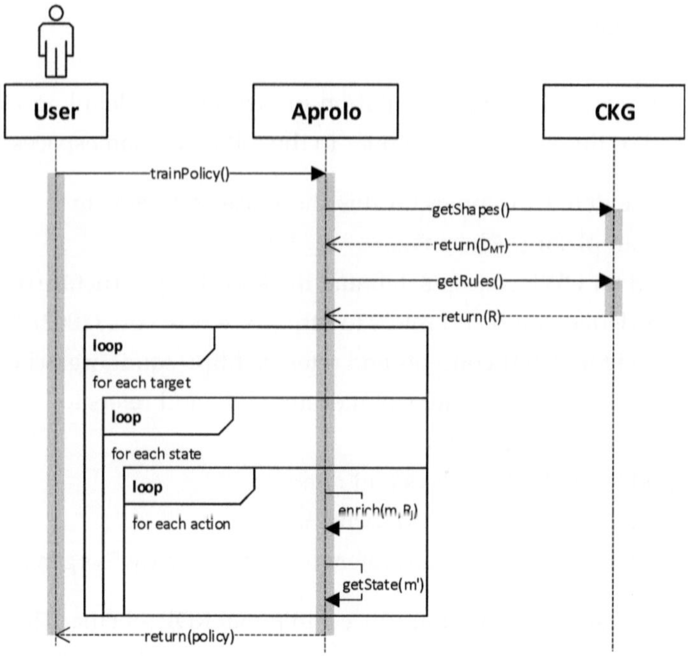

Figure 5.5: Sequence for training a policy to reach varying target states starting from a random initial state.

Train policy: The sequence for the use case of training a policy is shown in Figure 5.5. For training a policy, Aprolo retrieves all shapes D_{MT} of possible states and all rules R that can be employed for actions that affect the state of an observation from the corporate knowledge graph. To train a policy, each defined action is applied to each possible state. As the policy varies for each target state, this process has to be repeated for each possible target state.

In the following Section 5.4.2 we provide a showcase that demonstrates an exemplary implementation of the Aprolo approach.

5.4.2 Showcase

In order to showcase the implementation of Aprolo, we detail an example in Section 5.4.2. For this showcase, we refer to the following namespaces:

- **ex:** used to define examples for this showcase and refers to http://example.org/schema#.
- **owl:** used for OWL concepts defining the knowledge structure of the corporate knowledge graph and refers to http://www.w3.org/2002/07/owl#.
- **qudt:** used for QUDT concepts and refers to http://qudt.org/schema/qudt/.
- **unit:** used by QUDT for units of measurement and refers to http://qudt.org/vocab/unit/.
- **xsd:** used for XML data types and refers to http://www.w3.org/2001/XMLSchema#.
- **sh:** used for SHACL rules and refers to http://www.w3.org/ns/shacl.

Schema: For this showcase, we introduce a minimal RDF schema. This schema is used to define observation messages m of varying states and a set of rules R for the corporate knowledge graph that can be applied as actions to change the state of an observation. The schema includes the following four important properties:

- **ex:quantity** - We define *ex:quantity* as an instance of *owl:DatatypeProperty*. The range of this property is a literal value of type *xsd:string*. This property is the super property for all properties that define a quantity, independently from units that may be used. The units are encoded within the literal value together with the numeric value of the quantity in the form "*<numeric value> <unit symbol>*". Quantities that are described that way contain an explicitly modeled information about the observed quantity. The applicable unit can be retrieved by evaluating the unit symbol contained within the value string.
- **ex:quantity.unit** - In contrast to property *ex:quantity*, we define the range of the property *ex:quantity.unit* as a literal value of type *xsd:decimal*. This ensures that values can be evaluated as decimal values that allow for mathematical aggregations and indexing operations. Furthermore, sub properties of *ex:quantity.unit* also contain explicitly modeled information about the applicable unit of measurement in addition to explicitly modeled information

about the observed quantity. Therefore, units are distinct and do not have to be disambiguated from a given symbol or abbreviation.

- **ex:rangeQuantity** - To identify the observed quantity for sub properties of *ex:quantity* and *ex:quantity.unit*, the property *ex:rangeQuantity* points to the class of applicable units using the definition of QUDT. Therefore, the observed quantity is distinct and does not have to be disambiguated.
- **ex:rangeUnit** - Only sub properties of *ex:quantity.unit* imply explicitly the unit used for observed quantities. This unit is a unique instance of QUDT and tied to a sub property of *ex:quantity.unit* by specifying a value for *ex:rangeUnit*.

States: In the following, we show an exemplary implementation of states for observation messages as introduced in Section 5.3.3. All state definitions include examples for quantities using a *qudt:LengthUnit*, *qudt:TemperatureUnit* and *qudt:MassUnit*. For a consistent demonstration of the states, we assume that the target units for those three quantities are *unit:MilliM*, *unit:DEG_C* and *unit:GRAM* respectively. States of observations are distinguished by their model (string, float, QUDT) and their units of measurement (target, base, different), stated as *model/unit*.

- **S0** *string/different:* Observed quantities are encoded using sub properties of *ex:quantity*. Units are not contained within the property definition derived from the schema. Therefore, the symbol of the applicable unit has to be encoded within the literal value together with the numeric value. In state $S0$, units are neither the base units for their quantity, nor their target unit:
  - ◇ ex:length "65.2 in" ;
  - ◇ ex:temp "100.3 °F" ;
  - ◇ ex:weight "53.3 lbm" ;
- **S1** *float/different*: Similar to state $S0$, units in state $S1$ are neither the base units for their quantity, nor their target unit. However, in contrast to $S0$, observed quantities are encoded using sub properties of *ex:quantity.unit*. Therefore, the units are explicitly contained within the property definition derived from the schema. Numeric values are given as float values rather than strings:
  - ◇ ex:length.in 65.2 ;
  - ◇ ex:temp.degF 100.3 ;
  - ◇ ex:weight.lbm 53.3 ;

- **S2** *QUDT/different*: The quantities of state $S2$ are described in the most expressive semantic form defined for this showcase using the QUDT ontology. Rather than a property of the implementation specific schema, quantities of state $S2$ are modeled using the *qudt:hasQuantity* property that links to individual instances of *qudt:Quantity*. Each instance of *qudt:Quantity* explicitly states the kind of observed quantity and an arbitrary number of instances of *qudt:QuantityValue*. Each instance of *qudt:QuantityValue* in turn explicitly states the numeric value and applicable unit. Although the modeling of quantities in QUDT seems to be unnecessary complex at first glance, the included schema knowledge helps us to easily deal with such quantities using standard libraries such as jqudt[9]. Similar to states $S0$ and $S1$, the units used within the instances of *qudt:QuantityValue* in state $S2$ are neither the base units for their quantity, nor their target unit. The three instances of *qudt:QuantityValue* are therefore serialized as follows:
  - ◇ qudt:numericValue 65.2 ; qudt:unit unit:IN ;
  - ◇ qudt:numericValue 100.3 ; qudt:unit unit:DEG_F ;
  - ◇ qudt:numericValue 53.3 ; qudt:unit unit:LBM ;
- **S3** *string/base*: The properties used for quantities in state $S3$ are the same as in state $S0$. However, the literal values for the quantities are significantly different. In state $S3$, the literal values for quantities only contain symbols of units which are the base units of their respective quantity:
  - ◇ ex:length "1.656 m" ;
  - ◇ ex:temp "311.093 K" ;
  - ◇ ex:weight "24.176 kg" ;
- **S4** *float/base*: State $S4$ contains quantities with properties that are sub properties of *ex:quantity.unit* and numeric values as float values which is similar to state $S1$. However, state $S4$ contains only sub properties of *ex:quantity.unit* that use the respective base unit but not the target unit of the quantity. For example, the base unit for *ex:length* describing the quantity length is meter, abbreviated with m. The resulting sub property of *ex:quantity.unit* is therefore *ex:length.m* that explicitly links to *qudt:LengthUnit* as its quantity and *unit:M* as its unit. In the same way, the properties *ex:temp.K* and *weight.kg*

[9]https://github.com/egonw/jqudt

are used for the respective temperature and mass observation together with a numeric value:

- ◇ ex:length.m 1.656 ;
- ◇ ex:temp.K 311.093 ;
- ◇ ex:weight.kg 24.176 ;

- **S5** *QUDT/base*: Similar to state $S2$, the quantities of state $S5$ are also described in the most expressive semantic form using the QUDT ontology. The only difference to state $S2$ is that the units used within the instances of *qudt:QuantityValue* are the base units for their respective quantity. However, they are not the target units of the quantity as explained before. The three instances of *qudt:QuantityValue* are therefore serialized as follows:
  - ◇ qudt:numericValue 1.656 ; qudt:unit unit:M ;
  - ◇ qudt:numericValue 311.093 ; qudt:unit unit:K ;
  - ◇ qudt:numericValue 24.176 ; qudt:unit unit:KG ;
- **S6** *string/target*: The properties used for quantities in state $S6$ are the same as in states $S0$ and $S3$. However, the literal values for the quantities are significantly different. In state $S6$, the literal values for quantities only contain symbols of units which are the target units of their respective quantity. If the target unit is equal to the base unit for the quantity, the observation is considered in state $S6$ rather than state $S3$ if the unit is detected for a quantity:
  - ◇ ex:length "1656 mm" ;
  - ◇ ex:temp "37.943 °C" ;
  - ◇ ex:weight "24176 g" ;
- **S7** *float/target*: Similar to states $S1$ and $S4$, the properties used for quantities of state $S7$ are sub properties of *ex:quantity.unit* and numeric values are float values. However, only properties that link to the defined target units for each quantity are used. If the target unit is equal to the base unit for the quantity, the observation is considered in state $S7$ rather than state $S4$ if the unit is detected for a quantity:
  - ◇ ex:length.mm 1656 ;
  - ◇ ex:temp.degC 37.943 ;
  - ◇ ex:weight.g 24176 ;

- **S8** *QUDT/target*: The quantities of state $S8$ are described using the QUDT ontology, similar to states $S5$ and $S2$. The difference to states $S5$ and $S2$ is that the units used within the instances of *qudt:QuantityValue* are the target units of the quantity. The three instances of *qudt:QuantityValue* are therefore serialized as follows:
  - ◇ qudt:numericValue 1656 ; qudt:unit unit:MilliM ;
  - ◇ qudt:numericValue 37.943 ; qudt:unit unit:DEG_C ;
  - ◇ qudt:numericValue 24176 ; qudt:unit unit:GRAM ;

Actions: In order to change the state of an observation, we define nine generic SPARQL construct queries. Each query performs a small, dedicated task and can be applied to any state with different results. To provide a set of rules R for the corporate knowledge graph, these queries are encoded as *sh:SPARQLRule* as detailed in Section 4.4.2. Aprolo employs these rules as actions using the SHACL API. These actions affect the state of an observation message m as proposed in Section 5.3.4.

- **Query A0** represents a neutral action. It has no effect on the state of an observation.
- **Query A1** extracts all sub properties of *ex:quantity.unit* (float model) and creates a new observation message using a sub property of *ex:quantity* (string model). The state of the new message could be $S0$, $S3$, $S6$, or none, depending on the input used for this action and the target unit defined for the target state.
- **Query A2** extracts all sub properties of *ex:quantity.unit* (float model) and creates a new observation message using new instances of *qudt:Quantity* (QUDT model). The state of the new message could be $S2$, $S5$, $S8$, or none, depending on the input used for this action and unit defined for the target state.
- **Query A3** extracts all sub properties of *ex:quantity* (string model) and creates a new observation message using a sub property of *ex:quantity.unit* (float model). The state of the new message could be $S1$, $S4$, $S7$, or none, depending on the input used for this action and unit defined for the target state.

- **Query A4** extracts all sub properties of *ex:quantity* (string model) and creates a new observation message using new instances of *qudt:Quantity* (QUDT model). The state of the new message could be $S2$, $S5$, $S8$, or none, depending on the input used for this action and unit defined for the target state.
- **Query A5** extracts all instances of *qudt:Quantity* (QUDT model) and creates a new observation message using a sub property of *ex:quantity.unit* (float model). The state of the new message could be $S1$, $S4$, $S7$, or none, depending on the input used for this action and unit defined for the target state.
- **Query A6** extracts all instances of *qudt:Quantity* (QUDT model) and creates a new observation message using a sub property of *ex:quantity* (string model). The state of the new message could be $S0$, $S3$, $S6$, or none, depending on the input used for this action and unit defined for the target state.
- **Query A7** extracts all instances of *qudt:Quantity* (QUDT model) and creates a new observation message using similar instances of *qudt:Quantity*. However, the new instances are linked only to instances of *qudt:QuantityValue* that use the base unit for each quantity as their *qudt:unit*. To achieve this, the numeric value of the existing value is converted to the base unit using conversion multiplier and conversion offset of the existing unit. The state of the new message could be $S5$ or none, depending on the input used for this action and unit defined for the target state.
- **Query A8** extracts all instances of *qudt:Quantity* (QUDT model) and creates a new observation message using similar instances of *qudt:Quantity*. However, the new instances are linked only to instances of *qudt:QuantityValue* that use the target unit for each quantity as their *qudt:unit*. To achieve this, the numeric value of the base unit value is converted to the target unit using conversion multiplier and conversion offset of the target unit. The state of the new message could be $S8$ or none, depending on the input used for this action and unit defined for the target state.

In Section 5.5, we show how states, actions, and execution environment defined in Section 5.4 are used to perform an evaluation of research question RQ3.

5.5 Evaluation of the Aprolo Approach

Based on the implementation introduced in Section 5.4, we provide an evaluation for the research question of how preprocessing workflows for environmental observations can be composed automatically based on the contextual knowledge of an observation (RQ3) in Section 5.5.

5.5.1 Setup and Data

To evaluate the automated service composition, we perform a controlled laboratory evaluation. For this evaluation, we train a policy for the MDP by reinforcement learning using the Q-learning algorithm as introduced in Section 5.3.5. For this evaluation, we perform the following steps:

1.) choose target state S_{target} randomly
2.) perform actions randomly on every possible state until S_{target} is reached (*random approach, see Section 5.5.2*)
3.) train reward and action matrices R_{target} and A_{target} for S_{target}
4.) train quality matrix Q_{target} for reward matrix R_{target}
5.) infer policy P_{target} from quality matrix Q_{target}
6.) perform actions based on policy P_{target} to reach S_{target} (*policy approach, see Section 5.5.3*)

These steps are executed repeatedly to determine the average computational effort for random trials vs. training and executing a policy. For the MDP, we employ the set of states S and the set of actions A as defined in Section 5.4.2. To address the issue of varying data requirements of different data consuming applications, we use a subset of S to simulate different target states. As the incoming data could be in any state of S, we choose subjects randomly and classify the initial state before starting the evaluation process.

5.5.2 Random Approach

The first part of the evaluation process is trial and error. On a random initial state, actions of A are performed randomly until the target state is reached. Each iteration is logged to retrace the process afterwards. To illustrate this process, we detail two random examples. In the first example, the target state is defined to be $S8$. Aprolo determines the state of an incoming observation message as $S8$. In this case, the incoming data is by pure chance already in the desired target state $S8$. Therefore, no action is performed to reach the target state. For the second example, the target state is defined to be $S6$. Aprolo determines the state of an incoming observation message as $S4$. An exemplary result of randomly applying actions f_A is shown as follows:

1.) $f_{A1}(S4) = S3$
2.) $f_{A0}(S3) = S3$
3.) $f_{A5}(S3) = \emptyset$
4.) $f_{A4}(S3) = S5$
5.) $f_{A1}(S5) = \emptyset$
6.) $f_{A5}(S5) = S4$
7.) $f_{A8}(S4) = \emptyset$
8.) $f_{A5}(S4) = \emptyset$
9.) $f_{A3}(S4) = \emptyset$
10.) $f_{A5}(S4) = \emptyset$
11.) $f_{A6}(S4) = \emptyset$
12.) $f_{A3}(S4) = \emptyset$
13.) $f_{A2}(S4) = S5$
14.) $f_{A3}(S5) = \emptyset$
15.) $f_{A8}(S5) = S8$
16.) $f_{A6}(S8) = S6$

In this example, it took 16 iterations of randomly chosen actions before the target state is reached. Nine out of 16 iterations do not produce a valid result, therefore another action has to be chosen randomly. In iteration 6 we can see that the result falls back to the initial state $S4$, although other states have been reached in between. This is because the actions are not chosen wisely but randomly. However, although using this naive approach, the target state is reached in iteration 16 due to selecting the appropriate action by chance. Therefore, we use these results as reference and research how we can employ a more efficient process of automated service composition in Section 5.5.3.

5.5.3 Policy Approach

In contrast to the random approach of Section 5.5.2, a dedicated policy cannot be employed without prior training. Therefore, the first step towards a more efficient service composition is to train matrices of actions and rewards that can be performed in each possible state as introduced in Section 5.3.5. Both matrices are initialized with -1 values which indicates that there is no know action and therefore no possibility to reach any other state from an initial state. To train the matrices, all possible actions are performed on each possible state and the reward and action matrices are updated based on the result of the action. If a new state can be reached from an initial state, the element with the coordinates of this connection is updated from -1 to 0 in the reward matrix. If the new state is equal to the target state, the reward is updated to 100. At the same time, the ID of the action that successfully transforms one state to another updates the element of the action matrix with the coordinates of this connection. When performing the training with target state $S6$, the results are the reward matrix R_{S6} and the action matrix A_{S6}.

$$R_{S6} = \begin{pmatrix} 0 & 0 & 0 & -1 & -1 & -1 & -1 & -1 & -1 \\ 0 & 0 & 0 & -1 & -1 & -1 & -1 & -1 & -1 \\ 0 & 0 & 0 & -1 & -1 & 0 & -1 & -1 & -1 \\ -1 & -1 & -1 & 0 & 0 & 0 & -1 & -1 & -1 \\ -1 & -1 & -1 & 0 & 0 & 0 & -1 & -1 & -1 \\ -1 & -1 & -1 & 0 & 0 & 0 & -1 & -1 & 0 \\ -1 & -1 & -1 & -1 & -1 & -1 & 100 & 0 & 0 \\ -1 & -1 & -1 & -1 & -1 & -1 & 100 & 0 & 0 \\ -1 & -1 & -1 & -1 & -1 & 0 & 100 & 0 & 0 \end{pmatrix}$$

Reward matrix: The reward matrix R_{S6} contains all rewards for all possible action results in all possible states. As the reward is given for reaching a new state, regardless of the action that was performed to reach that state, the reward matrix shows all states that can be reached from an initial state indicated by the value 0 and also if the new state is the target state indicated by the value 100. For example, according to the reward matrix R_{S6}, starting from initial state $S0$ only the states

$S0$, $S1$ and $S2$ can be reached. None of them is the target state. In contrast, starting from initial state $S8$, states $S5$, $S6$, $S7$ and $S8$ can be reached. In addition, state $S6$ is defined as the target state indicated by the value 100.

$$A_{S6} = \begin{pmatrix} 0 & 3 & 4 & -1 & -1 & -1 & -1 & -1 & -1 \\ 1 & 0 & 2 & -1 & -1 & -1 & -1 & -1 & -1 \\ 6 & 5 & 0 & -1 & -1 & 7 & -1 & -1 & -1 \\ -1 & -1 & -1 & 0 & 3 & 4 & -1 & -1 & -1 \\ -1 & -1 & -1 & 1 & 0 & 2 & -1 & -1 & -1 \\ -1 & -1 & -1 & 6 & 5 & 7 & -1 & -1 & 8 \\ -1 & -1 & -1 & -1 & -1 & -1 & 0 & 3 & 4 \\ -1 & -1 & -1 & -1 & -1 & -1 & 1 & 0 & 2 \\ -1 & -1 & -1 & -1 & -1 & 7 & 6 & 5 & 0 \end{pmatrix}$$

Action matrix: The trained action matrix A_{S6} has one major characteristic in common with the reward matrix R_{S6}: Wherever there is a -1 value for the coordinates [x][y] in the reward matrix, there is also a -1 value for the action matrix with the same coordinates. This is because there is no action available to reach state Sy from state Sx. As a consequence, there is also no reward for the coordinates [x][y] in the reward matrix. The action matrix can be read as follows: In state $S0$, action $A0$ can be performed to reach state $S0$, action $A3$ to reach state $S1$ and action $A4$ to reach state $S2$. Another state can not be reached. In state $S8$, state $S5$ can be reached by performing action $A7$, state $S6$ by action $A6$, state $S7$ by action $A5$ and state $S8$ by action $A0$.

$$Q_{S6} = \begin{pmatrix} 20 & 27 & 51 & 0 & 0 & 0 & 0 & 0 & 0 \\ 23 & 24 & 51 & 0 & 0 & 0 & 0 & 0 & 0 \\ 5 & 7 & 22 & 0 & 0 & 63 & 0 & 0 & 0 \\ 0 & 0 & 0 & 13 & 22 & 63 & 0 & 0 & 0 \\ 0 & 0 & 0 & 10 & 25 & 63 & 0 & 0 & 0 \\ 0 & 0 & 0 & 14 & 0 & 5 & 0 & 0 & 79 \\ 0 & 0 & 0 & 0 & 0 & 0 & 99 & 0 & 0 \\ 0 & 0 & 0 & 0 & 0 & 0 & 99 & 0 & 0 \\ 0 & 0 & 0 & 0 & 0 & 0 & 100 & 0 & 0 \end{pmatrix}$$

Quality matrix: Using the trained matrices of reward R_{S6} and actions A_{S6}, we can train the quality matrix Q_{S6} by involving the Q-learning algorithm. The training of the quality matrix exploits the findings of the reward matrix. Starting from a random state, all states that can be reached from this state, indicated by a reward value of 0 or more, are extracted from the reward matrix as valid moves. Depending on the reward for reaching a new state, the quality matrix is updated with the new quality value calculated. The process of calculating the reward for each possible move is repeated until the target state is reached, which is indicated by a reward value of 100. After reaching the target state from the initial state, another initial state is chosen randomly for the next iteration of the quality training process. After 10^4 iterations, we gain quality matrix Q_{S6}. The trained quality matrix Q_{S6} shows the quality value for reaching a new state from each initial state. In this example, reaching state $S0$ from state $S0$ has a quality value of 20, reaching state $S2$ a quality value of 27 and state $S3$ a quality value of 51. As the other states cannot be reached, the quality value is 0. For initial state $S8$, reaching state $S6$ has a quality value of 100 as state $S6$ is the target state with a reward value of 100. All other states therefore have a quality value of 0, regardless whether they could be reached or not.

Policy: From the trained quality matrix, we can easily derive a policy of which state should be reached from an initial state by getting the coordinates with the maximum quality value for each row of the quality matrix. Based on the action matrix, we can identify the action that has to be performed to reach the desired state. The policy that is inferred for target state S6 based on the training quality and action matrices can be interpreted as follows:

- in state $S0$ perform action $A4$ to reach intermediate state $S2$
- in state $S1$ perform action $A2$ to reach intermediate state $S2$
- in state $S2$ perform action $A7$ to reach intermediate state $S5$
- in state $S3$ perform action $A4$ to reach intermediate state $S5$
- in state $S4$ perform action $A2$ to reach intermediate state $S5$
- in state $S5$ perform action $A8$ to reach intermediate state $S8$
- in state $S6$ perform action $A0$ to reach target state $S6$
- in state $S7$ perform action $A1$ to reach target state $S6$
- in state $S8$ perform action $A6$ to reach target state $S6$

By following the policy, we can easily perform the most efficient service composition for the evaluation task.

The execution framework for actions on initial states in order to reach a given target state is basically the same as introduced in Section 5.5.2. However, rather than applying random actions until the target state is reached, each performed action is derived from the policy P depending on current state and target state. This ensures the most efficient service composition to reach any target state from any initial state:

1.) $f_{A2}(S4) = S5$
2.) $f_{A8}(S5) = S8$
3.) $f_{A6}(S8) = S6$

Where the random approach of Section 5.5.2 required 16 iterations from initial state $S4$ to target state $S6$, the approach following the trained policy of Section 5.5.3 performs the same task with a much more efficient service composition requiring only three iterations.

5.5.4 Discussion of Results

For a valid evaluation of the training and applying a policy in comparison to the random approach, the evaluation process described in Section 5.5 was executed 2.579 times on a virtual server node with a Intel®Xeon®E5-2650 v3 CPU at 2.30GHz and 32 GB memory. As explained in Section 5.5.3, the first task towards an efficient service composition based on a dedicated policy is to train a reward matrix for each target state. The times needed to train the reward matrix for target state $S6$ are shown in Figure 5.6. The times for training the reward matrices of target states $S7$ and $S8$ are shown in Figure 5.7 and Figure 5.8 respectively.

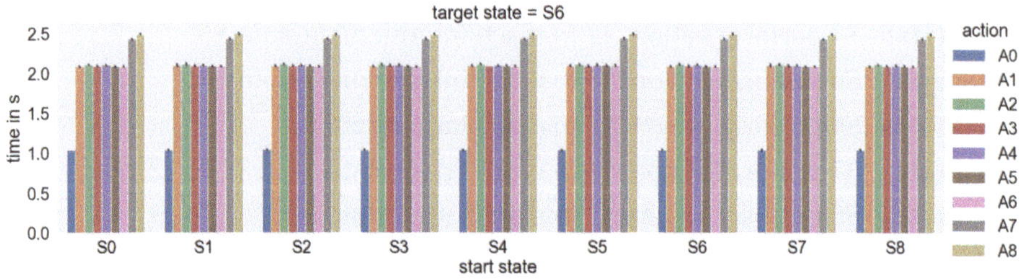

Figure 5.6: Training the reward matrix for target state $S6$.

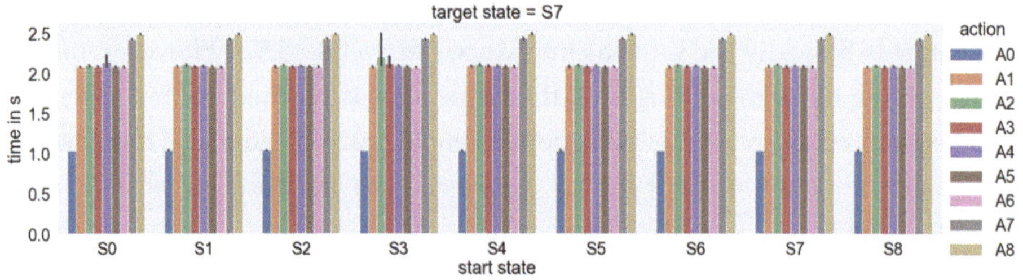

Figure 5.7: Training the reward matrix for target state $S7$.

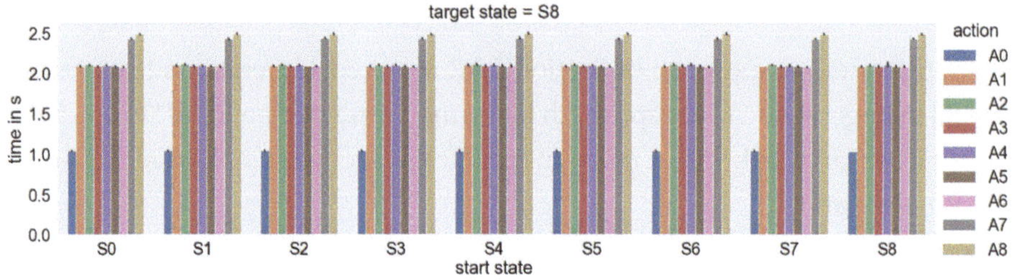

Figure 5.8: Training the reward matrix for target state $S8$.

As can be seen from the plots, the most costly actions for the reward training are actions $A7$ and $A8$ which both takes almost 2.5 seconds. The cheapest action is the $A0$ action, which simply creates a new graph by inserting all triples of the given graph unchanged and takes about one second for the given data. All other actions take around two seconds to perform. These findings apply to all target states, which leads to a training time for the reward matrices of about 18 seconds in total.

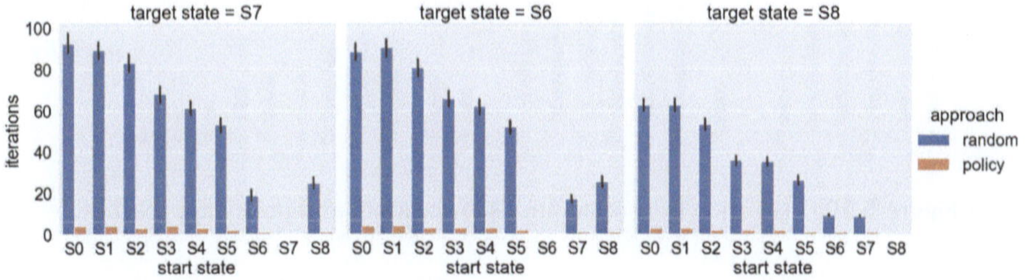

Figure 5.9: Number of iterations for random and policy approaches.

A comparison of the number of iterations for the random approach versus the policy approach is shown in Figure 5.9. As expected, the most iterations are required to reach target states $S6$, $S7$ and $S8$ when starting from states $S0$, $S1$ or $S2$ as initial states. The random approach requires 80 to 90 iteration in average for target states $S6$ and $S7$ where the policy approach requires only three respectively four iterations and 60 to 70 iteration for target state $S8$ where the policy approach requires two respectively three iterations. The least iterations are required when starting with states $S6$, $S7$ or $S8$ as the target state can always be reached with only one iteration or even zero, if the initial state is equal to the target state. The latter applies to both, the policy approach but also to the random approach, as no further action is performed as soon as the target state is reached. Therefore, there is no plot for initial state $S6/S7/S8$ when training for target state $S6/S7/S8$ respectively. However, the random approach still requires about 20 iteration in average to reach the target state when starting from initial states $S6/S7/S8$ if they are not the target states as well. The total time used for performing all these iterations is shown in Figure 5.10.

According to the number of iterations shown in Figure 5.9, the required time for these iterations shown in Figure 5.10 evolves almost proportionally. Remarkable difference is that the deviation for the timing is much higher than for the number of iterations. The total execution times for all iterations using the random approach starting from initial states $S0$, $S1$ or $S2$ is around 300 seconds for target states $S6$ and $S7$, still almost 200 seconds in average for target state $S8$. At the same time, the policy approach completes all tasks in about 10 seconds or less. The break

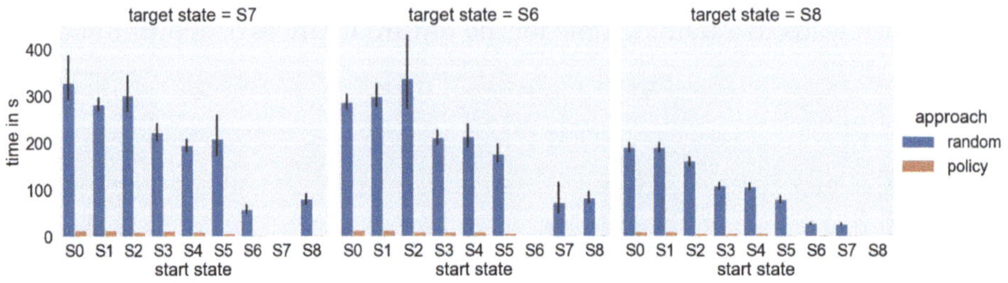

Figure 5.10: Execution time of iterations for random and policy approaches.

even point for training and executing the policy approach in comparison to the random approach which does not require any training in advance is shown in Figure 5.11.

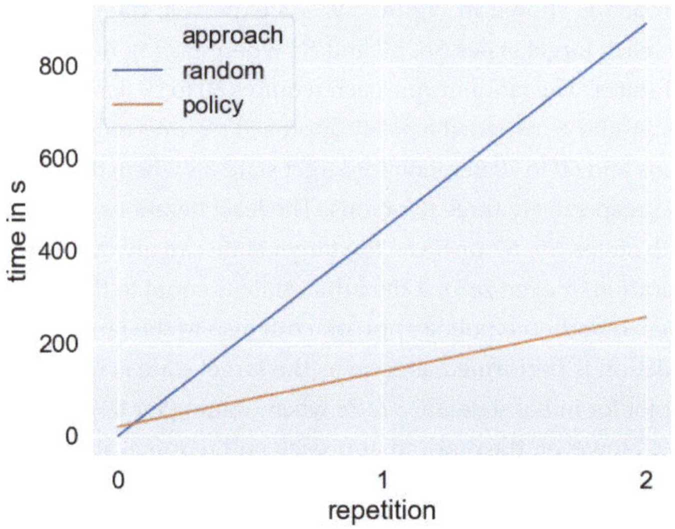

Figure 5.11: Comparison of total processing time for repetitive runs of random actions to training and applying a policy.

Although the policy approach requires some effort for training reward, action and quality matrices and deriving the policy before performing a single iteration of the test data, this time can be more than compensated starting from the first execution of the service composition as this can be performed much more efficient by the trained policy approach. While it takes more than 400 seconds to compose and execute the 27 workflows that are required for all nine initial and three target states using the random approach, the same task can be completed by the policy approach in less than 200 seconds including the required training time. Once the policies are trained, only the execution time for the most efficient sequence of actions is needed in order to preprocess any observation message m for any target state $state_{target}$, regardless of the initial state of the message. To conclude Chapter 5, we summarize this chapter in Section 5.6.45

5.6 Conclusion of Chapter 5

In Chapter 5, we have evaluated the research question of how preprocessing workflows for environmental observations can be composed automatically based on the contextual knowledge of an observation (RQ3). To answer this research question, we have proposed the Aprolo approach, a self-learning preprocessing workflow for linked observations that dynamically employs a set of predefined actions in order to meet varying requirements on demand (C3). We employ the approach to explicitly define possible states of observation messages for GIS in a machine interpretable way (C3.1), explicitly define the target state for all observations as required by a data consumer (C3.2), explicitly define actions and apply these actions to messages in order to change their state (C3.3), and provide an algorithm to learn the most efficient sequence of actions to reach a certain target state (C3.4).

Aprolo foundations: In Section 5.1, we have motivated our research with the demand of preprocessing of environmental sensor observations for a new generation of GISs. We have discussed related work in Section 5.2 and pointed out the lacking support for collaborative information integration based on explicit semantics for spatio-temporal data in a way that addresses provenance, veracity, velocity, structural and semantic dissimilarities of spatio-temporal data, especially for GIS. To overcome this limitation, we introduced the Aprolo approach in Section 5.3 which aims to exploit explicit semantics derived from a collaboratively maintained corporate knowledge graph for explicit definitions of states and rules for environmental observation messages. Exploitation and integration of big spatio-temporal data in a new generation of GIS strongly depend on a common understanding of concepts across heterogeneous data sources.

Evaluation: For the evaluation of the Aprolo approach we have modeled a MDP of possible states and actions that are semantically described within a corporate knowledge graph. We have shown how preprocessing workflows for environmental observations can be composed automatically based on the context knowledge of an observation. Further, we have shown that the effort of training a policy pays off even with one single execution of the training set compared to random actions.

Outcome: The results indicate that the Aprolo approach enables users even without a web engineering background to easily add sources and services for an existing GIS to a corporate knowledge graph and leads to a reduced workload in the context-dependent preprocessing of observation messages. Therefore, we consider the hypothesis that contextual knowledge of observations makes it possible to meet the requirements of different data consumers automatically (H3) as confirmed.

In the following Chapter 6, we conclude this thesis and discuss the results with respect to the hypotheses and research questions introduced in Chapter 1.

6 Conclusion

In Chapter 6, we conclude this thesis with a summary of results and an outlook on future work.

6.1 Summary of Results

In this thesis, we have developed and discussed methods to exploit LOD for automated and meaningful processing of heterogeneous environmental observations. Based on the hypothesis that Linked Open Data provides sufficient knowledge to automate the harmonization of sensor observations (principal hypothesis), we raised the principal research question for this thesis:

How can Linked Open Data be exploited for a knowledge-driven harmonization of sensor observations?

In particular, we have discussed the following research questions:

Research Question RQ1: In Chapter 3, we presented our findings for answering the research question of identifying and sufficiently addressing the challenges in exploiting Linked Open Data as a lever for the knowledge contained in corporate knowledge graphs (RQ1). We have introduced the LD-Wiki approach to assist users of organizational wikis in establishing and curating meaningful relations to LOD concepts by building adequate SPARQL queries based on the user's input and the given context. We pointed out the missing support for leveraging organizational knowledge bases with LOD of current approaches. To overcome this limitation, we introduced the LD-Wiki approach which aims to separate knowledge management and knowledge representation in order to gain a consistent knowledge base that also covers statements from LOD while keeping track of the provenance of each statement. Further, we have presented queries adopted to Wikidata and DBpedia as two major representatives of LOD sources and also the results we got from these sources. We have shown how we can assist users of organizational wikis with creating new links to LOD entities. By executing queries on common concepts such as instances of cities, we have shown that adequate LOD records exist to leverage organizational knowledge bases. Further, we have shown that the LD-Wiki approach can not only be applied to common concepts, but also to domain-specific concepts. We have tracked additional statements of provenance, especially for facts derived from LOD that leverage an organizational knowledge base. By evaluating the provenance information in PS, software agents can take the provenance of statements into account to estimate the trustworthiness of statements in CKG' in order to increase the informative value of a corporate knowledge graph. Therefore, we consider the hypothesis that the comprehensive knowledge which is provided as Linked Open Data can be exploited to leverage the knowledge represented in a corporate knowledge graph (H1) as confirmed.

Research Question RQ2: In Chapter 4, we presented our findings for answering the research question of how a stream of continuous environmental observations can be mapped, validated, and enriched on-the-fly based on contextual knowledge from a corporate knowledge graph (RQ2). For this evaluation, we have shown how collaboratively created annotations from a semantic wiki platform can be exploited to map non-semantic data streams of public and private observation stations to a representation with explicit semantic information of observations, measured quantities, measuring units, and context information. Furthermore, we have shown how data shape constraints can be defined on a collaborative wiki platform and employed for constraint validation of observation data streams on-the-fly. To evaluate our approach, we have measured the time interval for creation, serialization and validation of messages from a continuous data stream using the message format of exemplary public and private environmental observation stations. The results show that our generic approach for mapping non-semantic streams of observation messages to a meaningful representation with explicit semantic information and validating the shape constraints of messages can be done efficiently on-the-fly without adopting the code to specific data sources. We have introduced the LSane approach for collaborative definitions of semantic shapes and enrichment rules for heterogeneous message streams. We have discussed related work in the fields of heterogeneity and semantics of sensor streams, semantic annotations for sensor streams and semantic validation and enrichment of sensor streams and identified the research gap for collaborative definitions of shapes and rules for observation messages. Based on these findings, we have provided a formal description of a semantic validation and enrichment functions which both exploit collaboratively created semantic annotations of domain experts. For the implementation of LSane, we have extended an existing annotation platform based to define constraints for observation messages using SHACL, implemented a validation engine for observation messages and semantic stream enrichment based on the SHACL API. For the evaluation of LSane, we have used the shapes of concrete public and private environmental observation stations to generate streams of observation messages and validate these streams with shape definitions from the annotation platform. With our work we have shown that heterogeneous messages of environmental observations can be collaboratively validated using semantic annotations of SHACL shapes and also that collaboratively created annotations of rules can be exploited for semantic enrichment of heterogeneous messages of environmental observations. Therefore, we consider the hypothesis that a well-curated corporate knowledge graph enables automated mapping, validation, and enrichment of ambiguous sensor observations based on explicit semantics (H2) as confirmed.

Research Question RQ3: In Chapter 5, we presented our findings for answering the research question of how preprocessing workflows for environmental observations can be composed automatically based on the contextual knowledge of an observation (RQ3). To address the lacking support for collaborative information integration based on explicit semantics for spatio-temporal data, we introduced the Aprolo approach which aims to exploit explicit semantics derived from a collaboratively maintained corporate knowledge graph for explicit definitions of states and rules for environmental observation messages. Exploitation and integration of big spatio-temporal data in a new generation of GIS strongly depend on a common understanding of concepts across heterogeneous data sources. We have shown how to address this issue by combining the dynamics of a collaborative approach with the expressive power of established ontologies. For the evaluation of the Aprolo approach we have modeled a MDP of possible states and actions that are semantically described within a corporate knowledge graph. We have shown how preprocessing workflows for environmental observations can be composed automatically based on the contextual knowledge of an observation. The results indicate that the Aprolo approach enables users even without a web engineering background to easily add sources and services for an existing GIS and leads to a reduced workload in the context-dependent preprocessing of observation messages. Therefore, we consider the hypothesis that contextual knowledge of observations makes it possible to meet the requirements of different data consumers automatically (H3) as confirmed.

Based on the findings that *i*) *the comprehensive knowledge which is provided as Linked Open Data can be exploited to leverage the knowledge represented in a corporate knowledge graph* (H1), *ii*) *a well-curated corporate knowledge graph enables automated mapping, validation, and enrichment of ambiguous sensor observations based on explicit semantics* (H2), and *iii*) *contextual knowledge of observations makes it possible to meet the requirements of different data consumers automatically* (H3), we conclude that the principal hypothesis that Linked Open Data provides sufficient knowledge to automate the harmonization of sensor observations is confirmed as well.

6.2 Outlook

Based on our findings, future work can be seen with focus on at least three topics:

Data privacy for triples: The balancing act of sharing corporate knowledge with partners, suppliers or customers as LOD while ensuring data privacy of confidential corporate knowledge requires awareness on a organizational and also technical level. The privacy for confidential data on the one hand while publishing parts of the corporate knowledge base as LOD on the other hand requires a proper implementation of Access Control Lists (ACLs) with carefully designed access roles for each statement in the knowledge base.

Performance of queries on LOD: Our research has pointed out that current LOD resources can be exploited to leverage corporate knowledge and increase the informative value. However, it can also be learned that performing complex queries on such hugh amounts of triples within complex and heterogeneous ontologies on distributed endpoints can easily exceed the technical capabilities of LOD providers. Therefore, new solutions are required for indexing LOD at a large scale.

Shared services for common environmental observations: We have shown that annotating heterogeneous environmental observations with shared semantic concepts can lead to meaningful interpretations, independently of the technical origin of the observation. By providing shared services with pre-annotated environmental observations, synergistic effects could reduce the costs of preprocessing and increase the informative value of observations across various application domains.

Bibliography

Aasman, Jans (2017). 'Transmuting Information to Knowledge with an Enterprise Knowledge Graph'. In: *IT Professional* 19.6, pp. 44–51. ISSN: 1520-9202. DOI: 10.1109/MITP.2017.4241469.

Abele, Andrejs; McCrae, John P.; Buitelaar, Paul; Jentzsch, Anja; Cyganiak, Richard (2017). *Linking Open Data cloud diagram*. URL: http://lod-cloud.net/.

Ackoff, Russell Lincoln (1989). 'From Data to Wisdom'. In: *Journal of Applied Systems Analysis* 16, pp. 3–9.

Amiguet-Vercher, Juan; Wombacher, Andreas; Klifman, Tim E. (2010). 'Annotations: dynamic semantics in stream processing'. In: *Proceedings of the Third Ph.D. Workshop on Information and Knowledge Management, PIKM 2010, Toronto, Ontario, Canada, October 30, 2010*. Ed. by Anisoara Nica; Aparna S. Varde. ACM, pp. 1–8. DOI: 10.1145/1871902.1871904.

Arora, C. P. (1998). *Thermodynamics*. New Delhi: Tata McGraw-Hill Pub. 762 pp. ISBN: 978-0-07-462014-4.

Atemezing, Ghislain A.; Abadie, Nathalie; Troncy, Raphael; Bucher, Bénédicte (2014). 'Publishing Reference Geodata on the Web: Opportunities and Challenges for IGN France'. In: *TC-SSN 2014 - Terra Cognita - Semantic Sensor Networks*.

Auer, Sören (2011). 'Creating knowledge out of interlinked data: making the web a data washing machine'. In: *Proceedings of the International Conference on Web Intelligence, Mining and Semantics, WIMS 2011, Sogndal, Norway, May 25 - 27, 2011*. Ed. by Rajendra Akerkar. ACM, p. 4. DOI: 10.1145/1988688.1988693.

Auer, Sören; Herre, Heinrich (2007). 'A Versioning and Evolution Framework for RDF Knowledge Bases'. In: *Perspectives of Systems Informatics*. Ed. by Irina Virbitskaite; Andrei Voronkov. Vol. 4378. Lecture Notes in Computer Science. Berlin, Heidelberg: Springer Berlin Heidelberg, pp. 55–69. ISBN: 978-3-540-70880-3. DOI: 10.1007/978-3-540-70881-0_8.

Auer, Sören; Jungmann, Berit; Schönefeld, Frank (2007). 'Semantic Wiki Representations for Building an Enterprise Knowledge Base'. In: *Reasoning Web*. Vol. 4636. Lecture Notes in Computer Science. Berlin, Heidelberg: Springer Berlin Heidelberg, pp. 330–333. ISBN: 978-3-540-74613-3.

Aveiro, David; Pinto, Duarte (2013). 'Implementing Organizational Self Awareness - A Semantic Mediawiki based Enterprise Ontology Management Approach'. In: *KEOD 2013 - Proceedings of the International Conference on Knowledge Engineering and Ontology Development, Vilamoura, Algarve, Portugal, 19-22 September, 2013*. Ed. by Joaquim Filipe; Jan L. G. Dietz. SciTePress, pp. 453–461. ISBN: 978-989-8565-81-5.

Baader, Franz; Calvanese, Diego; McGuinness, Deborah; Nardi, Daniele; Patel-Schneider, Peter (2003). *The Description Logic Handbook: Theory, Implementation and Applications*. Cambridge University Press. ISBN: 0521781760.

Barnaghi, Payam M.; Wang, Wei; Dong, Lijun; Wang, Chonggang (2013). 'A Linked-Data Model for Semantic Sensor Streams'. In: *2013 IEEE International Conference on Green Computing and Communications (GreenCom) and IEEE Internet of Things (iThings) and IEEE Cyber, Physical and Social Computing (CPSCom), Beijing, China, August 20-23, 2013*. IEEE, pp. 468–475. ISBN: 978-0-7695-5046-6. DOI: 10.1109/GreenCom-iThings-CPSCom.2013.95.

Bellman, Richard (1957). 'A Markovian Decision Process'. In: *Indiana Univ. Math. J.* 6.4, pp. 679–684. ISSN: 0022-2518.

Bellomarini, Luigi; Gottlob, Georg; Pieris, Andreas; Sallinger, Emanuel (2017). 'Swift Logic for Big Data and Knowledge Graphs'. In: *Proceedings of the Twenty-Sixth International Joint Conference on Artificial Intelligence, IJCAI 2017, Melbourne, Australia, August 19-25, 2017*. Ed. by Carles Sierra. ijcai.org, pp. 2–10. DOI: 10.24963/ijcai.2017/1.

Bergman, Michael K. (2009). 'The Fundamental Importance of Keeping an ABox and TBox Split'. In: *AI3 series on ontology best practices.*

Bergman, Michael K. (2018). *A Knowledge Representation Practionary - Guidelines Based on Charles Sanders Peirce*. Springer. ISBN: 978-3-319-98091-1. DOI: 10.1007/978-3-319-98092-8.

Berners-Lee, Tim (1994). *Universal Resource Identifiers in WWW: A Unifying Syntax for the Expression of Names and Addresses of Objects on the Network as used in the World-Wide Web*. URL: http://tools.ietf.org/html/rfc1630 (visited on 05/08/2020).

Berners-Lee, Tim (2006). *Linked Data - Design Issues*. URL: http://www.w3.org/DesignIssues/LinkedData.html (visited on 05/08/2020).

Berners-Lee, Tim (2007). *Giant Global Graph*. URL: http://dig.csail.mit.edu/breadcrumbs/node/215 (visited on 10/07/2014).

Berners-Lee, Tim (2009). *Linked-data design issues*. W3C design issue document June http://www.w3.org/DesignIssue/LinkedData.html. URL: http://www.w3.org/DesignIssues/LinkedData.html (visited on 05/08/2020).

Berners-Lee, Tim; Fielding, Roy; Masinter, Larry (2005a). *Uniform Resource Identifier (URI): Generic Syntax*. URL: http://tools.ietf.org/html/rfc3986#section-1.1.3 (visited on 05/08/2020).

Berners-Lee, Tim; Fielding, Roy; Masinter, Larry (2005b). *Uniform Resource Identifier (URI): Generic Syntax*. URL: http://tools.ietf.org/html/rfc3986#section-3 (visited on 05/08/2020).

Berners-Lee, Tim; Hendler, James; Lassila, Ora (2001). 'The Semantic Web'. In: *Scientific American: Feature Article*.

Birbeck, Mark; McCarron, Shane (2009). *CURIE Syntax 1.0*. URL: http://www.w3.org/TR/2009/CR-curie-20090116/ (visited on 05/15/2020).

Bizer, Christian (2006). *Semantic Web Publishing Vocabulary. User Manual*.

Bizer, Christian; Heath, Tom; Berners-Lee, Tim (2009). 'Linked Data - The Story So Far'. In: *Int. J. Semantic Web Inf. Syst.* 5.3, pp. 1–22. DOI: 10.4018/jswis.2009081901.

Bok, Kyoungsoo; Yoon, Sangwon; Yoo, Jaesoo (2019). 'Trust evaluation of multimedia documents based on extended provenance model in social semantic web'. In: *Multimedia Tools and Applications* 78.20, pp. 28681–28702. ISSN: 1573-7721. DOI: 10.1007/s11042-018-6243-7.

Brachman, Ronald J.; Levesque, Hector J. (2004). *Knowledge Representation and Reasoning*. Elsevier. ISBN: 978-1-55860-932-7.

Breitman, K. K.; Casanova, Marco Antonio; Truszkowski, Walt (2007). *Semantic Web: Concepts, technologies and applications*. NASA monographs in systems and software engineering. New York and London: Springer. ISBN: 9781846285813.

Brickley, Dan; Guha, R. V. (2014). *RDF Vocabulary Description Language 1.0: RDF Schema*. W3C Recommendation. URL: http://www.w3.org/TR/rdf-schema/# (visited on 05/15/2020).

Brown, Danny (2013). *Without Context, Data is Meaningless*. URL: https://www.business2community.com/big-data/without-context-data-is-meaningless-0585837 (visited on 05/15/2020).

Calbimonte, Jean-Paul; Sarni, Sofiane; Eberle, Julien; Aberer, Karl (2015). 'XGSN: An Open-source Semantic Sensing Middleware for the Web of Things'. In: *Int. Workshop on the Foundations, Technologies and Applications of the Geospatial Web, TC*

2014, and 7th International Workshop on SSN 2014 (Riva del Garda, Trentino, Italy, Oct. 20, 2014). Ed. by Kostis Kyzirakos; Rolf Grütter; Dave Kolas; Matthew Perry; Michael Compton; Krzysztof Janowicz; Kerry Taylor. CEUR-WS.org, pp. 51–66.

Cao, Hung; Wachowicz, Monica (2019). 'Analytics Everywhere for Streaming IoT Data'. In: *Sixth International Conference on Internet of Things: Systems, Management and Security, IOTSMS 2019, Granada, Spain, October 22-25, 2019*. Ed. by Mohammad A. Alsmirat; Yaser Jararweh. IEEE, pp. 18–25. DOI: 10.1109/IOTSMS48152.2019.8939171.

Caronni, Germano (2000). 'Walking the Web of Trust for Collaborative Enterprises (WETICE 2000), 4-16 June 2000, Gaithersburg, MD, USA'. In: *9th IEEE International Workshops on Enabling Technologies: Infrastructure for Collaborative Enterprises (WETICE 2000), 4-16 June 2000, Gaithersburg, MD, USA*. IEEE Computer Society, pp. 153–158. ISBN: 0-7695-0798-0. DOI: 10.1109/ENABL.2000.883720.

Carroll, Jeremy J. (2003). 'Signing RDF Graphs'. In: *The Semantic Web - ISWC 2003, Second International Semantic Web Conference, Sanibel Island, FL, USA, October 20-23, 2003, Proceedings*. Ed. by Dieter Fensel; Katia P. Sycara; John Mylopoulos. Lecture Notes in Computer Science 2870. Springer, pp. 369–384. ISBN: 3-540-20362-1. DOI: 10.1007/978-3-540-39718-2_24.

Carroll, Jeremy J.; Bizer, Christian; Hayes, Patrick J.; Stickler, Patrick (2005). 'Named graphs, provenance and trust'. In: *Proceedings of the 14th international conference on World Wide Web, WWW 2005, Chiba, Japan, May 10-14, 2005*. Ed. by Allan Ellis; Tatsuya Hagino. ACM, pp. 613–622. ISBN: 1-59593-046-9. DOI: 10.1145/1060745.1060835.

Carroll, Jeremy J.; Stickler, Patrick (2004). *TriX : RDF Triples in XML*. Ed. by Hewlett-Packard Company.

Chadwick, David W.; Hibbert, Mark (2013). 'Towards Automated Trust Establishment in Federated Identity Management'. In: *Trust Management VII - 7th IFIP WG 11.11 International Conference, IFIPTM 2013, Malaga, Spain, June 3-7, 2013. Proceedings*. Ed. by M. Carmen Fernández Gago; Fabio Martinelli; Siani Pearson; Isaac Agudo. IFIP Advances in Information and Communication Technology 401. Springer, pp. 33–48. ISBN: 978-3-642-38322-9. DOI: 10.1007/978-3-642-38323-6_3.

Cherfi, Samira Si-Said; Akoka, Jacky; Comyn-Wattiau, Isabelle (2011). 'Federating Information System Quality Frameworks Using A Common Ontology'. In: *Inter-*

national Conference on Information Quality. November. Adelaide, New Zealand, pp. 160–173.

Compton, Michael; Barnaghi, Payam M.; Bermudez, Luis; Garcia-Castro, Raul; Corcho, Óscar; Cox, Simon J. D.; Graybeal, John; Hauswirth, Manfred; Henson, Cory A.; Herzog, Arthur; Huang, Vincent A.; Janowicz, Krzysztof; Kelsey, W. David; Le Phuoc, Danh; Lefort, Laurent; Leggieri, Myriam; Neuhaus, Holger; Nikolov, Andriy; Page, Kevin R.; Passant, Alexandre; Sheth, Amit P.; Taylor, Kerry (2012). 'The SSN ontology of the W3C semantic sensor network incubator group'. In: *J. Web Sem.* 17, pp. 25–32. DOI: 10.1016/j.websem.2012.05.003.

Cowen, David J. (1988). 'GIS versus CAD versus DBMS: What Are the Differences?' In: *Photogrammetric Engineering and Remote Sensing* 54, pp. 1551–1554.

Cox, Simon (2013). 'Geographic information - Observations and measurements'. In: *OGC Abstract Specification*.

Cruz, Isabel F.; Ganesh, Venkat R.; Caletti, Claudio; Reddy, Pavan (2013). 'GIVA: a semantic framework for geospatial and temporal data integration, visualization, and analytics'. In: *21st International Conference on Advances in Geographic Information Systems (SIGSPATIAL 2013)*. Ed. by Craig A. Knoblock; Markus Schneider; Peer Kröger; John Krumm; Peter Widmayer. ACM, pp. 534–537. ISBN: 978-1-4503-2521-9. DOI: 10.1145/2525314.2525324.

Cyganiak, Richard; Jentzsch, Anja (2014). *The Linking Open Data cloud diagram*. URL: http://lod-cloud.net/ (visited on 05/15/2020).

Daniele, Laura; den Hartog, Frank; Roes, Jasper (2015). 'Created in close interaction with the industry: the smart appliances reference (SAREF) ontology'. In: *International Workshop Formal Ontologies Meet Industries*. Springer, pp. 100–112.

Das, Souripriya; Sundara, Seema; Cyganiak, Richard (2012). *R2RML: RDB to RDF Mapping Language*. W3C Recommendation September. URL: http://www.w3.org/TR/r2rml/.

Davis, Randall; Shrobe, Howard E.; Szolovits, Peter (1993). 'What Is a Knowledge Representation?' In: *AI Magazine* 14, pp. 17–33.

De Dauw, Jeroen (2014). *Wikibase. The Software behind Wikidata*. Vienna.

Demirkan, Haluk; Delen, Dursun (2013). 'Leveraging the capabilities of service-oriented decision support systems: Putting analytics and big data in cloud'. In: *Decis. Support Syst.* 55.1, pp. 412–421. DOI: 10.1016/j.dss.2012.05.048.

Diefenbach, Dennis; Thalhammer, Andreas (2018). 'PageRank and Generic Entity Summarization for RDF Knowledge Bases'. In: *The Semantic Web - 15th International Conference, ESWC 2018, Heraklion, Crete, Greece, June 3-7, 2018, Proceedings*. Ed. by Aldo Gangemi; Roberto Navigli; Maria-Esther Vidal; Pascal Hitzler; Raphaël Troncy; Laura Hollink; Anna Tordai; Mehwish Alam. Lecture Notes in Computer Science 10843. Springer, pp. 145–160. ISBN: 978-3-319-93416-7. DOI: 10.1007/978-3-319-93417-4_10.

Dimou, Anastasia; Vander Sande, Miel; Colpaert, Pieter; Verborgh, Ruben; Mannens, Erik; Van de Walle, Rik (2014). 'RML: A Generic Language for Integrated RDF Mappings of Heterogeneous Data'. In: *Proceedings of the 7th Workshop on Linked Data on the Web*.

Dimou, Anastasia; Verborgh, Ruben; Vander Sande, Miel; Mannens, Erik; Van de Walle, Rik (2015). 'Machine-interpretable dataset and service descriptions for heterogeneous data access and retrieval'. In: *Proceedings of the 11th International Conference on Semantic Systems (SEMANTICS 2015)*. Ed. by Axel Polleres; Tassilo Pellegrini; Sebastian Hellmann; Josiane Xavier Parreira. ACM, pp. 145–152. ISBN: 978-1-4503-3462-4. DOI: 10.1145/2814864.2814873.

Doherty, Patrick; Lukaszewicz, Witold; Szalas, Andrzej (2000). 'Efficient Reasoning Using the Local Closed-World Assumption'. In: *Artificial Intelligence: Methodology, Systems, and Applications*. Berlin, Heidelberg: Springer Berlin Heidelberg, pp. 49–58. ISBN: 978-3-540-45331-4.

Duerst, M.; Suignard, M. (2005). *Internationalized Resource Identifiers (IRIs)*. URL: http://tools.ietf.org/html/rfc3987#section-1 (visited on 12/22/2014).

Duy, T. K.; Quirchmayr, G.; Tjoa, A.; Hanh, H. H. (2017). 'A semantic data model for the interpretion of environmental streaming data'. In: *2017 Seventh International Conference on Information Science and Technology (ICIST)*. April, pp. 376–380. DOI: 10.1109/ICIST.2017.7926788.

Ehrlinger, Lisa; Wöß, Wolfram (2016). 'Towards a Definition of Knowledge Graphs'. In: *Joint Proceedings of the Posters and Demos Track of the 12th International Conference on Semantic Systems - SEMANTiCS2016 and the 1st International Workshop on Semantic Change & Evolving Semantics (SuCCESS'16) co-located with the 12th International Conference on Semantic Systems (SEMANTiCS 2016), Leipzig, Germany, September 12-15, 2016*. Ed. by Michael Martin; Martí Cuquet; Erwin Folmer. Vol. 1695. CEUR Workshop Proceedings. CEUR-WS.org.

Elsaleh, Tarek; Enshaeifar, Shirin; Rezvani, Roonak; Acton, Sahr Thomas; Janeiko, Valentinas; Marúdez-Edo (2020). 'IoT-Stream: A Lightweight Ontology for Internet of Things Data Streams and Its Use with Data Analytics and Event Detection Services'. In: *Sensors* 20.4, p. 953. DOI: 10.3390/s20040953.

Fafalios, Pavlos; Baritakis, Manolis; Tzitzikas, Yannis (2015). 'Exploiting Linked Data for Open and Configurable Named Entity Extraction'. In: *International Journal on Artificial Intelligence Tools* 24.2. DOI: 10.1142/S0218213015400126.

Färber, Michael; Bartscherer, Frederic; Menne, Carsten; Rettinger, Achim (2018). 'Linked data quality of DBpedia, Freebase, OpenCyc, Wikidata, and YAGO.' In: *Semantic Web* 9.1, pp. 77–129. DOI: 10.3233/SW-170275.

Fensel, Dieter; Simsek, Umutcan; Angele, Kevin; Huaman, Elwin; Kärle, Elias; Panasiuk, Oleksandra; Toma, Ioan; Umbrich, Jürgen; Wahler, Alexander (2020). *Knowledge Graphs - Methodology, Tools and Selected Use Cases*. Springer. ISBN: 978-3-030-37438-9. DOI: 10.1007/978-3-030-37439-6.

Frank, Matthias (2016). 'Integrating Big Spatio-Temporal Data Using Collaborative Semantic Data Management Switzerland, June 6-9, 2016. Proceedings'. In: *Web Engineering - 16th International Conference, ICWE 2016, Lugano, Switzerland, June 6-9, 2016. Proceedings*. Ed. by Alessandro Bozzon; Philippe Cudré-Mauroux; Cesare Pautasso. Lecture Notes in Computer Science 9671. Springer, pp. 507–512. ISBN: 978-3-319-38790-1. DOI: 10.1007/978-3-319-38791-8_38.

Frank, Matthias T.; Bader, Sebastian R.; Simko, Viliam; Zander, Stefan (2018). 'LSane: Collaborative Validation and Enrichment of Heterogeneous Observation Streams'. In: *Proceedings of the 14th International Conference on Semantic Systems, SEMANTICS 2018, Vienna, Austria, September 10-13, 2018*. Ed. by Anna Fensel; Victor de Boer; Tassilo Pellegrini; Elmar Kiesling; Bernhard Haslhofer; Laura Hollink; Alexander Schindler. Procedia Computer Science 137. Elsevier, pp. 235–241. DOI: 10.1016/j.procs.2018.09.022.

Frank, Matthias T.; Simko, Viliam (2018). 'Semantic Data Stream Mapping and Shape Constraint Validation Based on Collaboratively Created Annotations Spain, June 5-8, 2018, Proceedings'. In: *Web Engineering - 18th International Conference, ICWE 2018, Cáceres, Spain, June 5-8, 2018, Proceedings*. Ed. by Tommi Mikkonen; Ralf Klamma; Juan Hernández. Lecture Notes in Computer Science 10845. Springer, pp. 321–329. ISBN: 978-3-319-91661-3. DOI: 10.1007/978-3-319-91662-0_26.

Frank, Matthias T.; Zander, Stefan (2017a). 'The Linked Data Wiki: Leveraging Organizational Knowledge Bases with Linked Open Data'. In: *Knowledge Discovery, Knowledge Engineering and Knowledge Management - 9th International Joint Conference, IC3K 2017, Funchal, Madeira, Portugal, November 1-3, 2017, Revised Selected Papers*. Ed. by Ana L. N. Fred; David Aveiro; Jan L. G. Dietz; Kecheng Liu; Jorge Bernardino; Ana Salgado; Joaquim Filipe. Vol. 976. Communications in Computer and Information Science. Springer, pp. 294–319. DOI: 10.1007/978-3-030-15640-4_15.

Frank, Matthias; Zander, Stefan (2016a). 'Pushing the CIDOC-Conceptual Reference Model towards LOD by Open Annotations'. In: *Modellierung 2016, 2.-4. März 2016, Karlsruhe*. Ed. by Andreas Oberweis; Ralf H. Reussner. LNI 254. GI, pp. 13–28. ISBN: 978-3-88579-648-0.

Frank, Matthias; Zander, Stefan (2016b). 'Smart Web Services for Big Spatio-Temporal Data in Geographical Information Systems'. In: *Proceedings of the 4th Workshop on Services and Applications over Linked APIs and Data co-located with the 13th Extended Semantic Web Conference (ESWC 2016), Crete, Greece, May 29, 2016*. Ed. by Maria Maleshkova; Ruben Verborgh; Felix Leif Keppmann. CEUR Workshop Proceedings 1629. CEUR-WS.org.

Frank, Matthias; Zander, Stefan (2017b). 'Exploiting Linked Open Data for Enhancing MediaWiki-based Semantic Organizational Knowledge Bases'. In: *Proceedings of the 9th International Joint Conference on Knowledge Discovery, Knowledge Engineering and Knowledge Management - (Volume 2), Funchal, Madeira, Portugal, November 1-3, 2017*. Ed. by David Aveiro; Jan L. G. Dietz; Joaquim Filipe. SciTePress, pp. 98–106. DOI: 10.5220/0006587900980106.

Frank, Matthias; Zander, Stefan (2017c). 'Linked Open Data for Organizational Knowledge Bases. Towards a Linked Data Wiki'. In: *Collaborative European Research Conference*. Ed. by Udo Bleimann; Bernhard Humm; Robert Loew; Stefanie Regier; Ingo Stengel; Paul Walsh, pp. 50–57.

Frischmuth, Philipp; Martin, Michael; Tramp, Sebastian; Riechert, Thomas; Auer, Sören (2015). 'OntoWiki - An authoring, publication and visualization interface for the Data Web'. In: *Semantic Web* 6.3, pp. 215–240. DOI: 10.3233/SW-140145.

Gemmeke, Philipp; Maleshkova, Maria; Philipp, Patrick; Götz, Michael; Weber, Christian; Kämpgen, Benedikt; Nolden, Marco; Maier-Hein, Klaus H.; Rettinger, Achim (2014). 'Using Linked Data and Web APIs for Automating the Pre-processing of Medical Images'. In: *Proceedings of the 5th International Workshop on Consuming Linked Data (COLD 2014) co-located with the 13th International Semantic Web Conference (ISWC 2014), Riva del Garda, Italy, October 20, 2014*. Ed. by Olaf Hartig; Aidan Hogan; Juan F. Sequeda. Vol. 1264. CEUR Workshop Proceedings. CEUR-WS.org.

Ghidini, Chiara; Rospocher, Marco; Serafini, Luciano; Kump, Barbara; Pammer, Viktoria; Faatz, Andreas; Zinnen, Andreas; Guss, Joanna; Lindstaedt, Stefanie (2008). 'Collaborative Knowledge Engineering via Semantic MediaWiki'. In: *International Conference on Semantic Systems (I-SEMANTICS '08)*. Ed. by S. Auer; S. Schaffert; T. Pellegrini. september 3-5. Graz, Austria, pp. 134–141.

Gil, Yolanda; González-Calero, Pedro A.; Kim, Jihie; Moody, Joshua; Ratnakar, Varun (2011). 'A semantic framework for automatic generation of computational workflows using distributed data and component catalogues'. In: *J. Exp. Theor. Artif. Intell.* 23.4, pp. 389–467. DOI: 10.1080/0952813X.2010.490962.

Gil, Yolanda; Michel, Felix; Ratnakar, Varun; Hauder, Matheus (2015). 'A Semantic, Task-Centered Collaborative Framework for Science'. In: *The Semantic Web: ESWC 2015 Satellite Events - ESWC 2015 Satellite Events Portorož, Slovenia, May 31 - June 4, 2015, Revised Selected Papers*. Ed. by Fabien Gandon; Christophe Guéret; Serena Villata; John G. Breslin; Catherine Faron-Zucker; Antoine Zimmermann. Lecture Notes in Computer Science 9341. Springer, pp. 58–61. ISBN: 978-3-319-25638-2. DOI: 10.1007/978-3-319-25639-9_11.

Golbeck, Jennifer; Parsia, Bijan; Hendler, James A. (2003). 'Trust Networks on the Semantic Web'. In: *Cooperative Information Agents VII, 7th International Workshop, CIA 2003, Helsinki, Finland, August 27-29, 2003, Proceedings*. Ed. by Matthias Klusch; Sascha Ossowski; Andrea Omicini; Heimo Laamanen. Lecture Notes in Computer Science 2782. Springer, pp. 238–249. ISBN: 3-540-40798-7. DOI: 10.1007/978-3-540-45217-1_18.

Gruber, Tom (2009). 'Ontology'. In: *Encyclopedia of Database Systems*. Ed. by Ling Liu; M. Tamer Özsu. Springer US, pp. 1963–1965. DOI: 10.1007/978-0-387-39940-9_1318.

Haller, Armin; Janowicz, Krzysztof; Cox, Simon J. D.; Lefrançois, Maxime; Taylor, Kerry L.; Le Phuoc, Danh; Lieberman, Joshua; García-Castro, Raúl; Atkinson, Rob; Stadler, Claus (2019). 'The modular SSN ontology: A joint W3C and OGC standard specifying the semantics of sensors, observations, sampling, and actuation'. In: *Semantic Web* 10, pp. 9–32.

Harris, Steve; Seaborne, Andy (2013a). *SPARQL 1.1 Query Language*. URL: http://www.w3.org/TR/sparql11-query/ (visited on 05/15/2020).

Harris, Steve; Seaborne, Andy (2013b). *SPARQL 1.1 Query Language: 10.2 VALUES: Providing inline data*. URL: http://www.w3.org/TR/sparql11-query/#inline-data (visited on 05/15/2020).

Harth, Andreas; Hose, Katja; Schenkel, Ralf, eds. (2014). *Linked Data Management*. Chapman and Hall/CRC. ISBN: 978-1-4665-8240-8.

Harth, Andreas; Knoblock, Craig A.; Stadtmüller, Steffen; Studer, Rudi; Szekely, Pedro A. (2013). 'On-the-fly Integration of Static and Dynamic Sources Data'. In: *Fourth International Workshop on Consuming Linked Data (COLD 2013)*. Ed. by Olaf Hartig; Juan Sequeda; Aidan Hogan; Takahide Matsutsuka. CEUR Workshop Proceedings 1034. CEUR-WS.org.

Hausenblas, Michael (2009). 'Exploiting Linked Data to Build Web Applications'. In: *IEEE Internet Computing* 13.4, pp. 68–73.

Hayes, Patrick (2004). *RDF Semantics. W3C Recommendation 10 February 2004*. URL: https://www.w3.org/TR/rdf-mt/ (visited on 05/15/2020).

Heath, Tom; Bizer, Christian (2011). *Linked Data: Evolving the Web into a Global Data Space*. Synthesis Lectures on the Semantic Web. Morgan & Claypool Publishers. DOI: 10.2200/S00334ED1V01Y201102WBE001.

Hebeler, John (2009). *Semantic Web programming*. Indianapolis, IN: Wiley. ISBN: 9780470418017.

Herman, Ivan; Adida, Ben; Sporny, Manu; Birbeck, Mark (2015). *RDFa 1.1 Primer - Third Edition. Rich Structured Data Markup for Web Documents*. W3C Working Group Note 17 March 2015. URL: https://www.w3.org/TR/rdfa-primer/ (visited on 06/10/2020).

Hitzler, Pascal; Krötsch, Markus; Rudolph, Sebastian; Sure, York, eds. (2008). *The semantic web: Grundlagen*. eXamen.press. Berlin, Heidelberg, and New York, NY: Springer. ISBN: 9783540339939.

Hitzler, Pascal; Krötzsch, Markus; Rudolph, Sebastian (2010). *Foundations of Semantic Web technologies*. Chapman & Hall/CRC textbooks in computing. Boca Raton, Fla: CRC Press. ISBN: 978-1-4200-9050-5.

Hogan, Aidan; Blomqvist, Eva; Cochez, Michael; d'Amato, Claudia; Melo, Gerard de; Gutierrez, Claudio; Gayo, José Emilio Labra; Kirrane, Sabrina; Neumaier, Sebastian; Polleres, Axel; Navigli, Roberto; Ngomo, Axel-Cyrille Ngonga; Rashid, Sabbir M.; Rula, Anisa; Schmelzeisen, Lukas; Sequeda, Juan F.; Staab, Steffen; Zimmermann, Antoine (2020). 'Knowledge Graphs'. In: *CoRR* abs/2003.02320.

Hubauer, Thomas; Lamparter, Steffen; Haase, Peter; Herzig, Daniel Markus (2018). 'Use Cases of the Industrial Knowledge Graph at Siemens'. In: *Proceedings of the ISWC 2018 Posters & Demonstrations, Industry and Blue Sky Ideas Tracks co-located with 17th International Semantic Web Conference (ISWC 2018), Monterey, USA, October 8th - to - 12th, 2018*. Ed. by Marieke van Erp; Medha Atre; Vanessa López; Kavitha Srinivas; Carolina Fortuna. CEUR Workshop Proceedings 2180. CEUR-WS.org.

Iancu, Bogdan; Sandu, Cristian (2016). 'A Cryptographic Approach for Implementing Semantic Web's Trust Layer'. In: *Innovative Security Solutions for Information Technology and Communications - 9th International Conference, SECITC 2016, Bucharest, Romania, June 9-10, 2016, Revised Selected Papers*. Ed. by Ion Bica; Reza Reyhanitabar. Lecture Notes in Computer Science 10006, pp. 127–136. ISBN: 978-3-319-47237-9. DOI: 10.1007/978-3-319-47238-6_9.

Ismayilov, Ali; Kontokostas, Dimitris; Auer, Sören; Lehmann, Jens; Hellmann, Sebastian (2015). 'Wikidata through the Eyes of DBpedia'. In: *CoRR* abs/1507.04180.

Jamali, Mohammad Ali Jabraeil; Bahrami, Bahareh; Heidari, Arash; Allahverdizadeh, Parisa; Norouzi, Farhad (2020). *Towards the Internet of Things - Architectures, Security, and Applications*. Springer. ISBN: 978-3-030-18467-4. DOI: 10.1007/978-3-030-18468-1.

Janowicz, Krzysztof; Hitzler, Pascal; Adams, Benjamin; Kolas, Dave; Vardeman, Charles (2014). 'Five stars of Linked Data vocabulary use'. In: *Semantic Web* 5.3, pp. 173–176.

Kämpgen, Benedikt; Ell, Basil; Paslaru Bontas Simperl, Elena; Vrandecic, Denny; Dengler, Frank (2011). 'Enterprise Wikis: Technical Challenges and Opportunities'. In: *Wissensmanagement 2011*.

Kämpgen, Benedikt; Harth, Andreas (2014). 'OLAP4LD - A Framework for Building Analysis Applications Over Governmental Statistics'. In: *The Semantic Web: ESWC 2014 Satellite Events - ESWC 2014 Satellite Events, Anissaras, Crete, Greece, May 25-29, 2014, Revised Selected Papers*. Ed. by Valentina Presutti; Eva Blomqvist;

Raphaël Troncy; Harald Sack; Ioannis Papadakis; Anna Tordai. Lecture Notes in Computer Science 8798. Springer, pp. 389–394. ISBN: 978-3-319-11954-0. DOI: 10.1007/978-3-319-11955-7_54.

Kämpgen, Benedikt; Stadtmüller, Steffen; Harth, Andreas (2014). 'Querying the Global Cube: Integration of Multidimensional Datasets from the Web'. In: *Knowledge Engineering and Knowledge Management - 19th International Conference, EKAW 2014, Linköping, Sweden, November 24-28, 2014. Proceedings*. Ed. by Krzysztof Janowicz; Stefan Schlobach; Patrick Lambrix; Eero Hyvönen. Lecture Notes in Computer Science 8876. Springer, pp. 250–265. ISBN: 978-3-319-13703-2. DOI: 10.1007/978-3-319-13704-9_20.

Kasten, Andreas (2016). 'Secure semantic web data management: confidentiality, integrity, and compliant availability in open and distributed networks'. University of Koblenz and Landau, Germany.

Khalili, Ali; Auer, Sören (2013). 'WYSIWYM Authoring of Structured Content Based on Schema.org'. In: *Web Information Systems Engineering - WISE 2013 - 14th International Conference, Nanjing, China, October 13-15, 2013, Proceedings, Part II*. Ed. by Xuemin Lin; Yannis Manolopoulos; Divesh Srivastava; Guangyan Huang. Lecture Notes in Computer Science 8181. Springer, pp. 425–438. ISBN: 978-3-642-41153-3. DOI: 10.1007/978-3-642-41154-0_32.

Klein, Michel Christiaan Alexander (2004). *Change Management for Distributed Ontologies*. Vol. 2004-11. SIKS dissertation series. 196 pp. ISBN: 90-9018400-7.

Kleiner, Frank; Abecker, Andreas (2010). 'Semantic MediaWiki as an Integration Platform for IT Service Management'. In: *Informatik 2010: Service Science - Neue Perspektiven für die Informatik, Beiträge der 40. Jahrestagung der Gesellschaft für Informatik e.V. (GI), Band 2, 27.09. - 1.10.2010, Leipzig, Deutschland*. Ed. by Klaus-Peter Fähnrich; Bogdan Franczyk. Vol. 176. LNI 176. GI, pp. 73–78. ISBN: 978-3-88579-270-3.

Klyne, Graham; Carroll, Jeremy J. (2004). *Resource Description Framework (RDF): Concepts and Abstract Syntax*. W3C Recommendation. World Wide Web Consortium. URL: http://www.w3.org/TR/2004/REC-rdf-concepts-20040210/ (visited on 06/08/2020).

Knublauch, Holger; Kontokostas, Dimitris (2017). *Shapes Constraint Language (SHACL). W3C Recommendation 20 July 2017*. URL: https://www.w3.org/TR/shacl/.

Koivunen, Marja-Riitta; Miller, Eric (2001). *W3C Semantic Web Activity.* URL: https://www.w3.org/2001/12/semweb-fin/w3csw (visited on 06/08/2020).

Kolozali, Sefki; Marúdez-Edo; Puschmann, Daniel; Ganz, Frieder; Barnaghi, Payam M. (2014). 'A Knowledge-Based Approach for Real-Time IoT Data Stream Annotation and Processing'. In: *2014 IEEE International Conference on Internet of Things, IEEE Green Computing and Communications, and IEEE Cyber, Physical and Social Computing, iThings/GreenCom/CPSCom 2014, Taipei, Taiwan, September 1-3, 2014.* IEEE Computer Society, pp. 215–222. ISBN: 978-1-4799-5967-9. DOI: 10.1109/iThings.2014.39.

Kopecký, Jacek; Vitvar, Tomas; Pedrinaci, Carlos; Maleshkova, Maria (2011). 'RESTful Services with Lightweight Machine-readable Descriptions and Semantic Annotations'. In: *REST: From Research to Practice.* Ed. by Erik Wilde; Cesare Pautasso. Springer, pp. 473–506. ISBN: 978-1-4419-8302-2. DOI: 10.1007/978-1-4419-8303-9_22.

Koren, Yaron (2015). 'Cargo and the future of Semantic MediaWiki'. In: *SMWCon Spring 2015. St. Louis, MO, USA.*

Krötzsch, Markus; Vrandečić, Denny; Völkel, Max (2006). 'Semantic MediaWiki'. In: *ISWC 2006.* Vol. 4273. Lecture Notes in Computer Science. Berlin, Heidelberg: Springer Berlin Heidelberg, pp. 935–942. ISBN: 978-3-540-49029-6.

Krötzsch, Markus; Vrandecic, Denny; Völkel, Max; Haller, Heiko; Studer, Rudi (2007). 'Semantic Wikipedia'. In: *J. Web Sem.* 5.4, pp. 251–261. DOI: 10.1016/j.websem.2007.09.001.

Lanthaler, Markus (2013). 'Creating 3rd generation web APIs with hydra'. In: *22nd International World Wide Web Conference* (*WWW '13*). Ed. by Leslie Carr; Alberto H. F. Laender; Bernadette Farias Lóscio; Irwin King; Marcus Fontoura; Denny Vrandecic; Lora Aroyo; José Palazzo M. de Oliveira; Fernanda Lima; Erik Wilde. International World Wide Web Conferences Steering Committee, ACM, pp. 35–38. ISBN: 978-1-4503-2038-2.

Lanthaler, Markus; Guetl, Christian (2013). 'Hydra: A Vocabulary for Hypermedia-Driven Web APIs'. In: *Workshop on Linked Data on the Web* (*WWW2013*). Ed. by Christian Bizer; Tom Heath; Tim Berners-Lee; Michael Hausenblas; Sören Auer. CEUR Workshop Proceedings 996. CEUR-WS.org.

Lanthaler, Markus; Gütl, Christian (2012). 'Seamless Integration of RESTful Services into the Web of Data'. In: *Adv. in MM* 2012, 586542:1–586542:14. DOI: 10.1155/2012/586542.

Lanthaler, Markus; Gütl, Christian (2013). 'Model your application domain, not your JSON structures'. In: *22nd International World Wide Web Conference (WWW '13)*. Ed. by Leslie Carr; Alberto H. F. Laender; Bernadette Farias Lóscio; Irwin King; Marcus Fontoura; Denny Vrandecic; Lora Aroyo; José Palazzo M. de Oliveira; Fernanda Lima; Erik Wilde. International World Wide Web Conferences Steering Committee, ACM, pp. 1415–1420. ISBN: 978-1-4503-2038-2.

Leach, Paul; Mealling, Michael; Salz, Rich (2005). *A Universally Unique IDentifier (UUID) URN Namespace*. URL: http://tools.ietf.org/html/rfc4122 (visited on 06/08/2020).

Lebo, Timothy; Sahoo, Satya; McGuinness, Deborah (2013). *PROV-O: The PROV Ontology. W3C Recommendation 30 April 2013*. URL: https://www.w3.org/TR/prov-o/.

Lefort, Laurent; Bobruk, Josh; Haller, Armin; Taylor, Kerry; Woolf, Andrew (2012). 'A Linked Sensor Data Cube for a 100 Year Homogenised Daily Temperature Dataset'. In: *International Workshop on Semantic Sensor Networks (SSN 2012)*. Ed. by Cory A. Henson; Kerry Taylor; Óscar Corcho. CEUR Workshop Proceedings 904. CEUR-WS.org, pp. 1–16.

Lehmann, Jens; Isele, Robert; Jakob, Max; Jentzsch, Anja; Kontokostas, Dimitris; Mendes, Pablo N.; Hellmann, Sebastian; Morsey, Mohamed; van Kleef, Patrick; Auer, Sören; Bizer, Christian (2015). 'DBpedia - A large-scale, multilingual knowledge base extracted from Wikipedia'. In: *Semantic Web* 6, pp. 167–195.

Li, Wenwen; Li, Linna; Goodchild, Michael F.; Anselin, Luc (2013). 'A Geospatial Cyberinfrastructure for Urban Economic Analysis and Spatial Decision-Making'. In: *ISPRS Int. J. Geo-Information* 2.2, pp. 413–431. DOI: 10.3390/ijgi2020413.

Maleshkova, Maria; Philipp, Patrick; Sure-Vetter, York; Studer, Rudi (2016). 'Smart Web Services (SmartWS) - The Future of Services on the Web'. In: *IPSI BgD Transactions on Advanced Research (TAR)* 12.1. Januar Article, pp. 15–26.

Manola, Frank; Miller, Eric (2004). *RDF Primer. W3C Recommendation 10 February 2004*. URL: https://www.w3.org/TR/rdf-primer/ (visited on 06/08/2020).

Markovic, Milan; Edwards, Peter (2016). 'Semantic Stream Processing for IoT Devices in the Food Safety Domain'. In: *Joint Proceedings of the Posters and Demos Track of the 12th International Conference on Semantic Systems - SEMANTiCS2016 and the 1st International Workshop on Semantic Change & Evolving Semantics (SuCCESS'16) co-located with the 12th International Conference on Semantic Systems (SEMANTiCS 2016), Leipzig, Germany, September 12-15, 2016.* Ed. by Michael Martin; Martıí Cuquet; Erwin Folmer. CEUR Workshop Proceedings 1695. CEUR-WS.org.

Markovic, Milan; Edwards, Peter; Kollingbaum, Martin J.; Rowe, Alan (2016). 'Modelling Provenance of Sensor Data for Food Safety Compliance Checking'. In: *Provenance and Annotation of Data and Processes - 6th International Provenance and Annotation Workshop, IPAW 2016, McLean, VA, USA, June 7-8, 2016, Proceedings.* Ed. by Marta Mattoso; Boris Glavic. Lecture Notes in Computer Science 9672. Springer, pp. 134–145. ISBN: 978-3-319-40592-6. DOI: 10.1007/978-3-319-40593-3_11.

Marúdez-Edo; Elsaleh, Tarek; Barnaghi, Payam M.; Taylor, Kerry (2017). 'IoT-Lite: a lightweight semantic model for the internet of things and its use with dynamic semantics'. In: *Personal and Ubiquitous Computing* 21.3, pp. 475–487. DOI: 10.1007/s00779-017-1010-8.

Masuch, Lukas (2014). *Enterprise Knowledge Graph. One graph to connect them all.* SAP AG. URL: https://www.managementexchange.com/hack/enterprise-knowledge-graph-one-graph-connect-them-all (visited on 06/08/2020).

Moats, R. (1997). *URN Syntax.* URL: http://tools.ietf.org/html/rfc2141 (visited on 07/08/2020).

Moreau, Luc (2010). 'The Foundations for Provenance on the Web'. In: *Foundations and Trends in Web Science* 2.2-3, pp. 99–241. DOI: 10.1561/1800000010.

Moreira, João L. R.; Daniele, Laura; Pires, Luis Ferreira; van Sinderen, Marten; Wasielewska, Katarzyna; Szmeja, Pawel; Pawlowski, Wieslaw; Ganzha, Maria; Paprzycki, Marcin (2017). 'Towards IoT Platforms' Integration Semantic Translations between W3C SSN and ETSI SAREF'. In: *Joint Proceedings of SEMANTiCS 2017 Workshops co-located with the 13th International Conference on Semantic Systems (SEMANTiCS 2017), Amsterdam, Netherlands, September 11 and 14, 2017.* Ed. by Anna Fensel; Laura Daniele; Lora Aroyo; Victor de Boer; Sándor Darányi; Omar Elloumi; Raúl Garc-Castro; Laura Hollink; Oana Inel; Gerard Kuys; Maria Maleshkova; Munir Merdan; Albert Meroño-Peñuela; Thomas Moser; Felix Leif Keppmann; Efstratios Kontopoulos; Lodewijk Petram; Enrico Scarrone; Ruben Verborgh. Vol. 2063. CEUR Workshop Proceedings. CEUR-WS.org.

Nolle, Andreas; Chekol, Melisachew Wudage; Meilicke, Christian; Nemirovski, German; Stuckenschmidt, Heiner (2017). 'Automated Fine-Grained Trust Assessment in Federated Knowledge Bases'. In: *The Semantic Web - ISWC 2017 - 16th International Semantic Web Conference, Vienna, Austria, October 21-25, 2017, Proceedings, Part I*. Ed. by Claudia d'Amato; Miriam Fernández; Valentina A. M. Tamma; Freddy Lécué; Philippe Cudré-Mauroux; Juan F. Sequeda; Christoph Lange; Jeff Heflin. Lecture Notes in Computer Science 10587. Springer, pp. 490–506. ISBN: 978-3-319-68287-7. DOI: 10.1007/978-3-319-68288-4_29.

Ogden, Charles K.; Richards, Ivor A. (1956). *The meaning of meaning. A study of the influence of language upon thought and of the science of symbolism*. 10. ed., 4. impr. International library of psychology, philosophy and scientific method. London: Routledge and Kegan Paul.

Ogden, Charles Kay; Richards, Ivor Armstrong; Malinowski, Bronislaw; Crookshank, F. G. (1923). *The meaning of meaning. A study of the influence of language upon thought and of the science of symbolism*. Vol. 0029. A Harvest book. New York: Harcourt, Brace and World. 363 pp. ISBN: 9780156584463.

Pellegrini, Tassilo, ed. (2006). *Semantic Web: Wege zur vernetzten Wissensgesellschaft*. X.media.press. Berlin, Heidelberg, and New York: Springer. ISBN: 3540293248.

Prud'hommeaux, Eric; Seaborne, Andy (2004). *SPARQL Query Language for RDF*. URL: http://www.w3.org/TR/2004/WD-rdf-sparql-query-20041012/ (visited on 06/08/2020).

Ram, Sudha; Liu, Jun (2012). 'A Semantic Foundation for Provenance Management'. In: *J. Data Semantics* 1.1, pp. 11–17. DOI: 10.1007/s13740-012-0002-0.

Rautenberg, Sandro; Ermilov, Ivan; Marx, Edgard; Auer, Sören; Ngomo, Axel-Cyrille Ngonga (2015). 'LODFlow. A Workflow Management System for Linked Data Processing'. In: *Proceedings of the 11th International Conference on Semantic Systems, SEMANTICS 2015, Vienna, Austria, September 15-17, 2015*. Ed. by Axel Polleres; Tassilo Pellegrini; Sebastian Hellmann; Josiane Xavier Parreira. ACM, pp. 137–144. ISBN: 978-1-4503-3462-4. DOI: 10.1145/2814864.2814882.

Razniewski, Simon; Nutt, Werner (2014). 'Databases under the Partial Closed-world Assumption: A Survey'. In: *Proceedings of the 26th GI-Workshop Grundlagen von Datenbanken, Bozen-Bolzano, Italy, October 21st to 24th, 2014*. Ed. by Friederike Klan; Günther Specht; Hans Gamper. Vol. 1313. CEUR Workshop Proceedings. CEUR-WS.org, pp. 59–64.

Razniewski, Simon; Savkovic, Ognjen; Nutt, Werner (2016). 'Turning The Partial-Closed World Assumption Upside Down'. In: *Proceedings of the 10th Alberto Mendelzon International Workshop on Foundations of Data Management, Panama City, Panama, May 8-10, 2016*. Ed. by Reinhard Pichler; Altigran Soares da Silva. Vol. 1644. CEUR Workshop Proceedings. CEUR-WS.org.

Richardson, Matthew; Agrawal, Rakesh; Domingos, Pedro M. (2003). 'Trust Management for the Semantic Web'. In: *The Semantic Web - ISWC 2003, Second International Semantic Web Conference, Sanibel Island, FL, USA, October 20-23, 2003, Proceedings*. Ed. by Dieter Fensel; Katia P. Sycara; John Mylopoulos. Lecture Notes in Computer Science 2870. Springer, pp. 351–368. ISBN: 3-540-20362-1. DOI: 10.1007/978-3-540-39718-2_23.

Ross, Sheldon M.; Birnbaum, Z. W.; Lukacs, E. (2014). *Introduction to Stochastic Dynamic Programming*. eng. Burlington: Elsevier Science. 179 pp. ISBN: 0-12-598420-0.

Rowley, Jennifer E. (2007). 'The wisdom hierarchy: representations of the DIKW hierarchy'. In: *Journal of Information Science* 33.2, pp. 163–180. DOI: 10.1177/0165551506070706.

Sacco, Owen; Breslin, John G. (2014). 'In users we trust: towards social user interactions based Trust Assertions for the Social Semantic Web'. In: *Social Network Analysis and Mining* 4.1, p. 229. ISSN: 1869-5469. DOI: 10.1007/s13278-014-0229-x.

Sanderson, Robert; Ciccarese, Paolo; Young, Benjamin (2017). *Web Annotation Data Model. W3C Recommendation 23 February 2017*. URL: https://www.w3.org/TR/annotation-model/ (visited on 10/04/2019).

Sapot, Bryan (2016). *Sensor Data is Meaningless without Context*. SensrTrx Manufacturing Analytics. URL: https://www.sensrtrx.com/sensor-data-meaningless-without-context/ (visited on 08/09/2019).

Schied, Manfred; Köstlbacher, Anton; Wolff, Christian (2010). 'Connecting Semantic Mediawiki to different Triple Stores Using RDF2Go'. In: *SemWiki@ESWC*.

Schreiber, Guus; Raimond, Yves (2014). *RDF 1.1 Primer. W3C Working Group*. URL: http://www.w3.org/TR/rdf11-primer/#section-Introduction (visited on 06/08/2020).

Segaran, Toby; Evans, Colin; Taylor, Jamie (2009). *Programming the Semantic Web*. 1st ed. Beijing and Sebastopol, CA: O'Reilly. ISBN: 9780596153816.

Shirgahi, Hossein; Mohsenzadeh, Mehran; Haj Seyyed Javadi, Hamid (2017). 'Trust estimation of the semantic web using semantic web clustering'. In: *Journal of Experimental & Theoretical Artificial Intelligence* 29.3, pp. 537–556. ISSN: 0952-813X. DOI: 10.1080/0952813X.2016.1199601.

Sholarin, Ebenezer A.; Awange, Joseph L. (2015). *Environmental Project Management. Principles, Methodology, and Processes*. eng. Environmental Science and Engineering. Sholarin, Ebenezer A. (VerfasserIn) Awange, Joseph L. (VerfasserIn). Cham and s.l.: Springer International Publishing. 32 pp. ISBN: 9783319276496. DOI: 10.1007/978-3-319-27651-9.

Sowa, John F. (2000). 'Knowledge representation: logical, philosophical, and computational foundations'. In: *Computational Linguistics* 27, pp. 286–294.

Sprague, Ralph H. (1980). 'A Framework for the Development of Decision Support Systems'. In: *MIS Quarterly* 4.4, pp. 1–26.

Stojanovic, Ljiljana (2004). *Business-process oriented knowledge management: concepts, methods, and tools*. DOI: 10.5445/IR/1000003270.

Stolz, Alex; Hepp, Martin (2013). 'Currency Conversion the Linked Data Way'. In: *First Workshop on Services and Applications over Linked APIs and Data (ESWC 2013)*. Ed. by Ruben Verborgh; Maria Maleshkova; Steffen Stadtmüller; Thomas Steiner; Pedro A. Szekely. CEUR Workshop Proceedings 1056. CEUR-WS.org, pp. 44–55.

Thalhammer, Andreas; Lasierra, Nelia; Rettinger, Achim (2016). 'LinkSUM: Using Link Analysis to Summarize Entity Data'. In: *16th International Conference on Web Engineering (ICWE 2016)*. Ed. by Alessandro Bozzon, Philippe Cudré-Mauroux, Cesare Pautasso. Vol. 9671. Lecture Notes in Computer Science. Springer, pp. 244–261.

Theoharis, Yannis; Fundulaki, Irini; Karvounarakis, Grigoris; Christophides, Vassilis (2011). 'On Provenance of Queries on Semantic Web Data'. In: *IEEE Internet Computing* 15.1, pp. 31–39. DOI: 10.1109/MIC.2010.127.

Tommasini, Riccardo; Della Valle, Emanuele; Mauri, Andrea; Brambilla, Marco (2017). 'RSPLab: RDF Stream Processing Benchmarking Made Easy'. In: *The Semantic Web - ISWC 2017 - 16th International Semantic Web Conference, Vienna, Austria, October 21-25, 2017, Proceedings, Part II*. Ed. by Claudia d'Amato; Miriam Fernández; Valentina A. M. Tamma; Freddy Lécué; Philippe Cudré-Mauroux;

Juan F. Sequeda; Christoph Lange; Jeff Heflin. Vol. 10588. Lecture Notes in Computer Science. Springer, pp. 202–209. DOI: 10.1007/978-3-319-68204-4_21.

Tsvetkova, Milena; García-Gavilanes, Ruth; Floridi, Luciano; Yasseri, Taha (2017). 'Even good bots fight: The case of Wikipedia'. In: *PLoS ONE 12(2): e0171774.*

Tu, Doan Quang; Kayes, A. S. M.; Rahayu, Wenny; Nguyen, Kinh (2020). 'Integration of IoT Streaming Data With Efficient Indexing and Storage Optimization'. In: *IEEE Access* 8, pp. 47456–47467. DOI: 10.1109/ACCESS.2020.2980006.

Tummarello, Giovanni; Morbidoni, Christian; Puliti, Paolo; Piazza, Francesco (2005). 'Signing Individual Fragments of an RDF Graph'. In: *Proceedings of the 14th international conference on World Wide Web, WWW 2005, Chiba, Japan, May 10-14, 2005 - Special interest tracks and posters*. Ed. by Allan Ellis; Tatsuya Hagino. ACM, pp. 1020–1021. ISBN: 1-59593-051-5. DOI: 10.1145/1062745.1062848.

Vandenbussche, Pierre-Yves; Vatant, Bernard (2014). 'Linked Open Vocabularies'. In: *ERCIM News* 2014.96.

Vettor, Pierre De; Mrissa, Michael; Benslimane, Djamal; Berbar, Salim (2014). 'A Service Oriented Architecture for Linked Data Integration'. In: *8th IEEE International Symposium on Service Oriented System Engineering, SOSE 2014, Oxford, United Kingdom, April 7-11, 2014*. IEEE Computer Society, pp. 198–203. DOI: 10.1109/SOSE.2014.30.

Völkel, Max; Groza, Tudor (2006). 'SemVersion: An RDF-based ontology versioning system'. In: *Proceedings of the IADIS International Conference WWW/Internet 2006. Murcia, Spain, October 5 - 8, 2006*. Ed. by Pedro Isaías. Murcia. ISBN: 972-8924-19-4.

Vrandecic, Denny; Krötzsch, Markus (2006). 'Reusing Ontological Background Knowledge in Semantic Wikis'. In: *SemWiki2006, First Workshop on Semantic Wikis - From Wiki to Semantics, Proceedings, co-located with the ESWC2006, Budva, Montenegro, June 12, 2006*. Ed. by Max Völkel; Sebastian Schaffert. Vol. 206. CEUR Workshop Proceedings 206. CEUR-WS.org.

Vrandecic, Denny; Krötzsch, Markus (2014). 'Wikidata. A free collaborative knowledgebase'. In: *Communications of the ACM* 57.10, pp. 78–85.

Watkins, Christopher J. C. H. (1989). *Learning from Delayed Rewards.*

Watkins, Christopher J. C. H.; Dayan, Peter (1992). 'Technical Note Q-Learning'. In: *Machine Learning* 8, pp. 279–292. DOI: 10.1007/BF00992698.

Webster, Jane; Watson, Richard T. (2002). 'Analyzing the Past to Prepare for the Future: Writing a Literature Review'. In: *MIS Quarterly* 26.2.

Wiener, Patrick; Stein, Manuel; Seebacher, Daniel; Bruns, Julian; Frank, Matthias; Simko, Viliam; Zander, Stefan; Nimis, Jens (2016). 'BigGIS: A continuous refinement approach to master heterogeneity and uncertainty in spatio-temporal big data (vision paper)'. In: *Proceedings of the 24th ACM SIGSPATIAL International Conference on Advances in Geographic Information Systems, GIS 2016, Burlingame, California, USA, October 31 - November 3, 2016*. Ed. by Siva Ravada; Mohammed Eunus Ali; Shawn D. Newsam; Matthias Renz; Goce Trajcevski. ACM, 8:1–8:4. ISBN: 978-1-4503-4589-7. DOI: 10.1145/2996913.2996931.

Wood, David; Marsha Zaidman; Luke Ruth, eds. (2014). *Linked Data. Structured data on the Web*. Shelter Island, NY: Manning. ISBN: 9781617290398.

Zander, Stefan; Ahmed, Nadia; Frank, Matthias T. (2017). 'A Survey about the Usage of Semantic Technologies for the Description of Robotic Components and Capabilities'. In: *Proceedings of the 1st International Workshop on Science, Application and Methods in Industry 4.0 co-located with (i-KNOW 2016), Graz, Austria, October 19, 2016*. Ed. by Roman Kern; Gerald Reiner; Olivia Bluder. CEUR Workshop Proceedings 1793. CEUR-WS.org.

Zander, Stefan; Merkle, Nicole; Frank, Matthias (2016a). 'Enhancing the Utilization of IoT Devices Using Ontological Semantics and Reasoning'. In: *The 7th International Conference on Emerging Ubiquitous Systems and Pervasive Networks (EUSPN 2016) / The 6th International Conference on Current and Future Trends of Information and Communication Technologies in Healthcare (ICTH-2016) / Affiliated Workshops, September 19-22, 2016, London, United Kingdom*. Ed. by Elhadi M. Shakshuki. Procedia Computer Science 98. Elsevier, pp. 87–90. DOI: 10.1016/j.procs.2016.09.015.

Zander, Stefan; Swertz, Christian; Verdú, Elena; Pérez, Mariía Jesús Verdú; Henning, Peter (2016b). 'A Semantic MediaWiki-Based Approach for the Collaborative Development of Pedagogically Meaningful Learning Content Annotations'. In: *Semantic Web Collaborative Spaces - Second International Workshop, SWCS 2013, Montpellier, France, May 27, 2013, Third International Workshop, SWCS 2014, Trentino, Italy, October 19, 2014, Revised Selected and Invited Papers*. Ed. by Pascal Molli; John G. Breslin; Maria-Esther Vidal. Vol. 9507. Lecture Notes in Computer Science 9507. Springer, pp. 73–111. ISBN: 978-3-319-32666-5.

List of Figures

List of Tables

List of Code Examples

List of Abbreviations

ABox	Assertional Box. 23–25, 32, 36, 47, 49, 50, 61, 62, 81, 87
ACL	Access Control List. 182
API	Application programming interface. 3, 56, 100, 103, 108, 111, 126, 127, 132, 138, 144, 146–150, 166, 181
Aprolo	Automated processing of linked observations. 13, 14, 19, 151–155, 159–162, 166, 169, 177, 178, 181, 182, 206
ASCII	American Standard Code for Information Interchange. 27, 92
bnode	Blank node. 29, 40, 57, 58
BoI	Biodiversity of India. 84, 90, 96
CC	Creative Commons. 34
CCIS	Communications in Computer and Information Science. 18
CKG	Corporate knowledge graph. 5, 17, 98, *Glossary:* corporate knowledge graph
CRS	Coordinates reference system. 140, 145
CSV	Comma-separated values. 34, 105
CURIE	Compact URI expression. 28
DIKW	Data-information- knowledge-wisdom. 4
DL	Description logic. 19, 21, 23, 24, 53
DSS	Decision support system. i, 2–6, 9, 10, 14, 132, 141, 142, 155, 156, *Glossary:* decision support system
FOAF	Friend of a Friend. 56
GGG	Giant Global Graph. 25, 33, 35
GIS	Geographical information system. i, 2, 3, 5, 6, 9, 11, 18, 139–145, 147–152, 154, 156, 157, 177, 178, 181, 182, *Glossary:* geographical information system

GUI	Graphical user interface. 60
HTML	Hypertext Markup Language. 25, 28, 148
HTTP	Hypertext Transfer Protocol. 148
ID	Identifier. 2, 29, 40, 57, 61, 66, 73, 75–78, 116, 120, 170
IGN	French national mapping agency. 145
IoT	Internet of Things. i, 5, 107–110, *Glossary:* Internet of Things
IRI	Internationalized Resource Identifier. 27, 60, 74–76
IS	Information system. 5, 147, 150
ISO	International Organization for Standardization. 27
JSON	JavaScript Object Notation. 16, 105, 126–128, 131, 132, 135, 136
KR	Knowledge representation. 21, 47
LD-Wiki	Linked Data Wiki. 12–14, 17–19, 64, 70–76, 78–85, 90, 91, 94, 96, 97, 102, 116, 122, 137, 179, 180, 205
LDaMM	Linked Data Management Module. 72–77, 79–82
LOD	Linked Open Data. i, 1–7, 9–12, 16, 17, 19, 21, 31, 33–37, 39, 41–43, 46–52, 54–58, 60–69, 72, 74–77, 79–84, 86–88, 90, 91, 93, 94, 96, 97, 105, 108, 112, 117, 122, 145, 179, 180, 182, 183, 207, *Glossary:* Linked Open Data
LOV	Linked Open Vocabulary. 4, 10, 49, 52, 54–58, 60–63, 71, 73, 80, 81
LSane	Linked Stream Annotation Engine. 12–14, 19, 102–104, 111, 114, 115, 121–129, 131, 132, 134–138, 181, 205
LUBW	Landesanstalt für Umwelt Baden-Württemberg. 14, 15
MDP	Markov decision process. 154, 158, 168, 178, 182
NEE	Named Entity Extraction. 62
NGO	Non-governmental organization. 5, 37, 45, 53
O&M	Observations and Measurements. 145
OADM	Open Annotation Data Model. 17, 62
OGC	Open Geospatial Consortium. 144

OWL	Web Ontology Language. 38, 59, 86, 162
QName	Qualified name. 2, 28, 41
QUDT	Quantities, Units, Dimensions and Data Types Ontologies. 123, 128, 130, 145, 155–157, 162–167
RDB	Relational database. 105
RDF	Resource Description Framework. 25, 28–31, 34–40, 42, 43, 47, 52–65, 70, 71, 73, 102, 105, 106, 108–110, 126–128, 132, 136, 145, 147, 162
RDFa	RDF in Attributes. 56
RDFS	RDF-Schema. 59
RFC	Request for Comments. 26, 27
RML	RDF Mapping Language. 105, 150
SAO	Stream Annotation Ontology. 108–110
SCA	Semantic content authoring. 60
SHACL	Shapes Constraint Language. 38, 39, 43, 125–130, 132, 136–138, 162, 166, 181, 209
SMW	Semantic MediaWiki. 53, 54, 56, 70–72, 80, 147, 205
SOS	Sensor Observation Service. 145
SPARQL	SPARQL Protocol and RDF Query Language. 16, 30, 34, 38, 47, 54–57, 61, 80, 82, 84, 86, 87, 97, 108, 127, 130, 148, 166, 179
SPIN	SPARQL Inferencing Notation. 38
SSN	Semantic Sensor Network. 106–108, 110, 123, 144, 147, 149
SWE	Sensor Web Enablement. 144
SWRL	Semantic Web Rule Language. 38, 39
TBox	Terminological Box. 23–25, 32, 47, 49, 52, 61, 62, 80, 86
URI	Uniform Resource Identifier. 23, 26–30, 34, 40, 41, 43, 48, 50, 57, 66, 78, 79, 82, 84, 93, 113–115, 117, 120, 128, 135

URIref	URI reference. 26
URL	Uniform Resource Locator. 27
URN	Uniform Resource Name. 27
UUID	Universally Unique IDentifier. 27, 57
VGI	Volunteered geographic information. 140
W3C	World Wide Web Consortium. 30, 34, 38, 53, 144
WaterML	Water Model Language. 145
WGS84	World Geodetic System 1984. 15, 16
WWW	World Wide Web. 25, 26, 35
WYSIWYG	What-you-see-is-what-you-get. 59
WYSIWYM	What-you-see-is-what-you-mean. 60, 63
XML	Extensible Markup Language. 105, 162
XSD	XML Schema Definition. 38

Glossary

closed-world assumption
: The closed-world assumption is the assumption that the truth value of a statement is only true if it is known to be true, otherwise it is considered as false. 7, 36, 37

concept
: A concept is the set of statements that every human associates with a real-world subject. It is to be assumed that this set is varying for every human, wherefore no unique overall concept can be applied to a subject. Within the scope of this thesis, a concept is defined as the subset of shared formal statements about that subject. 4, 5, 10, 11, 16, 19, 22–24, 31, 33, 37, 40, 43, 46–52, 54–56, 58, 60–69, 75–82, 84–94, 96–98, 107–110, 114, 117, 128, 135, 140, 142, 147, 149, 150, 152, 162, 178, 209

context knowledge
: Context knowledge provides the explicit semantics of observation messages and therefore enables rule based evaluation. i, 4, 5, 9, 12, 13, 17, 18, 40, 47, 106, 111, 121, 130, 138, 178

corporate knowledge graph
: A corporate knowledge graph within the context of this thesis is defined as a knowledge base modelled as locally closed environment. It includes curated triples from LOD and may also contain curated triples from other sources. 2, 5, 7–12, 16, 37, 39, 42, 43, 45–52, 54–56, 61, 63–66, 68–73, 80, 82–84, 88–91, 93–99, 101, 111, 112, 114–121, 131, 137, 138, 141, 153, 154, 160–162, 166, 177–182, 207

decision support system
: Service-oriented DSSs enable efficient and effective decision making processes with right data that is transformed to be meaningful information with data-driven discoveries. i, 2, 5

geographical information system
: A geographical information system is a special type of information system that is used to input, store, retrieve, process, analyze and visualize geospatial data and information in order to support decision making. i, 2, 5

Internet of Things

A network of things that is empowered by sensors, identifiers, software intelligence, and internet connectivity. i, 5

IoT data stream

Data streams of sensor observations available on the internet. i, 1–3, 5–10, 12–14, 16–18, 98, 99, 101, 106

knowledge

For practical reasons, we define knowledge in this thesis as a theoretical understanding of a subject, formalized as explicit statements about this subject. It cannot always be ensured whether these formalised statements are true or false. i, 1, 2, 4, 5, 9, 10, 12, 15, 17–19, 21–25, 29, 30, 32, 33, 35, 37, 43, 47–49, 52–65, 67, 72, 74, 75, 83, 101, 116, 117, 122, 141, 162, 164, 180, 182, 183, 207

Linked Open Data

The global 'web of data', which is described and interlinked in meaningful and machine-processable ways and follows well-defined grammar and language constructs. i, 1, 4, 7–9, 13, 18, 34, 45, 46, 72, 74, 77, 83, 90, 91, 96, 98, 179, 180, 182, 205

locally closed environment

A locally closed environment refers to a knowledge base that is treated under closed-world semantics, although the underlying concepts are derived from an open domain under an open-world assumption. This allows for completeness assertions as required for our approach. 5, 7, 36, 37, 46

observation

An observation is the act of measuring or otherwise determining the value of a property. It includes method, time, place and result of determining the value. In the context of this thesis, the result is always a numerical value observed by a sensor and has to be evaluated by a GIS. i, 1–18, 36, 37, 43, 94, 99–143, 145, 149, 151–163, 165–167, 169, 177–183, 205–207, 209, 216

open-world assumption

The open-world assumption is the assumption that the truth value of a statement may be true irrespective of whether or not it is known to be true. 2, 3, 5, 7, 36, 48, 65